T4-ADN-292

P. F. M. FONTAINE

THE LIGHT
AND
THE DARK

A CULTURAL HISTORY OF DUALISM

VOLUME V

J.C. GIEBEN, PUBLISHER
AMSTERDAM

THE LIGHT AND THE DARK

/ Fontaine, P.F.M.

THE LIGHT AND THE DARK

A CULTURAL HISTORY OF DUALISM

VOLUME V

DUALISM IN ANCIENT IRAN, INDIA, AND CHINA

J.C. GIEBEN, PUBLISHER
AMSTERDAM 1990

To my son Filip,
electrotechnical engineer,
able drawer of maps,
amateur musician

No part of this book may be translated or reproduced in any form, by print, photoprint, microfilm, or any other means, without written permission from the publisher.

© by P.F.M. Fontaine / ISBN 90 5063 051 0 / Printed in The Netherlands

"For all things are called
light and darkness"

Parmenides

CONTENTS

Preface		xiii
I	PERSICA POSTALEXANDRICA	1
1.	The Seleucid Empire	1
	a. The division of Alexander's heritage	1
	b. The decay of the Seleucid Empire	2
2.	The Parthian Empire	4
	a. 'The frontier of Europe'	4
	b. A head brought to the king	5
	c. A delicate balance	6
	d. Trajan retraces Alexander's footsteps	8
3.	The Sasanian Empire	10
	a. The Persian renaissance	10
	b. A Roman emperor down on his knees	12
	c. A brother kept at bay	14
	d. The last apogee of Sasanian power	16
4.	Orthodox Zorastrianism: a recapitulation	18
5.	The Zervanite heresy	21
	a. What about 'Ormuzd and Ahriman'?	21
	b. The Zervanite myth	22
	c. Finite and infinite deities	25
	d. The Magians	26
	e. The role of the Magi in the history of Zoroastrianism	28
	f. Zervanism under the Sasanian emperors	29
6.	Mandaeism and Manichaeism	30
	a. Mandaeism	31
	b. Manichaeism	32
7.	A mosaic of religions	33
Appendix to Chapter I: on Mazdakism		35
Notes to Chapter I		37
II	INDICA	40
1.	India between particularism and the drive to unity	40
	a. India from the inside and from the outside	40
	b. Prehistoric man and nature	41
	c. The Indus civilization	42
	d. The coming of the Aryans	45
2.	The first power centre	48
	a. The Vedic period	48
	b. Magadha's bid for power	50

3.	Persians and Greeks in India	53
	a. Persian influence	53
	b. Alexander beyond the Indus	54
4.	The Mauryan Empire	55
	a. The foundation of the empire	55
	b. Chandragupta's power test	57
	c. Asoka	58
	d. The Bactrian menace	60
5.	Nomad incursions	62
6.	Particularism or unity	64
7.	The Gupta dynasty	66
8.	The Harappa culture	69
9.	The Aryans, their kings, and the conquered peoples	71
10.	The emperors	73
11.	Empire and unity	75
12.	The three great Indian concepts	76
	a. Dharma	77
	b. Samsara	78
	c. Karman	79
13.	Slavery as a divisive element	80
	a. A Greek observer	80
	b. Who became slaves	81
	c. Utterly different	82
14.	Women as the lesser sort	83
	a. Harappan matriarchate	83
	b. The 'macho' Aryans	83
	c. The greater importance of the sons	84
	d. Polygamy	86
	e. The sad fate of the widow	88
	f. Child marriages	90
	g. The dualistic relationship of women and women	92
	h. Buddhist attitudes to the female sex	93
15.	The caste system and the lesser breeds	95
	a. The word 'caste'	96
	b. The origin of the caste system	96
	c. What is a caste?	97
	d. The castes and the varnas	98
	e. Outcastes and pariahs	99
	f. Mutual exclusivity	100
	g. The Shudras	101
	h. Conclusion	104
16.	Dualistic tendencies in Indian philosophy	104
	a. The Indian conception of existence	105
	b. Unity and diversity	106
	c. Male and Female	107
	d. Matter and Spirit	108

17.	Dualistic tendencies in Indian mythology	109
	a. Vedic devas	109
	b. Rifts and fissures in the Vedic pantheon	111
	c. Demons	112
18.	The Brahmanic religion	113
	a. The difference between Vedism and Brahmanism	113
	b. Brahma, Brahmanas, and Brahmans	114
	c. Brahma(n) as the highest principle	115
	d. The Brahmanic idea of unity in the cosmos	116
	e. Theism and pantheism	118
	f. The importance of ritual	119
19.	The superiority of the Brahmans	121
	a. The Brahmans as sacrificial experts	121
	b. The purohita	122
	c. Brahmanic wealth	123
	d. A highly privileged class	125
20.	Dualistic tendencies in Hinduism	126
	a. Vishnu and Krishna	126
	b. Contradictory statements about women	128
	c. The Hindu mother cult	128
	d. Mother-Goddesses	129
	e. The come back of the female divinities	130
	f. The dual(istic) character of Maha-Devi	131
	g. The Linga and the Yoni: an uneasy balance	132
21.	Yoga dualism	136
	a. The way of the atman	136
	b. The 'via negativa'	137
	c. What is yoga?	138
	d. Yoga's philosophical background	139
	e. Yoga practice	141
22.	Jainism	143
	a. The founder, Vardhamana	143
	b. Jainism's relation to the Parshva creed	143
	c. The annihilation of karma	145
	d. The arduous road upwards	147
	e. Jainism to-day	148
23.	Buddhism	149
	a. The life of the Buddha	149
	b. The corpus of Buddhist scripture	151
	c. The spread of Buddhism	151
	d. Buddhism a 'non-theistic religion'?	153
	e. The road to Nirvana	155
	f. The Lesser Vehicle	157
	g. The Great Vehicle	158
24.	Looking back	160
Notes to Chapter II		163

| III | SINENSIA | 174 |

1.	The cradle of Chinese civilization	174
2.	Times of legend	175
3.	The Shang dynasty	176
4.	Zhou rule	178
5.	The Eastern Zhou	180
	a. The position of the ruler	180
	b. Chinese imperialism	181
	c. The ruler and his vassals	183
6.	Qin, the first unified Chinese empire	185
	a. Qin and China	185
	b. The foundation of the Chinese empire	186
	c. The promotion of national unity	187
	d. Qin authoritarianism	188
7.	The foundation of Han rule	190
8.	Some thoughts on the unification of China and on history writing	191
9.	Early problems of the Han regime	195
	a. The initial situation	195
	b. Modernists and reformists	196
	c. The beginnings of Chinese bureaucracy	197
10.	The showdown with the Xiongnu	199
11.	The Son of Heaven and his Celestial Mandate	202
12.	The unhappy end of the First Han Period	203
13.	The Latter Han Period	204
14.	A time of disunion	206
15.	Chinese philosophical concepts	210
	a. A universe in three parts	210
	b. Heaven as the supreme godhead	210
	c. The square earth	211
	d. Pairs of oppositions	212
	e. Yin and Yang	215
16.	The life of Master Kong	217
17.	Not a religious reformer	219
18.	Confucius the humanist	220
19.	Confucians and Legalists	222
20.	The Qin and Han emperors and Confucianism	223
21.	Confucian education	225
22.	Mohist pessimism	225
	a. Mo's puritanism	225
	b. Mo's concept of universal love	226
	c. Mohism and Confucianism at loggerheads	228
23.	Mengzi's optimism	229
24.	One of the Hundred Schools	230
25.	Dao, the Way	232
	a. What is Dao?	232

b. About Laozi		233
c. Dao, what it means		234
d. Once again, the One and the Many		235
e. The gods of Daoism		237
f. A doctrine of salvation		238
g. Daoist practices		239
h. The Daoist 'Church'		242
26. A final overview		243
Notes to Chapter III		244
Bibliography		251
General Index		260

Time Table of Indian history			43
Map I	The Seleucid Empire	opposite p.	2
Map II	The Parthian Empire	opposite p.	4
Map III	The Sasanian Empire	opposite p.	10
Map IV	The Indus Civilization	opposite p.	42
Map V	The Vedic Period	opposite p.	48
Map VI	The Empire of Magadha	opposite p.	51
Map VII	The Mauryan Empire under Asoka	opposite p.	56
Map VIII	The Gupta Empire	opposite p.	68
Map IX	The Shang and Zhou realms	opposite p.	176
Map X	The Qin Empire	opposite p.	186
Map XI	The Han Empire	opposite p.	200

PREFACE

One of my reviewers, Mr. R.W. Jordan, writing in the 'Classical Review', 1989, X, pp. 268 - 269, of Volumes II and III that are dealing with dualism in the Greek classical world, showed himself partly content, partly dissatisfied. In his opinion I argued convincingly that there are (his underlining) dualistic tendencies in Greek thought in this period. In his view, I am also right when I stated that Plato, without any doubt, was a person with a distinct proclivity towards dualism. But what makes him feel discontented is that I did not say very clearly what I mean by dualism. This astonished me. For in the preface of every volume I repeat my original definition; in many passages in the books I make this formula still more explicit. Here it is (and in almost the same words it is quoted by my reviewer).

The term dualism, as used by me, refers to two utterly opposed conceptions, principles, systems, groups of people, or even worlds, without any intermediate terms between them. They cannot be reduced to one another; in some cases they are not even dependent on each other. The opposites are considered to be of different quality - so much so that one of them is always seen as distinctly inferior, and hence must be neglected, repudiated, or, if needs be, destroyed. This same definition will serve as a premise for the discussions in this volume.

Although I feel that in stating this, I expressed my notion of dualism clearly enough, and although I honestly believe that I demonstrated it by a host of examples, Mr. Jordan, nevertheless, speaks of 'a continuing unclarity about the central ideas'. True enough, he says,

I admit that there is thinking that is non-dualistic in character, but I do not try to place dualistic thought in the context of non-dualistic or antidualistic thinking. I show myself, he continues, altogether too optimistic in hoping that my readers will simply take it that the several dualistic tensions (he cites a few of them) are interrelated in any interesting way, or understand what they have to do with one another. My main failure seems to be that I did not present (Greek) dualism as a coherent system (or anti-system). In my reviewer's own words, I did not make out my case that 'dualism' is a key-concept for historians of culture. This makes me think of what one correspondent wrote to me with respect to the chapter on India in this volume, that I had brought out the opposition between dualism and monism so well. Here again I am supposed, but this time with approval, to confront dualism as a system or concept with another system or concept.

Now it is not my intention to attack Mr. Jordan whose review I consider as, on the whole, positive. But I want to seize this opportunity to say some basic things about dualism and about my notion of it. Let me first of all state that nothing is more normal than thinking in oppositions. We have at our disposal two ways of ordering the multifarious phenomena that confront us. One of these is to subsume similar or connected phenomena under one heading that may indicate a whole group or complex. I am referring now to words like tree, dog, France, multinationals, opera. The other way we have is to oppose phenomena in contrasting pairs like cold and warm, old and young, quick and slow, and innumerable others. Both manners of ordering are perfectly legitimate; everybody unthinkingly makes use of them hundreds of times a day.

With regard to ordering the world by means of opposing or contrasting, there is normally no trace of dualism in it. Ice has to be cold, just as tea should be served hot. Somebody may be a slow learner but another is too quick with his tongue, while in dancing we have the slow waltz as well as the quickstep. The two halves of a pair usually are connected by intermediary stages; there is a central area where the one changes into the other, often imperceptibly. At dusk the day slowly gives way to the night; in springtime the winter step by step blends into summer, while in the autumn the summer little by little makes place for the winter.

Some oppositions, however, have a sterner character. Good and evil are much more different and opposed than, for instance, cold and warm, but, nevertheless, there sometimes is discussion how good or how bad something is. Nothing could be further apart than tyranny and democracy. In the months that I was writing the present volume, in the course of 1989, the world saw one autocratic regime after the other come toppling down. But soon it became evident that their place was not automatically taken by a democratic system. Here too intermediary stages have to be intercalated. A last example. What could be more opposed than love and hate? But all of us know relationships in which love and hate are so intermingled that we speak of a 'love-hate relationship'. For a long time it may hang in the balance before one of the two, for instance in a marriage, gains the upperhand.

So far we have been speaking only of contrasts that are useful and necessary, and, therefore, wholly innocuous, and of sharper oppositions with a problematic character, although, given good will and common sense, the parties concerned may be brought closer together. This is in accord with the idea all of us have of the world. I believe that in all periods of history and in all civilizations nearly everyone envisages the world as a whole. Perhaps schizophrenics are the sole exception but then they are considered insane. Normally, however, we are simply incapable of imagining the world as fragmented or parcelled into unconnected single phenomena or even into disconnected series of events or phenomena. The fundamental vision of the world all of us cherish is characterized by words like wholeness, harmony, stillness, peace, quiet.

Still deeper, in our innermost hearts, we wish, hoping against hope, that the world might be uneventful and unchanging, even unchangeable, that it would always present the picture of a perfect summer afternoon in which we sit in a shaded garden with no leaf stirring in incomparable tranquillity and in quiet harmony with the nature that surrounds us. The British novelist Angus Wilson in his short story 'More friend than lodger', expressed what I mean in the following way : "It would be so much nicer if there was no cause and effect in this life, no one thing leading inevitably to another but just everything being sufficient in itself". With these words this author does not mean that his ideal is a fragmented world but that there should be no change, no permanent rolling on of events. In short, there should be no history.

But there is history. The world is constantly changing, and we are changing with it, as the Latin saying goes. We might perhaps accept the changeableness of the world without demurring if only the changes were imperceptibly slow, so slow that they would remain unnoticed. I mean the kind of changes that the French historian Braudel classified under the 'longue durée', changes in the climate, for instance, that only become apparent after hundreds or even thousands of years. But we all know that changes can be very abrupt and sudden. That perfect summer afternoon I was speaking of a few moments ago may suddenly end in a thunderstorm. "Ever after thy calm look I for a storm", wrote Sir Thomas More meditating on the fickleness of fortune.

To put this in a more philosophical way, there is not only wholeness in the world but also discontinuity, and we somewhat suffer from it. At this point I must connect what I am saying here with the idea, as I stated earlier, that we use to think in contrasts or opposing pairs. The fact that phenomena, apart from being grouped together, can also be treated as separate and even as contrasted is the very first emergence of discontinuity. Our attitude to this discontinuity is ambiguous, and, at the same time, discontinuous itself. On the one hand, we laconically accept this state of affairs, being, however, sometimes evidently unhappy because of it; on the other, we try to plaster it over by denying or minimizing the oppositions. Some time ago a colleague confidently told me that he got along with everybody very well; what he conveniently forgot is that his own daughter had walked out on him and did not see him for years.

The wholeness of the world has our preference; to keep the picture intact we sacrifice part of reality to it, with the help of our short memory. Some people do this so assiduously that they become quite unrealistic. Goodhearted though they may be such people often are a nuisance in business or teamwork. But we must not be oblivious of the fact that all of us are inclined to be somewhat forgetful of reality when it comes to choosing between wholeness and disunity. We are favouring holism more than dualism.

Some people, however, show a tendency for preferring discrepancies. Who does not know a person without a talent for happiness and feeling at peace with people and life, somebody who is always complaining and whining about shortcomings real and imagined. Such a person is never content with his wife, his children, his home, his colleagues, his work, in short, with the world. A man or woman of this kind is, perhaps unconsciously, permanently comparing his or her obviously pitiful state with an ideal, that of the happy, harmonious existence. He or she is not only unhappy because the ideal seems unattainable but probably still more because he or she experiences this discrepancy so painfully and hopelessly.

In such people this unhappy feeling can easily develop into an antagonistic attitude to life. Normal and natural oppositions may become intensified into polarities, into very sharp oppositions that is. The Greeks were particularly fond of polarities, far more than Egyptians or Israelites, which enabled G.E.R. Lloyd to write a book on 'Polarity and Analogy' in Greek thought, and to call them 'two types of argumentation' (Cambridge, 1966). But we are not yet in the presence of dualism here. In a polarity there still are intermediate stages, the two terms having not become wholly disconnected. In the decades since 1945 the world has lived through the Cold War. This is a good example of a polarity. Of course, there exists a very sharp difference between peace and war but the Cold War, however much it opposed the two blocks, was neither war nor peace.

But finally, when all is said and done, the gap may become unbridgeable. Some people obviously feel an urge to push oppositions to extremes. Then the intermediary stages gradually phase out till nothing but a wide abyss remains. Then it is no longer possible to reduce the terms of the opposition to each other; there no longer is any relationship or connection. If this stage is reached, we are in the presence of dualism.

On one level dualism should be thought of as an historical phenomenon that appears and functions in historical contexts, that is, in human societies. However, it is not 'historical' in the narrower sense that it is typical for certain societies or historical situations only. This statement offers me an opportunity to explain why I did not start my series with an exposition of Iranian dualism. If dualism really were an historical phenomenon in the traditional sense of the word 'historical', I should have done so. To many people all dualism originates from Iran; according to them, Iranian dualism is the beginning and fountainhead of every type of dualism (see my Volume IV, Ch. IV, 4, on the 'the origins of dualism'). Historically minded as we are we feel that a thing like dualism must have a distinct origin in time, that it must originate in a definable place at a fixable time. For this is what modern historiography is about.

In my view, dualism is an anthropological phenomenon rather than an historical one. By this I mean that it can, and in fact does, occur everywhere and at any time in individual persons, in social groups, in societies, and in civilizations, be they primitive or highly developed, simple or sophisticated. This also implies that we must not restrict the study of dualism to the realms of philosophy or the history of religions. There really is no good reason why oppositions should occur only in these fields but nowhere else. We find it in every conceivable department of life, in history and politics, in literature and art, in social relationships and personal life. Everywhere we see people grappling with or suffering from or trying to accomodate themselves to unbridgeable oppositions. Let me repeat what I said on page

272 of Volume IV : we are here in the presence of a general human phenomenon forming part of our human make-up and therefore rightly termed anthropological. The origin of dualism is not to be found in history or in mythology, in religion or in philosophy, but in the human condition.

Having arrived at this point I must caution the reader against two serious misunderstandings of what I mean by dualism. First, varying a famous dictum by Karl Marx, I must state that, in my opinion, the history of mankind is not the history of dualism. When I am accused of not making out my case that dualism is a key-concept for historians of culture, I must retort that I did not set out to make such a case.

Linking up with that term 'key-concept' I come to my second point. This is that dualism is neither a concept nor an ideology. Aldous Huxley once wrote of 'the prevailing mania of the Middle Ages to turn everything into a concept' (in his 'The Doors of Perception'). We could equally say that the prevailing mania of our time is to turn everything into an ideology. We are fond of -isms. By coining the term 'dualism' we are putting it on a par with liberalism, marxism, nominalism, historicism, and other ideologies and intellectual systems ending on -ism. But it cannot be stressed often enough that dualism is nothing of this kind. It is not an intellectual system, not an ideology, not a philosophy, not a concept, not a religion. It is something quite different. Therefore, it cannot be set against non-dualistic systems, for then we would be comparing things of a totally different order.

Some of my reviewers and correspondents, while admitting that my indication of dualistic trends is quite right, nevertheless say that my view is one-sided. To a certain extent this doubtless is true. At several points in my series I expressly state that I omit this development or skip that system because they are not dualistic. After all, I am writing a history of dualism, and not of something else. My subtitle makes this perfectly clear. It honestly is no quid pro quo (or cheap revenge) when I say that other works are 'one-sided' too because they primarily and preferably document coherence. What they above all love to do is to draw long lines of development on which persons and events appear connected with each other. In my chapter on China in this volume, in section 8, I take the professional historians to task for knitting everything together so neatly. They can only achieve their aim by leaving out what does not fit. I am in no sense suggesting that they purposefully distort the picture. By no means! But 'success oriented' as they are, they often fail to detect failure and tragedy and appear not interested in the 'misfits'. I believe this applies to scholars in every field of history. The paramount proof of this 'success-orientedness' is the popularity of evolutionism - another modern -ism - in which ideology all lines are ascending, every stage being a step for the next higher stage; the failures are simply disregarded.

What I am doing is looking at the backside of the tapestry. People gaze admiringly at the beautiful picture presented to them by the frontside. They do not bother to look at the other side. And right they are, for they would not see anything else than a confused mass of threads. Now history, although no tapestry but a thing in movement, has its own loose threads. The 'backside' of history displays disconnectedness. I ask the reader to pay special attention to the following remark. Dualism may occur everywhere and at any time but dualistic trends always appear in dispersed order. Large segments of society may be 'holistic' but here and there some cracks, some deep fissures appear. However, these do not hang together nor do they offer a coherent picture of a dualistic contra-society. I believe that the expression 'dualistic society' would be a contradiction in terms since, when it really could be applied, there would be two different societies.

Dualistic elements can be combined into some sort of philosophy, as sometimes happens. This, however, remains a rare occurence. In the course of my study I found only a few dualistic systems : the Pythagorean fraternity (Vol. I, Ch. I, 15), the Orphic religion (Vol. I, Ch. IV, 10), the philosophies of Empedocles, Heraclitus, and, in particular, Parmenides (Vol. I, Ch. II, 6, 8 and 9), those elements in Plato's teaching that show a strong tendency towards dualism (Vol. III, Ch. III,

20, 21, and 22), Zoroastrianism (Vol. IV, Ch. IV, 8 and 9), and still more Iranian Zervanism (Vol. V, Ch. I, 4), in India in particular yoga (Vol. V, Ch. II, 22), and, finally, Chinese Daoism (Vol. V, Ch. III, 25). This is a rather meagre harvest for the long periods and the many civilizations I have studied. Furthermore, the impact of these systems was not great. Pythagoreans and Orphics were restricted groups, like Yogis and Daoists. Most dualistic philosophies did not become popular or widespread, and of these Plato had the greatest influence of them all. I believe that Zervanism came nearest to becoming a national religion for some time. This gives some substance to Duchesne-Guillemin's claim that Iran was 'the classical country of dualism'. As far as I can judge now, no dualistic system witnessed a greater success than Zervanism in Persia.

For the rest, we only find dispersed and isolated elements of dualism that fail to present a coherent picture and often differ widely from each other. To cite only a few instances, the opposition of Greeks and barbarians in Hellenic public opinion (Vol. II, Ch. III, 3), of desert and Nile valley in Egypt (Vol. IV, Ch. I, 1), of Jews and Samaritans in ancient Israel (Vol. IV, Ch. II, 14c), and the situation of outcastes and pariahs in India (Vol. V, Ch. II, 16). In describing trends and situations like these I willingly and consciously rob myself of the great advantage historians have, that of presenting a whole. I realize that in this way I am laying myself open to criticism from the side of those many writers and scholars who above all want coherence.

Some time ago a former student of mine asked me (and he was not the only one to do so) why I occupied myself with dualism. He flattered me by telling me that he had come to know me as an harmonious person, and, therefore, wondered why I was so constantly busy with unbridgeable oppositions. Perhaps there exist deep psychological reasons for my preoccupation with dualism, but having neither time nor fancy to stretch myself on the psychoanalyst's couch, the reader must remain content with the answer Edmund Hillery gave when asked why he had climbed the highest top of Mount Everest : 'because it is there'. Dualism is a thing that exists, that, furthermore, is far from rare in human history. But until now, nobody has bothered to write a history of it, although Ugo Bianchi once declared that a 'Weltgeschichte' of dualism would be possible (see my Volume I, p. 263). Perhaps historians shrink back from this undertaking because a 'history' of dualism in the strictly traditional sense of the presentation of a coherent story is impossible.

Let us now return to my remark of a few paragraphs back that dualism is something quite different from a conceptual system or an ideology, let alone a philosophy. Dualism is a psychological urge, an anthropological tendency, and as such part of the human condition. It is for this reason that some form of dualism may develop everywhere, at any time, in every person, in every social group. Contrasts come natural to us, and given the circumstances may be sharpened and deepened into unbridgeable oppositions. Most of the time this does not happen because of that other and stronger urge we all feel, that towards harmony and wholeness, an urge which usually triumphs over the opposite tendency. However, I believe that the proclivity to emphasize contrasts is more obviously present in some people (a minority) than in others. This urge to intensify contrasts to the extreme may, indeed, be innate in some human beings; given the favourable circumstances, it can get a fair chance to develop into some form of downright dualism.

When people ask me what I mean by dualism I often refer to Jesus' parable of the tares among the wheat (Mt.13:24-30). The corn was growing high when an enemy of the farmer came and sowed weeds between its ranks. When these had grown too, the labourers ran to their master and asked him : "Shall we gather them up?". But no, the farmer said, leave it thus till harvest time, for otherwise you will root up the wheat with the tares. Now in this short story the labourers are clean dualists : one term of the opposition (the tares, = evil) must be utterly destroyed. Their master, however, is thinking otherwise, for he realizes that in human life good and bad are inextricably bound together.

The narrator does not tell us how these labourers became such fierce dualists. Since, as I said, dualism is part of the human condition, we must look for some obvious duality, one that everyone is acquainted with, one that may be the general origin. In every human being there exists a rift between ideal and reality; one need not be a philosopher or a deeply religious person to feel this often in a very painful way. Nowhere in that part of human history we have perused until now does this come more strongly to the fore than in ancient India. Heesterman calls this 'the inner conflict of tradition'. Usually our attention is riveted by the conflict of modernity and tradition in India, one could also say by that of progress and conservatism. Heesterman ('The Inner Conflict of Tradition'. Essays in Indian Ritual, Kingship, and Society. Chicago and London, 1985. Ch. I) of course does not deny that such a conflict really exists but there is also another, perhaps stronger one, an inner conflict in 'the hard core of tradition'. This may be sketched in terms of 'Brahman' and 'king', or of the Brahmanic (ideal) and kingly order of things.

"The 'kingly' order is immanent in social relations." The king, his ministers, his officials, and all those who form part of the social order that is managed and administered by them, I mean the subjects or the citizens, apply themselves constantly to their daily rounds of affairs, be it warfare, commerce, or the tilling of the land. Not so much of this has a permanent character; they usually occupy themselves with things of a fleeting nature. In other words, "society is felt (by the Brahmans) to be based on the alternation of life and death, and consequently participation in society's web of relations is felt to be tantamount with continual involvement with death". In consequence Brahmans, wanting to be totally independent of all relations, turn their backs on society and utterly renounce the world. Heesterman states that the establishment of 'modernity' in no way resolves this inner conflict. It is easy enough to agree with this point of view, since the opposition between ideal and reality will never be resolved in human existence. This conflict will always remain a potential source of dualism.

Closely akin to this opposition is another, that of body and soul. True enough, modern holism and related anti-dualistic ways of thought rightly posit that body and soul form a whole, just as scholastic philosophy already taught that body is the matter of the soul, and soul the form of the body. Nevertheless, almost everyone of us from time to time painfully experiences the difference. Fatigue makes us miss our goal, illness keeps us from the work we want to do, disablement prevents us from enjoying many of the good things of life, sleep can overwhelm us when driving a car, passion may obscure our clear insight. The claims of the body, the need to eat, to drink, to sleep, press a certain pattern of life on us, however we feel about it.

Often the experience of body and soul being different is much more in accordance with our intuition than is preached by philosophy. In certain circumstances and in certain persons or social groups this sentiment may operate as a wedge that makes the gap wider and wider; the difference may grow into an opposition and the opposition into enmity - against the body that is. There are telling instances of this in the Indian chapter in this volume and in that on Plato in Volume III (Ch. III, 7-10). Here too we find a starting-point for dualism, the more so because the feeling that body and soul are not in complete accordance is common to all of us (see for instance Vol. IV, Ch. IV, 8g).

There is, however, yet a third reason, a psychological or anthropological one, why dualistic trends so readily emerge. I mean the man-woman duality. I myself believe this to be the most important source of dualism. Of course, man and woman, when married, are 'one flesh' as Gen. 2 : 24 says, that is, in modern terminology, they have but one existence. This oneness certainly is not meant in a merely metaphorical sense. But at the same time man and woman are different from one another. This too is expressed in the biblical words that "God created them man and woman" (Gen.1:27). Nevertheless, they are complementary beings since, without their coming together, the human race would die out.

But here again this duality, this being different may, starting from the famous 'petite différence', be intensified and developed into a growing distancing, and this into downright mutual contempt which, in the married state, can lead to 'living apart together'. In several of my volumes, instances of this dualistic attitude may be found. Neither Plato nor Aristotle were great admirers of women (Vol. III, Ch. III, 14c and 24a and b). Athenian society was not conspicuous for having the female sex in high regard (Vol. II, Ch. IV, 4; see also the sections on women in Greek tragedy and comedy in Vol. III, Ch. I, 6 and 7). In the present volume the chapter on India presents many examples of women being held in disdain (Ch. II, 15).

The duality of ideal and reality, of body and soul, and of man and woman, can give rise to a dualistic attitude in thought and action. As the five volumes I have published thus far abundantly prove, there is no society or culture without dualistic tendencies and trends, sometimes resulting in overtly dualistic systems, philosophies, and religions. In my opinion, the span runs between Israel and Iran, Israel being the least and Iran the most dualistic society we have studied thus far, with Egypt a good second to Israel, and ancient Hellas to Iran, while India too present a claim to this second place. But even Israel nor Egypt are without dualistic phenomena.

It must never be forgotten that dualism is not an automatism nor is it on an equal footing with the urge to wholeness. While this is always given pride of place as being the most natural and self-evident of things, there must, on the other hand, be special impulses for the development of dualism. These impulses are to be found in the life of individual persons or in the mode of existence of certain nations or groups. In Antiquity, alas, our data are too scarce for underpinning this statement safely. Here and there I ventured to offer a guess. I am not the only one to believe that the rampant dualism of Iran has something to do with the inclemency of her climate (Vol. IV, Ch. IV, 5).

The only dualistic personality in Antiquity of whom we know somewhat more than next to nothing is Plato. I am convinced that he was a man with an innate proclivity towards dualism. But this is no sufficient reason for his philosophy also being dualistic. This congenital tendency was activated by certain events or situations in his life. These must have been the realization that he was not talented enough to become a great tragedian, and next the shock of Socrates' execution. The normal road of a political career was henceforward closed to the young man. He then turned towards philosophy, but we must not forget that he did so as a doubly frustrated man. This works itself out in a philosophy that shows many dualistic aspects (Vol. III, Ch. IV, 1a).

There doubtless exist people for whom discontinuity is a way of life. Of the most radical or consequent of them it can be said that they live in two different worlds. A case in point would be Adolf Hitler. There is no doubt that for him there were indeed two worlds, a world of light, and a world of obscurity. The light world, in his view, was inhabited by the luminous Aryan people (this was a purely hypothetical race, more to be created than actually existing, and most certainly not to be identified with the Germans of his days). The dark world was the domain of the inferior, subhuman groups like the Jews and the Gypsies. We all know that his opinion of the people of darkness was so radically dualistic that he condemned it to the Holocaust.

Hitler, therefore, was a dualist if there ever was one. But what made him so? I do not doubt that he was born with a propensity to extremes. Already in his early youth he showed a tendency to harshness and an inclination to lord over his school-fellows. But from this to the final decision to exterminate all the Jews is a very far cry; his road through life is by no means punctuated by logical or natural stages. First of all, he bore the imprint of the dumb conflict between his father and mother, an ill-assorted pair. This means that the man-woman duality had a greater impact on him than on children in happier families. Furthermore, I have the impression that he loathed his own body; his extreme puritanism and his obsession with his personal hygiene are indications of this. Possibly the cause of this hatred is that he considered himself incomplete, or even mutilated, since he had only one testicle.

Then, when he was somewhat older, there was the lasting effect of his months of poverty in Vienna in the autumn of 1909; in that time he even slept out on a bank in the Hofgarten. Still more, there was the influence World War I had on him when he served for four years in the trenches. In this period he changed from a timid young man into a firebrand, as he said himself. Finally, I mention the suicide of Geli Raubal, the one and only love of his life (with the exception of his mother). This catastrophe not only for some time plunged him into utter despair but, still more, put a negative, a destructive sign on all his relations with all his fellow-men.

What I want to demonstrate by means of this short description (that I could easily elaborate in great detail) is that dualism originates in the personal or anthropological sphere, not in that of philosophy or ideology. But since 'no man is an island', everyone is also moving on quite a number of other levels, social, political, religious, for instance. Dualistically minded people introduce their private dualistic views and customs into these fields. There really exists no domain of human thought or action that is impervious to dualism. What specific form dualism will take depends on the interests, the education, and the life-story of the persons concerned. For Hitler it became politics and ideology, for Plato philosophy, for Zoroaster religion. If such people are domineering personalities - as the three men cited certainly were -, they will have no difficulty in finding a following or founding a movement. There always have been and there always shall be people who feel attracted by radical positions.

To conclude. Dualism is not a phenomenon like, say, scholasticism or national-socialism (bien étonnés de se trouver ensemble). By this I mean that dualism is not a neatly circumscribable philosophy or ideology with a limited radius of action and situated in a definable period of history. Scholasticism has long been an historical phenomenon, and national-socialism is on the way out (Hitler even said that it would not survive him). The reader will understand that this temporality applies to all other philosophical or ideological movements; witnessing the sudden demise of Marxism-Leninism he or she will not doubt this. But dualism, being nothing of the kind, will always accompany mankind. Since it may emerge anywhere and at any time, its history must needs be a world history. And since its emergence never is the result of a logical, rational, purely 'historical' process (in the sense of a concatenation of cause and effect), it is always found inscribed into a given historico-cultural context.

This makes the writing of a cultural history of dualism necessary. Or, in other words, dualistic phenomena have to be described as occurring in a non-dualistic context with which they are contrasting or that they try to encapsulate (as in ancient Iran). The necessity of placing dualistic phenomena in their proper context has as a consequence that this context has to be described although it is impossible to tell how much of it has to be presented. After all, I am not writing a history of the world but a world history of dualism. This means omitting much, even most, of history.

When confronted by the choice between dualistic and non-dualistic phenomena, my preference, of course, is dictated by the main subject of this work. On the whole, I feel that I may take the non-dualistic description of the world for granted. Historians of every kind describe history, and will continue to do so, from a non-dualistic point of view. This certainly is a laudable undertaking but in their eagerness to be 'holistic' historians tend to forget what Robert Musil, the Austrian novelist, said : "History does not originate from a centre but from the periphery, out of trifling causes"; and still more important "history grows out of a lack of happiness" (in his 'Der Mann ohne Eigenschaften', I 361 and II 1129, as published by Rowohlt 1981).

As far as I know I am the only one to tackle history from the side where 'rien ne va plus'. In doing so I find myself in a permanent dilemma between giving either too much or too little. There is self-evidently no hard and fast rule to help me out, the more so since

I am pioneering. Some commentators reproach me for giving too much. However, when forced to make the choice, I rather prefer giving too much since I do not keep my eye on the expert who, indeed, often will feel that he or she is led along a well-known road, but rather on the general reader who, I confidently assume, will be served with more information than the expert deems necessary. I gladly take the risk that here or there the main subject may become somewhat obscured by the amount of general information. This very pregnantly applies to the present volume in which such esoteric subjects as the history of ancient India and China are treated.

Although Chapter I on ancient Iran forms the sequel to Chapter IV of Volume IV, the present volume can be read independently of the foregoing work. I hope that the short summary of Zoroastrian religion will be sufficient to introduce the reader to the subject of later Iranian religious history. My faithful corrector, Dr. J.R. Dove, now retired and living definitely in his beloved Amsterdam, again took care of the linguistic aspect of my work that I wrote directly in English. I have all the more reason to be grateful to him since he has experienced considerable difficulties with his health. My daughter Resianne, philosophiae doctor, and Dr. A. Budé, a classical scholar, acting as 'general readers', read the whole book in typescript and supplied me with many a valuable remark.

Three learned persons invested their time and energy in a careful perusal of my chapters and saved me from a number of mistakes and omissions. I feel most thankful to them. Chapter I I submitted to Dr. Ph.G. Kreyenbroek, lecturer of Zoroastrianism in the Department of the Near and Middle East in the University of London School of Oriental and African Studies. Chapter II, on India, was read by Dr. J.C. Heesterman who holds the chair of Indian civilization at Leyden State University NL. Finally, Dr. E. Zürcher, professor of East Asian history at Leyden State University, took good care of Chapter III on China; he was kind enough to transcribe all the proper names in it into the pinyin spelling. Mr. J.C. Gieben, the publisher, saw to it that my brain-child is presented to the world.

My son Filip, to whom I dedicate this volume, now a qualified electro-technical engineer at his first job, again drew the maps very neatly; I am glad and thankful that he took this trouble off my hands. Last but not least - on the contrary -, there is my beloved wife Anneke who undertook the painstaking task of correcting the camera-ready typescript. However, as for the four foregoing volumes, I assume the full responsibility for the contents, the English text, and the typography.

I have already started work on Volume VI. In this I am returning to the West, that is to the Hellenistic world after Alexander.

Piet F.M. Fontaine
Amsterdam NL

CHAPTER I

PERSICA POSTALEXANDRICA

1. The Seleucid Empire

a. The division of Alexander's heritage

Alexander's great idea died with him. This was the foundation of an empire larger than the world had ever seen, stretching from the Danube to the Indus, from the Caucasus to the Nile, uniting Europe, Africa, and Asia, comprising Greeks, Egyptians, and Asians, and having one ruler, one language, and one civilization. Never before did anybody dream such a fantastic dream; it did not materialize. Certainly the Macedonian victor conquered the whole of the Persian Empire; he even went beyond its eastern frontiers by crossing the Indus and penetrating into the heart of India. Then again he inaugurated the process of cultural amalgamation by marrying an oriental princess and forcing thousands of his men, Macedonians and Greeks, into nuptial ties with Persian women. Had he succeeded in his grand design, the old dualism of Europe and Asia would have been dissolved, and a homogeneous world culture would perhaps have originated. But Alexander died suddenly in 323 B.C. at the age of only thirty-three years.

His generals could not equal his greatness. After much in-fighting between them, called 'the wars of the Diadochi', or successors, Alexander's heritage became divided among them. About twenty years of war found their apogee in the final Battle of Ipsus in 301 B.C. The result was the emergence of three monarchies, each with a Greek-

Macedonian dynasty : a Macedonian kingdom in Europe, the realm of the Ptolemaics in Egypt, and that of the Seleucids in Asia. At least originally, the Seleucid kingdom could, with good reason, claim to be the real empire since it comprised most of the domain Alexander had left behind him, and by far the larger part of the countries that had been under Persian rule. In the first period it stretched from the Aegean to the Indus. Its founder, Seleucus I, was very close to his master's ideas. He himself was married to a Persian noblewoman, Apamea, and in consequence, as Ghirshman points out, became the ancestor of a mixed Macedonian-Iranian dynasty. He integrated the fine cavalry which constituted the élite of the Persian army into his own fighting forces [1].

b. The decay of the Seleucid Empire

After his death in 280 B.C., the empire began to crumble. It is generally supposed that the old Persian heartland, Persia proper, made itself virtually independent during the reign of his successor, Antiochus I (280-261) [2]. Worse was to follow. During the reign of Antiochus II (261-246) the whole eastern half of the empire fell away. The Greek satrap of Bactria succeeded in shaking off the rule of the Seleucid monarch; his son began to style himself king and in doing so founded the Greek Kingdom of Bactria which, in its largest extent, comprised the territory of present-day Pakistan, Afghanistan, and some southern Soviet-republics. For two centuries it served as a focus of Greek culture radiating into India and Central Asia [3].

Then it was the turn of the Parthians to free themselves. They were a semi-nomadic people of Indo-European stock living in what is now the northern half of the Republic of Iran. This secession was indeed, as Ghirshman remarks, an evident proof of the fundamental weakness of the Seleucid Empire. However, there was as yet no sign that the Parthian nation was to revive the Persian imperial tradition. Yet Antiochus III (223-187) was a strong prince; he demonstrated Seleucid power on his eastern frontier and subjected Persia again to a state of vassalage. But the unfortunate idea of conquering Macedonia was to prove his ruin.

THE SELEUCID EMPIRE

-·-·- : the original extent
//// : conquests in Asia Minor and Syria
····· : empire of Antiochus IV

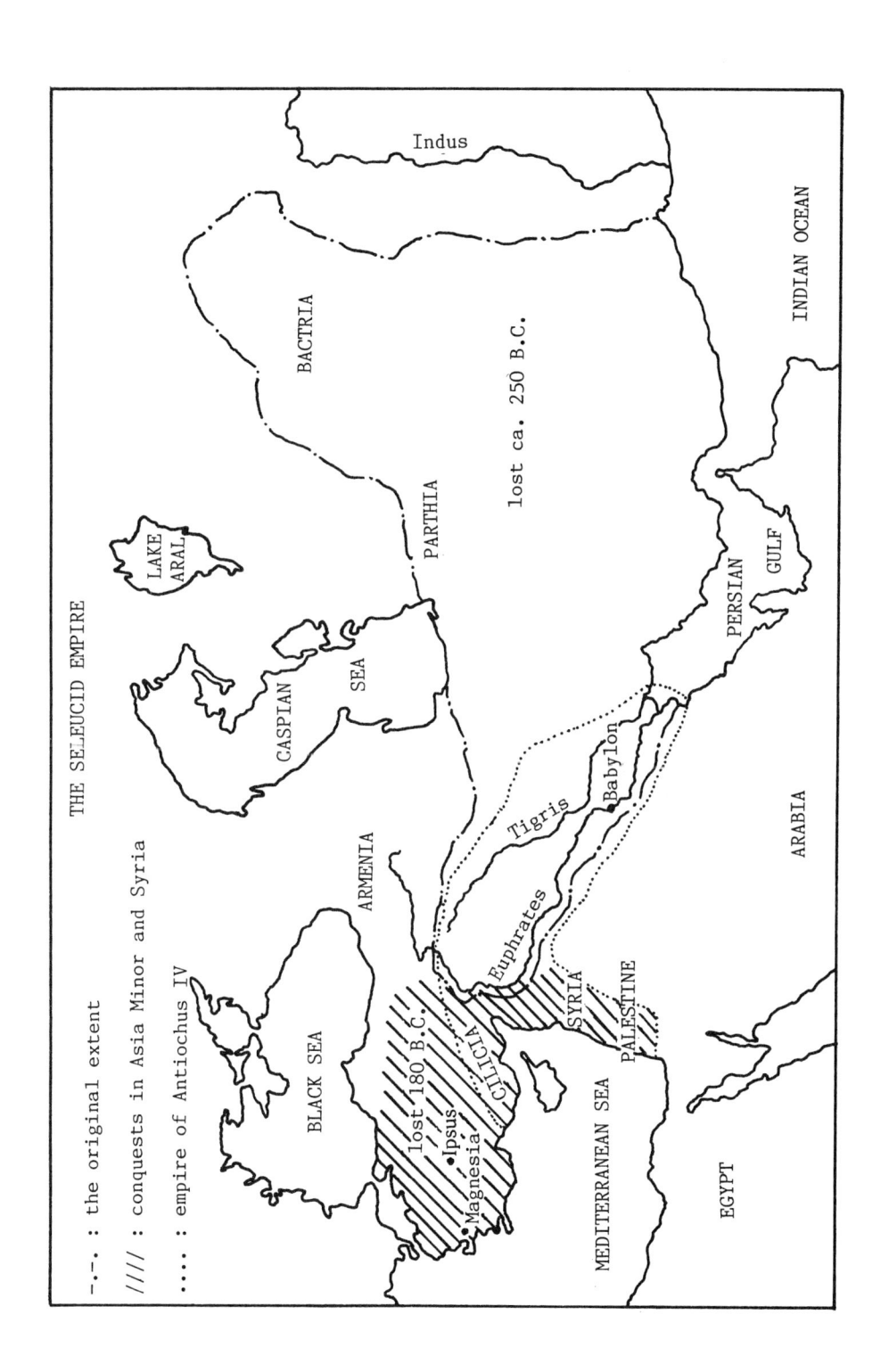

As if he were a new Xerxes he crossed to Europe where he was to encounter not only the stubborn resistance of the Macedonians but the full blast of Roman military power. Rome, extending her sphere of influence steadily eastward, had no need of a competitor in the Balkans. Antiochus was crushingly defeated by Scipio Africanus, the first Roman to make his way into these volumes, in the Battle of Magnesia; as a consequence the king was forced to recross the straits to Asia Minor. There he had to sign the Peace of Apamaea in 188 B.C. according to the terms of which he had to cede all his possessions west of the Taurus, that is virtually the whole of Asia Minor. This territory was divided into a number of smaller kingdoms with Greek dynasties dependent on the favour of Rome. In the wake of this humiliating defeat Armenia tore herself free from Seleucid rule.

The kingdom that Antiochus III the Great left to his successor Antiochus IV (175-164) was only a remnant of the original Seleucid Empire. Nevertheless, it still had a sizeable extent, comprising as it did Mesopotamia, Cilicia, Syria and Palestine, with the Euphrates and the Tigris running through it diagonally. Antiochus IV, the fierce persecutor of the Jews, of whom I have already spoken in Volume IV (Chapter II), squandered the forces he needed so much for keeping his patrimony intact, by ceding to the old imperial dream. His attack on Ptolemaic Egypt remained, however, unsuccessful. His still considerable kingdom did not survive his death for long. The Parthians succeeded in occupying Mesopotamia; Syria, which, unfortunately for the Jews, also included Palestine, was all that remained of the Seleucid Empire. This meant the end not only of a great empire but still more of all attempts to combine Greek and Persian civilization and to unite, politically, culturally, and intellectually, Europe and Asia. Now the old dualistic antagonism between the two continents could be revived again. It was, by the Parthians.

2. The Parthian Empire

a. 'The frontier of Europe'

The true founder of the Parthian Empire was King Mithridates I (163-138); he knew how to profit from the defeats the Seleucids had suffered. In about twenty years this ruler annexed large territories, Persia, Media and Mesopotamia, to his kingdom which, originally, only comprised the region to the south-east of the Caspian Sea between Bactria and Media. Mithridates' conquests made it as big as, in modern terms, the Republics of Iran and Iraq taken together. This king is sometimes compared to Cyrus, the founder of the Persian Empire. He too was a great administrator and legislator, an able commander in war, and, generally speaking, a magnanimous ruler, although he was, on occasion, ruthless and harsh. He doubtless considered himself the legitimate successor of the Persian emperors, since he too styled himself 'Great King'. The adoption of this title by Mithridates and his successors indicated that they intended to extend Parthian sway further and further westward.

Imperial dreams know no frontiers, and, as I explained in Volume IV (Chapter III), they recognize no other empires. In Toynbee's terms such an empire is 'universal'. In principle, it wants to absorb all the kingdoms and states that lie around it. In the foregoing volume I described the relationship between an empire and the states that do not belong to it as dualistic, since the empire, being a 'universal state', considers every other political entity as virtually non-existent. All those states can only acquire an existence of some sort by permitting themselves to be incorporated into the empire.

During the reign of Mithridates' successor Phraates II (138-128) the Seleucid king Antiochus VII Sidetes made a last attempt to recover Mesopotamia from Parthia. Initially successful he was finally beaten by his own incompetence, by the unpopularity of the Greeks with the Mesopotamians, and by the cunning military tactics of Phraates. He dealt Antiochus a crushing defeat and drove him from Mesopotamian

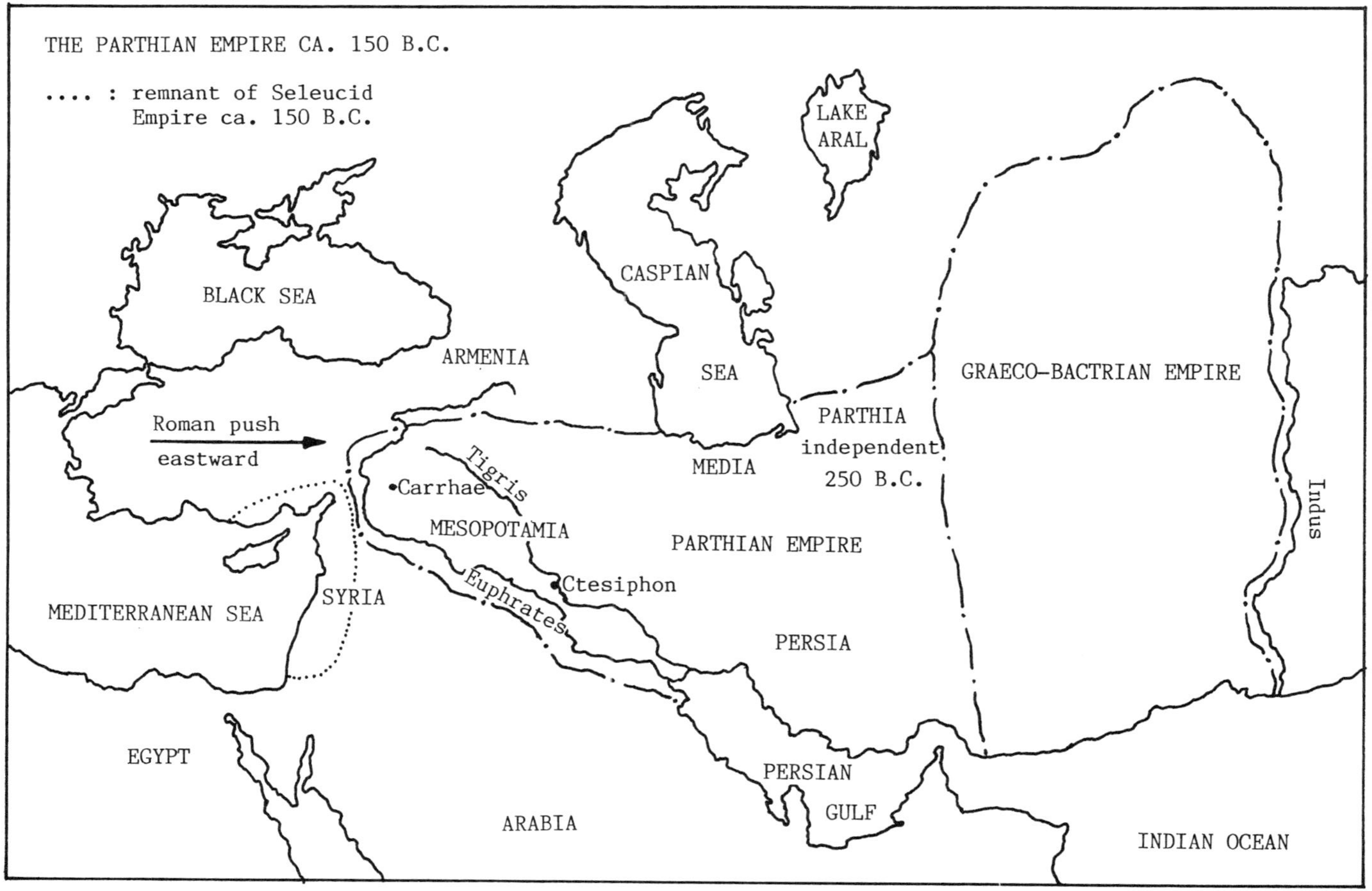
THE PARTHIAN EMPIRE CA. 150 B.C.
.... : remnant of Seleucid
Empire ca. 150 B.C.
LAKE
ARAL
CASPIAN
SEA
BLACK SEA
ARMENIA
Roman push
eastward
GRAECO–BACTRIAN EMPIRE
PARTHIA
independent
250 B.C.
MEDIA
Tigris
Carrhae
MESOPOTAMIA
PARTHIAN EMPIRE
Indus
Ctesiphon
Euphrates
SYRIA
MEDITERRANEAN SEA
PERSIA
EGYPT
PERSIAN
GULF
ARABIA
INDIAN OCEAN

soil. Ghirshman says that this date, 129 B.C., was 'a fateful date for Hellenism', for its cause in Mesopotamia and Bactria was definitely lost. As this author puts it : "The frontier of Europe was withdrawn to the Euphrates" [4].

Perhaps this frontier would have been pushed back still further westward but for the invasions of nomadic tribes in the northeast. They made an end of the Graeco-Bactrian kingdom and penetrated in force into Parthia; Phraates II fell in 128 B.C. when trying to resist them. But King Mithridates II (123-87) taught these Asian nomads such a lesson that neither he nor his successors had even to fear them again. In the politics of that period Mithridates II occupied a curious middle position, for he established relations with the Emperor of China with whom he concluded a commercial treaty, as well as with the Romans. In 92 B.C., when Roman power already extended to the Euphrates, this king sent an embassy to Lucius Sulla with the offer of a treaty of alliance. Sulla, an arrogant Roman if ever there was one, rejected this offer so contemptuously that the Great King not only felt deeply insulted but also realized that two such great powers never could become true allies [5]. From that moment onward the ferocious dualistic relationship of the two empires took its inexorable course.

b. A head brought to the king

In the next three decades Parthia was harassed by considerable internal strife. In consequence she failed to establish herself in Syria; the Romans became the masters of this country in the year 64/63 B.C., and also of the adjoining Palestine which had belonged to Syria for centuries. Parthia was also confronted with growing Roman strength in Asia Minor; from a sphere of Roman influence it was steadily turning into a conglomerate of Roman provinces. The coastal and western part of it, the highly civilized Kingdom of Pergamum (more or less the extent of the old Kingdom of Lydia), became a Roman province in 133 B.C., when its last king made Rome his heir. The adjoining regions on the southern coast fell into Roman hands after the defeat of Antiochus III; Cilicia, further east along the same coast, for so long a a part of Syria, became a Roman province in 102 B.C. On the coast of the Black Sea the western part, Bithynia, was annexed in 74 B.C., to be followed by Pontus, the eastern part, in 64 B.C. The old Hittite heartland in the centre of Anatolia was not yet a province of Rome, but there too, in Galatia and Cappadocia, the Roman presence was blatant.

All this meant that Rome was steadily creeping nearer and nearer to the Euphrates and was perhaps even looking beyond. For Crassus, the Roman proconsul of Syria, tried to profit from Parthia's weakness. Against the wishes of the Senate in Rome he crossed the Euphrates with his army believing that the weakened country, at grips with secessionist Armenia in the north, would fall an easy prey to him. A few weeks later very little remained of the too confident Roman army. The Battle of Carrhae, in 53 B.C., about sixty miles east of the river in Mesopotamia, became a horrible carnage in which more than half of the Roman soldiers perished, among them Crassus himself and his son; thousands of men were led away in captivity, and only a quarter of the invading force found their way back home.

Faced with the danger of annexation by Rome Parthia had suddenly rediscovered herself. Poor Crassus' head was brought to the Parthian king while he sat watching a performance of Euripides' 'The Bacchants'; the irony of the situation is that this play also is about a severed head. Obviously there were still some traces of Hellenic influence in Parthia. The captured eagles of the defeated legions were hung in Parthian temples. The hapless prisoners of war, according to Ghirshman, were settled in the oasis of Merv (now in the Soviet-Republic of Turcmenia), where a number of them became integrated into Parthian society [6].

c. A delicate balance

After this event Rome came to realize that, in spite of temporary setbacks, Parthia was a great power, the only one that was left in the Middle East. The reverse was also true. When a Parthian army tried to profit from the Roman disaster by invading Syria, it proved unable to maintain itself there. In the next ten years Rome and Parthia lived in a state of armed peace. But the Parthians would never feel at ease with the Romans so near. In 41 B.C. King Orodes II (57-37/36) decided to drive the Romans from Syria and Asia Minor. The first successes of the Parthian army were highly impressive. Syria and Palestine were conquered; Jerusalem too fell into their hands, and Herod I, a Roman vassal, was ousted. To the west the whole of Asia Minor was overrun; the Parthians even reached the Aegan coast. It looked as though Rome had lost all her Asian possessions. But once again the tables were turned, this time against the Parthians. Roman reinforcements were rapidly brought over to which the Parthian heavy cavalry proved no match. The Romans soon succeeded in recovering all that they had lost.

However, the balance was not restored. Thirsting after revenge for these humiliating defeats, Marc Antony, Caesar's one-time friend, appeared on the stage. When after the death of Orodes II Parthia again was plunged into confusion, he invaded Armenia in 34 B.C., penetrated as far as the Caucasus Mountains, and made this country into a Roman protectorate. Trying to outflank Parthia still more - perhaps in preparation for an all-out attack - he marched on eastward through Media. But it seemed to be fated that in this long struggle between Rome and Parthia both sides constantly tended to overrate their possibilities. The Parthians succeeded in capturing Antony's baggage and siege train; the Roman might consider himself lucky that he escaped with his life and that of his soldiers.

Once more Rome realized how strong Parthia really was; all dreams of repeating Alexander's drive to the Indus were given up. On the other hand the many internal conflicts in Parthia made Rome aware that this country never would be able to threaten her power in Asia Minor seriously. With Armenia definitely in Roman hands, in case of emergency Parthia could be invaded from Syria and Armenia at the same time, from the south and the north that is. This made the balance of power more stable. Both parties henceforward tried to behave themselves in a moderate way. The Romans did so under the guidance of their sensible emperor Augustus; that the Parthians also underwent a change of heart became evident in 20 B.C., when they returned the eagles of Carrhae to Rome.

Nevertheless, the Parthians felt some painful thorns in their side. Their kings, the last of the direct Arsacid line, without actually becoming vassals, were heavily leaning over to the Romans; one of their princes was even educated in Rome. In the eyes of his nobles this king was much too western, and this became his undoing; they murdered him in 10 A.D. This was in fact the end of the Arsacid dynasty; his successors came from a female line. Another circumstance that pained Parthian national sentiment was that Armenia remained under Roman influence; the last Arsacid princes were accused of being much too lenient on this score. In 66 A.D. an Armenian vassal king was triumphantly received in Rome where the emperor Nero personally put the crown on his head. The Roman presence in Armenia, although from time to time merely a token one, meant to the Parthians that Rome had not ceased to interfere in their affairs. However, in spite of certain oscillations in the balance of power, on the whole the first century A.D. was a peaceful one; the moderate Parthian policy of Augustus was pursued by his successors.

d. Trajan retraces Alexander's footsteps

A great change occurred with the advent of the emperor Trajan. The balance of power was completely overthrown when this Roman ruler got it into his head to revive the old imperial dream of Alexander and to become the successor of Cyrus and Darius at the same time. Under his rule the Roman Empire reached its greatest extent. It already was a threatening sign that he annexed the regions on the northern shores of the Black Sea - the so-called Kingdom of the Bosporus - and incorporated them in the Roman provinces of Asia Minor. In this way the Black Sea became a Roman inner sea. Then he descended in force on the peoples and tribes of the Caucasus region and subjected them; next he invaded Armenia where he made an end of the long line of vassal princes of Rome and made this country into a Roman province.

And now, in 114 B.C., what the Parthians had always feared would happen came to pass : the Roman legions invaded their country from the north. Without meeting much resistance Trajan crossed the country following the course of the Euphrates till he reached and captured Ctesiphon, the Parthians' proud capital, the ruins of which still stand. He then marched down the Tigris to the Persian Gulf. The whole country lay prostrate at his feet. The old dualistic antagonism of the two empires had now reached its most radical stage, since the total destruction of Rome's opposite pole, the Parthian Empire, seemed at hand. On his return march north-eastward Trajan visited Babylon where he meditated some time in the room where Alexander had died. Could anything have shown more clearly what was on his mind? He even seems to have been contemplating retracing the footsteps of the Macedonian army to India.

Trajan, however, made the same mistake as Crassus and Mark Antony. He had seriously underestimated the resilience of the Parthians and of the subjected peoples of the Middle East. Revolts broke out everywhere in the rear of the Roman army, in particular among the Jews and other Semitic peoples. Armenia too rose in rebellion; the Parthians themselves started a guerilla war against the invaders. Trajan hastily hurried back and died soon afterwards. What then followed in Parthia bore a great similarity to what happened in Germany in the wake of the Napoleonic wars : national feeling was strongly aroused. Trajan's successor Hadrian gave up this aggressive policy and restored the old balance, with the Euphrates as the traditional frontier.

This balance of power was as impossible to maintain in Antiquity as it was in eighteenth century Europe. The reinvigorated Parthians invaded Syria; a fierce Roman counter-attack followed that brought the legions under the eagle for the second time to Ctesiphon, which was burnt down in 165. But now the plague broke out, probably imported by the Roman legions themselves. In one of the first great bouts of this illness that was to scourge Europe and Asia regularly for centuries on end, the epidemic spread over the whole of the Middle East and over large parts of Europe. The decimated Roman army had to return. Another attempt, this time by the emperor Septimius Severus in 197, was an equal failure. Thus, as Ghirshman sums it up, "two and a half centuries (of) Roman attempts to reduce (Parthia) to vassalage had ended in failure" [7].

3. The Sasanian Empire

a. The Persian renaissance

Great national revivals often begin with what seems to be a retreat to the innermost core of the country. For a very long time the policy of the Arsacid kings and their successors from the female line was mainly directed westward; the continual struggle with the Roman Empire monopolized their attention. In consequence little is known of the history of the old Iranian heartland that the Greeks called 'Persis' and that we, following them, call 'Persia', but that was, and still is, dubbed 'Fars' by the inhabitants themselves. It was from there that the Persian expansion of the sixth and fifth centuries B.C. began. The memory of the famous Achaemenid emperors was kept alive by the names some later Persian rulers bore such as 'Daryav' = Darius, or 'Artakhshatr' in which we easily recognize the name of Artaxerxes [8].

The eponymous ancestor of the Sasanian dynasty is said to have been a certain Sasan (or Sassan) who lived in the second century A.D. and who was a fire priest in the Anahita temple at Istakhr, not far from the Persian Gulf. His son Papak (Papek, Pabagh) succeeded him in this calling, married the daughter of a local dynast in 208 and took on the role of a (still petty) worldy ruler. This is usually considered the beginning of the Sasanian era [9]. The move was not, however, condoned by his overlord, the Parthian Emperor, probably because bitter experience had taught him that local princelets could develop into mighty sovereigns. If this was his foreboding, it did not deceive him. Papak overthrew one of the vassal kings in the region and started to style himself 'king'.

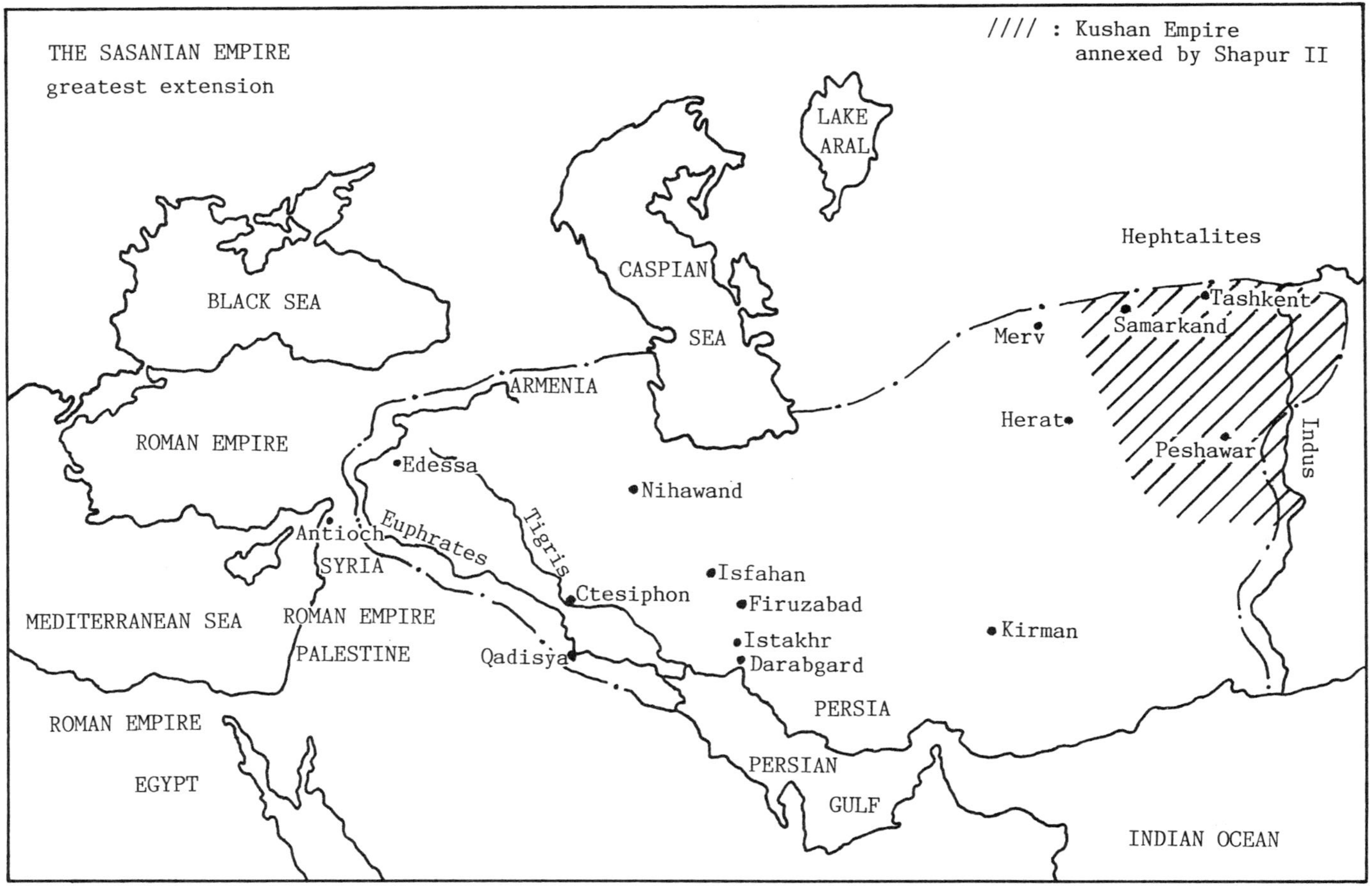
THE SASANIAN EMPIRE
greatest extension
//// : Kushan Empire
annexed by Shapur II
LAKE
ARAL
Hephtalites
BLACK SEA
CASPIAN
SEA
Tashkent
Samarkand
Merv
ARMENIA
ROMAN EMPIRE
Herat
Peshawar
Indus
Edessa
Nihawand
Antioch
Euphrates
Tigris
SYRIA
Isfahan
Ctesiphon
Firuzabad
MEDITERRANEAN SEA
ROMAN EMPIRE
Kirman
Istakhr
PALESTINE
Qadisya
Darabgard
PERSIA
ROMAN EMPIRE
PERSIAN
EGYPT
GULF
INDIAN OCEAN

One of his younger sons, Ardashir (Artakhshatr, Artaxerxes), fulfilled a high military function in the city of Darabgard (Darabjird), between Istakhr and the Persian Gulf. Operating from there on his own initiative, he defeated a number of provincial kinglets, taking good care to kill all of them. Fate came to his help when his elder brother, who was destined to succeed his father, died; on Papak's death, Ardashir became king. Although his other brothers acquiesced in the succession, this bloody man disposed of all of them with the sword. More at his ease now he began to extend his sway. First of all he captured Kirman far out to the east, and Gabai (now Isfahan) to the north of his own power base; these conquests brought the whole centre of Persis under his control. The littoral along the Persian Gulf followed. Not one of the small princes of Fars was able to withstand him. About 220 he was virtually master of old Persia, calling himself its king; in Gor, now Firuzabad, at no great distance from the former Achaemenid residences of Persepolis and Pasargadae, he erected his royal palace and an adjoining fire temple.

The then reigning emperor of Parthia, Artabanus V (Ardewan in Parthian), viewed this rapid rise to power with profound misgivings. He had refused the royal title to Papak; he refused it also to Ardashir. First the emperor sent one of his eastern satraps to meet the king in battle; having defeated this underling Ardashir marched westward seeking an armed encounter with his suzerain. Three times he was victorious, the last and decisive battle taking place near the old Persian capital of Susa on April 24, 224. Artabanus, the last Parthian emperor, was killed, as Sasanian tradition has it, by Ardashir, who smashed his enemy's head with his foot [10]. He is said to have taken the skin of the dead emperor with him, together with the heads of his other beaten enemies [11]. Ardashir victoriously entered Ctesiphon, the Parthian capital, where he was crowned king in 226; as Sasanian emperor we know him as Ardashir I. 370 years of Arsacid rule and Parthian supremacy were now over; five and a half centuries after the death of the last Achaemenid emperor, another Persian king had established himself on the imperial throne.

b. A Roman emperor down on his knees

Ardashir I had to begin his reign by bringing down a pro-Arsacid coalition mainly led by Armenia and supported by the Romans. In the end the new emperor remained victorious although it took him ten years of continuous fighting to subdue and annex Armenia. Roman power was firmly pushed back beyond the Euphrates. To his son, Shapur I (241-272), he left a well-organized new Persian Empire. In terms of modern states this empire, at the beginning of Shapur's reign, comprised Iraq, Iran, and most of Pakistan, its most eastern towns being Pattala, Herat, and Merv.

However stable this inheritance was, he must have viewed his situation with some uneasiness. Beyond the Euphrates the Romans were still firmly established; Shapur, of course, knew that they considered every power east of this river as a menace. North of the Caucasus there was considerable movement among the nomads who tried to descend through the passes and invade Armenia. Finally, far out to the east, a new power had arisen, that of the Kushans. In all probability these were Scythians who, coming from the steppes of Southern Russia, were gradually penetrating into eastern Iran and into India. In the first century A.D. they were firmly established along the Amu Darja and occupied a large part of Afghanistan including the region where the modern capital of Kabul is situated; they also settled themselves east of the Indus and along this river southward to the point where it flows into the Indian Ocean. They also pressed on westward into Iran. In this way a large Kushan Empire had originated that, in the second century A.D., knew how to profit from the commercial traffic between east and west. The last Parthian emperors already viewed these developments with dismay; the Kushanites were their commercial competitors, and, what was worse, the Romans tried to enter into contact with them, attempting in this way to exert pressure on Parthia from both the east and the west.

Probably Shapur thought the Kushan Empire the lesser danger of the two. To all intents and purposes its rulers do not seem to have dreamt of pushing westward through the arid Iranian desert. But although it did not constitute a military threat, it was a kind of Roman ally as well as a formidable competitor in commerce. Shapur marched eastward and had no great difficulty in making an end of Kushan power. The days of Alexander the Great seemed to have returned with the Sasanian emperor triumphantly entering cities as far away as Samarkand and Tashkent on the Syr Darja, both in Soviet-Uzbekistan. He also victoriously captured Peshawar in what is now Pakistan, one of the Kushanite royal residences. Finally he deposed the Kushan ruler and gave his realm over to vassal princes who had to recognize the Persian ruler as their suzerain. Thus nearly six hundred years after the death of the last Achaemenid, another Persian prince succeeded in establishing Iranian overlordship in the farthest eastern parts of the old empire, and, as the heir of Alexander, even in the regions beyond the Indus.

As a result of these relatively easy victories in the east, Shapur gave himself a curious but significant title : 'King of the Kings of Iran and of Non-Iran' [12]. This not only meant that the former Great Kings of Persia had found a worthy successor but, still more, that he was treading in the footsteps of all those claimants to universal power who had followed one another since the days of the earliest Sumerian kings. As I explained in Volume IV (Chapter III), these rulers all considered themselves 'universal'; in principle, all other states and tribes were theirs. These were, as I stated there, seen as 'non-existent', as having no political identity. The only fully real, authentic political entity was the 'universal state'. Shapur I expressed this by dubbing the rest of the world 'non-Iran'. In styling himself in this way he situated himself in the age-old tradition of radical political dualism that was characteristic of all the emperors since Sumer.

Having come back from the Indus Shapur then turned against what he considered his most dangerous enemy, Rome. Although he suffered some setbacks he was on the whole successful and succeeded in laying a firm hand on Mesopotamia in 244. But the greatest victories were still to come in the days of the Roman emperor Valerian.

Waging the war offensively Shapur invaded Syria, took Antioch, and defeated Valerian himself in 260 in the Battle of Edessa. The Roman emperor was taken prisoner, together with seventy thousand of his legionaries - a real 'dies ater' for the Roman Empire. Shapur put his prisoners to good use by settling them in specially built towns (on the model of a Roman military camp) and engaged them in a great building activity; according to Ghirshman, some of their works in Khuzistan, like bridges and roads, are still in use [13]. On a series of reliefs near Bichapur in the Fars country proud Shapur had himself pictured as the great victor, with the Roman emperor on his knees before him and the laurel crown still on his head [14]. Not much is known of Valerian after this event; very probably he died in capitivity.

c. A brother kept at bay

Great as this victory was, it by no means meant the end of hostilities with Rome; as of old Mesopotamia and Armenia remained the bones of contention between the two empires. When Bahram II (276-293) was coping with revolts in the eastern part of his state, the Romans succeeded in occupying the northern half of Mesopotamia and the adjoining Armenia; the Persian king had to acquiesce in this. During the reign of his successor, the Emperor Narseh (293-303), a still more serious defeat by the Romans resulted in the cession of every square mile west of the Tigris. Thus the two greatest events in the age-long struggle between the Parthians-Persians and Rome, the capture of a Roman emperor, and the loss of Mesopotamia-Armenia occurred within a life-time.

Hoping that the glorious name of Shapur would bring luck to the Sasanian Empire, King Shapur II (309-379) demonstrated Persian power in the east as well as in the west. On his eastern frontier he beat down attempts by the Kushanites to re-establish themselves; he annexed the territory of the old Kushan states which meant that Iranian sovereignty now reached to far beyond the Indus. Cultural expansion went still further; traces of it are found in Chinese Turkestan and in Chine herself [15]. Shapur profited from the internal troubles in the always unhappy country of Armenia for re-opening the war against the Romans. He experienced no difficulty in occupying Armenia but in Mesopotamia things went less smoothly. There were victories as well as defeats.

In 356 King Shapur II, as a response to a Roman peace offer, addressed a very telling letter to the Roman emperor Constantine II, the tone of which could not be more condescending. Presenting himself as 'Shapur, king of kings, companion of the stars, brother of the sun and the moon', he observed with satisfaction that 'his brother (the Roman emperor)' had rediscovered the right road. He reminded his brother that his (Shapur's) forefathers once extended their rule as far as Macedonia (by which words he claimed to be the legitimate successor to Xerxes and Darius). Being equal to the ancient kings and even their better, he felt it his duty to reoccupy Armenia and Mesopotamia which had both been fraudulently severed from his country. He, Shapur, could not believe that his fellow-emperor could be insolent enough to authorize conquests that were only the result of fraud and not of valour. In case the Iranian ambassadors should return without a satisfying answer, the Persian king would see himself forced to march against his brother with all his military resources. But his brother, presenting himself as 'always victorious on land an sea', curtly refused to give in; he admitted that the Romans had suffered some defeats but in the end they always proved the victors [16].

In consequence of this unfruitful exchange of letters hostilities were re-opened, this time by the Romans under the personal command of Julian the Apostate. This emperor fell fighting in 363. His successors left the contested areas to the Sasanian king who annexed Armenia. The dispute with Rome became still more complicated and embittered by the rise of Christianity in both empires; since Constantine the Great even the Roman emperors were Catholics. The new religion was steadily gaining ground in Armenia too which caused bitter rivalry between the Christian faction that was pro-Roman, and the non-Christian one that leaned towards Persia. Shapur did not welcome at all the establishment of Catholicism within his frontiers, since he saw it as a threat to the unity of his realm; very probably he suspected its adherents of being pro-Roman. Remaining himself 'the adorator of Mazdah the god', and 'the most glorious of the adorators of Ormuzd', that is remaining a faithful adherent of the old Iranian religion, he took to persecuting the Christians in the most cruel way.

d. The last apogee of Sasanian power

A bleak century followed. The Iranian kings were, as Ghirshman states, 'devoid of personality' [17]. The situation of the empire deteriorated from year to year. The emperors were, almost without exception, weak rulers; there was endless religious strife, the Huns were making incursions from the Caucasus southward, sometimes even threatening Antioch. In the east a new power was rising, the Hephtalite kingdom that was situated in the formerly Kushanite region; originally only federates of Iran they were now making themselves independent. One of the Sasanian kings, Peroz (459-484), even fell into their hands and had to be ransomed. These former vassals of the Sasanian Empire were now, at the end of the fifth century, behaving as masters exacting tribute from those who formally still were their suzerains, and interfering constantly in Iranian affairs. The Byzantine Empire which had succeeded in the meantime the Roman Empire in the west, did not profit from the disturbances in the neighbouring state since its rulers, also menaced by the Huns, thought it dangerous to weaken their rival too much.

The Sasanian Empire experienced its final apogee during the reign of King Chosroes I (531-579), surnamed 'Anosharvan', which means 'him with the immortal soul'. For the last time Persia had a ruler who knew how to impose his will on his country. He brought the warring factions to peace and re-ordered the political and religious affairs of the state in the most sensible way. In the north, building new fortresses, the king held the Huns at bay; in the south he pushed on in Arabia as far as the Yemen; in the east he crushed Hephtalite power and liberated Iran from the humiliating tribute. With the Huns now safely behind the Caucasus he could permit himself to ignore that subtle and tacit 'gentleman's agreement' of the fifth century with Byzantium and revive the old dualistic antagonism. Periods of war and peace followed each other; Syria and Mesopotamia saw much fighting and suffered much devastation without either of the two parties definitely gaining the upper hand. When Chosroes died in 579, matters were still undecided.

The end was at hand. Under his successor, less able than Chosroes I, the war with the Byzantines continued relentlessly, with both sides claiming successes. For a short time under King Chosroes II (590-628) the most glorious days of the old Achaemenid emperors seemed to have returned. In 611 his armies conquered Syria and Palestine, where in Jerusalem fifty thousand Christians were butchered, entered Egypt in 616, and followed the Nile to the frontiers of Ethiopia. Later his victorious generals crossed the whole of Asia Minor and even laid siege to Constantinople. The end of Roman power seemed to have come. But again, as always in the old, old struggle between east and west, flux and reflux closely followed each other. The Byzantine emperor, Heraclius, counter-attacked, reconquered Asia Minor, reached the Caucasus, and from there descended the Tigris valley till he could beleaguer Ctesiphon, the old capital, that had been made more splendid than ever by Chosroes I. There Chosroes II, hated by his subjects for his heavy taxes and his constant levying of men for his army, the persecutor of the Christians, was murdered. No less than twelve kings in fourteen years followed him, just as ghostlike as the eight kings conjured up by the witches for Macbeth.

Finally some semblance of order was restored when King Yazgard III in 632 succeeded to the throne. Not much of the ancient unity of the Sasanian Empire remained then. Actually the empire existed only on paper, the victorious generals ruling the provinces as though they were in fact kings. Then a storm arose from the side of the southern desert. The Arab caliph Omar, realizing very well how weak the once so powerful Sasanian Empire had become, sent out his Islamic forces against it. In 636 the last great Iranian general, Rustam, encountered the Arabs at Qadisiya in Mesopotamia where the battle raged for three whole days. Rustam was killed in the fighting; the imperial standard, the symbol of Sasanian power, fell into the victor's hands. Ctesiphon, with all her riches, was captured.

The Iranian army withdrew to the environs of Hamadan (Ecbatana) in Media, where Yazgard himself fought the last battle in the plain of Nihawand, in 642. Once again the royal army was crushed. The Arabs, under the green banner of the Prophet, then occupied Media and Armenia, and next invaded Fars, or Persia, from where both the Achaemenid and Sasanian dynasties had originated. The emperor, who had nothing left but his title 'king of kings' [18], fled northward till he reached Merv; it is said that he had four thousand courtiers and servants with him, but not a single soldier. Realizing, however, that the governor of Merv was trying to lay hands on him, he fled on, as legend tells us, clad in his mantle of gold-brocate, but all alone. Tired as he was he found a refuge in a mill. There the miller, not recognizing the emperor but coveting that fine mantle, assassinated his guest. Thus, in 651 or 652, the Sasanian Empire ended in the same way as its Achaemenid predecessor had ended [19].

4. Orthodox Zoroastrianism : a recapitulation

As it is possible that the reader has not had an opportunity for consulting my Volume IV, I feel obliged to recapitulate shortly the most essential part of its Chapter IV. This treats of ancient Persia, the main body of it being devoted to Zoroastrianism, the famous old religion of Iran.

Of its founder, Zoroaster - which name is the Greek version of his old Persian name 'Zarathustra' - we know precious little. Scholars suggest that he lived at some time in the eight centuries between 1400 and 600 B.C. He was very probably - although not all experts agree - born in Chorasmia, in the north-eastern part of Iran. Part of his life he spent with a tribe wandering between Lake Aral and the Oxus basin (the Oxus is now called the Amu Darya). He was married, perhaps more than once, and had several children. This prophet used to call himself a 'zaotar', that is a priest and, at the same time, a composer of hymns and a sacred poet. The possibility exists that a number of 'gathas' in the Avesta were composed by him; the gathas form the oldest and most authentically Zoroastrian part of the Avesta, the great collection of Iranian religious hymns, formulas, stories, and laws.

The core of Zoroaster's message is that, in the beginning, there was only one god, Ahura Mazda, the Wise Lord. Ahura Mazda is the Creator, he is good and he is holy, he is the father of all and everything; however, he did not bring forth what is evil. He is 'spenta' (an old Iranian word), that means he is 'working', causing effects that, self-evidently, are also good and holy. This supreme good 'spenta' is realized in a number of spirits that are called 'amesha spentas' which signifies something like 'Holy Immortals' or 'Bounteous Spirits'. These may be considered aspects of Ahura Mazda's being but then could equally well be independent gods. This last eventuality would mean an inroad on Zoroaster's apparently pure monotheism. Anyhow, the 'amesha spentas' are the godhead's gifts to man. The principal one of them is the 'Spenta Mainyu', the 'Holy Spirit'; there are places in the gathas where he too is an independent spirit or deity, and others where he is identified with Ahura Mazda himself. The latter version seems to have been preferred by the orthodox.

The Spenta Mainyu is one half of a twin, the other half being the 'Evil Spirit' or 'Angra (or Ahra) Mainyu'. Angra Mainyu too is an uncreated being existing from the beginning. From this it follows that, if Zoroaster's system is monotheistic, it is not seamlessly so; his was not a homogenous world. The word 'twins' would, on the face of it, mean that both spirits had the same father, this parent being Ahura Mazda. But since this divinity is not the origin of whatsoever kind of evil, we must very probably not take this word 'twins' in a strictly literal sense. The term 'twins' in all probablity means that both spirits are coeval but does not say that they are related. Its use betrays the problem with which the Prophet saw himself confronted : he could impossibly deny that there is evil in the world, but, at the same time, his sublime notion of Ahura Mazda forbade him to ascribe its origin to the Creator. So there was no other possibility left than to make evil into an independent spirit just as eternal as Ahura Mazda.

It will be clear that Zoroastrian religion shows a strongly dualistic character. In the Prophet's view Good and Evil, both uncreated, existed side by side in the universe. Angra Mainyu is a divine being who chose to be bad by his own choice. This means that his choice was made in the sphere of the divine, beyond and outside human history. In this way Zoroaster succeeded in solving his painful problem, that of combining his monotheistic (or monistic) starting-point with his dualistic views. The dual list of good and bad entities - the spentas and their opposites presents us with a clear case of dualism. Every good spenta has its bad counterpart; the elements of each pair are utterly irreconcilable.

In fact, the whole universe is split up into two halves, that of Spenta Mainyu, and that of Angra Mainyu; these two are involved in constant warfare. This means that the cosmos is dualistically divided into two parts each ruled by one of the leading mainyus. Human life forms no exception to this. Here too we find a permanent battle. Human beings have the moral obligation to choose between good and evil. Those who opt for the Good and side with Spenta Mainyu, or Ahura Mazda, will receive the bounteous gifts of this god as his spentas. Those who prefer to be bad will have all kinds of evil on their hands. Of the good spentas and their opposites I mention here only the Good Mind and the Bad one. To the Good Mind belong good opinions, praiseworthy thoughts, ennobling ideas, and also the actions that follow from them. The Evil Spirit leads to bad thoughts, wicked words, and blameworthy deeds. Another pair of opposed spentas is Truth and Lie (Drug). 'Drug' (or 'Druj') is the source of all possible social evils, of all that is crooked and not fair and square. But in the end Truth will triumph over Drug. It was the holy and stern duty of Zoroastrians to combat lies and untruth; in consequence they must, in social life, keep apart from the wicked as far as possible.

All this means that mankind is partioned into a good and a bad half which are fundamentally and inimically opposed. The same sharp dividing line that runs through the cosmos divides the good from the bad in this life and in the hereafter. This division will be sealed for ever in eternity when the good and the bad part ways for different abodes never to meet again. At the moment of death the good will definitely be separated from those who are evil. The wicked will find their eternal abode in a place of darkness; the good will attain eternal bliss in the 'House of Song'. It is at this point that Zoroaster's dualism shows its most stringent character. Good and Evil, the good and the wicked, will fight one another as long as the world lasts. But at the end the world will pass through the ordeal of fire. The flames of hell will consume all those who live the wicked way; their plight will be eternal. Then Ahura Mazda will establish on earth the 'second existence' over which he himself will reign. There the faithful will enjoy the perennial bliss of Paradise.

5. The Zervanite heresy

a. What about 'Ormuzd and Ahriman'?

It cannot be stressed often enough that orthodox Zoroastrianism starts with a monistic principle, to wit the existence of Ahura Mazda, the Creator. Let me repeat what I wrote in Volume IV, on page 298 : "The first principle of the universe is monistic, but just below this (highly abstract) level, dualism emerges. This dualism is relative for, in some form or other, it is dependent on Ahura Mazda who, in the end will have the last word". Zoroaster's world order is a spiritual order not to be expressed in terms of temporal logic (as we do). "In this order Ahura Mazda takes precedence over Angra Mainyu, simply because the Good is superior to Evil."

Up to this point I have studiously avoided to mention the names of 'Ormuzd and Ahriman'. What about them? Are not the dual entities of Zoroaster known in the west in this form? 'O(h)rmuzd' or 'O(h)rmazd' is a more recent form of 'Ahura Mazda'. 'Ahriman' too is a later (Pahlevi) rendering of an older name, this time that of 'Angra Mainyu'. From a linguistic point of view there is no compelling reason not to use the terms 'Ormuzd and Ahriman'. But there is another, more cogent argument. The west did not really feel at ease with Zoroaster's dualism of Good and Evil. As Mary Boyce writes, European scholars sought "to interpret Zoroastrianism according to their own ideas of a desirable monism". This meant that in their view Good and Evil should have a common origin - a notion that is abhorred by orthodox Zoroastrians. "It is, in essence, ... a heresy, ... evolved by unbelievers from a heresy (that was) a radical interpretation of Zoroaster's ancient and well-defined dualism" [20]. We shall now have to speak of this heresy.

b. The Zervanite myth

The Iranian doctrine that gave rise to this mutilated version of orthodox Zoroastrianism was 'Zervanism' (or 'Zurvanism'). Its full blast was felt only in the period after the Achaemenids, that is to say, after 330 B.C.; perhaps its development already began during the reigns of the later rulers of this dynasty, in the earlier periods of the fourth century B.C. However, in all matters regarding Zoroastrian chronology one must be treading very carefully. The word 'zervan' or 'zurvan', occurs in the Avesta; in its earlier sections it even denotes a minor deity called 'Zervan'. This Iranian word means 'time'. Although Zervan was no more than a very subordinate divine being, this personification meant, nevertheless, that time began to be hypostatized as 'Time'.

Zervanism had a slow growth the stages of which are unknown to us. It probably was important in the centuries after the birth of Christ, in the Sasanian period that is. Early Christian authors living in the eastern part of the Catholic Church which then was rapidly spreading were fierce opponents of the Persian religion that they knew in its Zervanite variety. Very probably the Greek speaking Christian theologian Theodorus of Mopsuestia (ca. 350-428, Mopsuestia being a town in Cilicia, near the south-east coast of Asia Minor, where he was bishop) polemized extensively against the Persian religion. Except for a few fragments, all the writings of Theodorus are lost, but we find the main part of his argument in a work of an Armenian theologian, Eznik of Kolb, who died in 439. The work in which he, in all probability, is transcribing Theodorus is called 'Against the sects' and is written in Armenian. In a shortened form and stripped of the polemical remarks inserted into it by Eznik it runs as follows.

Before anything existed, even heaven and earth, there was a being called Zervan. During a period of a thousand years it (or he) was offering sacrifices with the intention of begetting a son. This son Zervan would name Ormizd; he was to become the creator of all that exists. But at the end of this thousand years he began doubting whether all this sacrificing really made sense. In fact, two sons were born to him, Ormizd, the fruit of his sacrifices, and Ahriman (spelled 'Ahrmn' in Armenian), the result of his doubts. When still in the womb Ormizd told his brother that their father had promised that the first-born would become king and creator of the universe. On hearing this Ahriman tore up his mother's body and placed himself before his father. But his father did not recognize him and said : "Who are you? You are dark and you smell bad". While they were quarreling Ormizd was born and joined them. Zervan at once recognized him as the son he had prayed for and made him a sacrificial priest in his place. Ahriman, however, vociferously protested claiming that his father promised to make a king of the son who first appeared before him. Wishing to remain true to his promise Zervan solved the dilemma in this way. Ahriman would be king for nine thousand years; after that Ormizd would become the great ruler. "And everything that Ormizd made was good and just, but that Ahriman created was evil and corrupt" [21].

A short analysis of this myth yields the following results. First of all, as a proper name 'Zervan' means 'Time'. In order to beget a son he needed a wife whom he made pregnant. In spite of the fact that for a long time Zervan is the sole being existing, there is, nevertheless, also a woman present. Who she is and how she came into existence is not explained. It is very important to notice that Zoroaster's great god, Ahura Mazda (here called Ormizd), as the origin of everything is replaced by Zervan. Ormizd is relegated to the status of a secondary god who is not omnipotent but has to share power with his brother Ahriman.

Above all we must not overlook the fact that, although Ahriman is portrayed as the bad god, the real source of evil is Zervan. The dual principle already is present in him; Ahriman is representing the dark side of his father. As a consequence, the origin of evil is not to be found in mankind, not even in the universe; it dates from before the creation and is introduced into the cosmos from outside. Finally, the good and the bad are presented as equals; they have the same origin and the same rights (expressed by the fact that they are 'twins'). Both of them account for one half of the universe in which, therefore, good and evil are present in equal parts. Could anyone imagine a more tellingly dualistic story?

Nevertheless, some outstanding scholars contend that Zervanism is less dualistic than orthodox Zoroastrianism. They aver that, whereas in the orthodox version everything starts with a dual(istic) principle, Zervanism, with its one original god Zervan, has a monistic background. Several objections can be urged against this. First, as I already argued, original Zoroastrianism is primarily monistic since Ahura Mazda has pride of place in it; its unmistakable dualism is relative. Then, while it is true that in Zervanism everything depends on the Time god, his uniqueness is, nevertheless, somewhat impaired by the fact that there is an unexplainable woman about. Third, the god Zervan is not really important to Zervanites; the god whom they honour is Ahura Mazda (Ormuzd) for which reason they call themselves 'Mazdaites'. In other words, their so-called monism is so vague and abstract that it does not really play a role. To all intents and purposes, the Zervanite ideology is wholly dominated by the inexorable enmity of Ormuzd and Ahriman. In my opinion, therefore, Zervanism, in spite of appearances, is more radically dualistic than orthodox Zoroastrianism.

c. Finite and infinite deities

Like all heretics, Zervanites appealed to orthodox scripture to justify their opinion. In one of the gathas that are considered to stem from Zoroaster's own hand [22] we find it stated in as many words that the Good Spirit and the Destructive One are 'twins'. Now, as I already argued in Volume IV and as I repeated in this volume, it would be wholly contrary to the Prophet's thought to take this literally; this would make Ahura Mazda the real father of the Evil Spirit which, according to original Zoroastrian doctrine, is impossible. But later heretics seized upon this passage and explained it in a fundamentalistic sense. Since the Good and the Evil Spirits, called by the Zervanites Ormuzd (Ormizd) and Ahriman, were, according to them, biological twins, they must needs have a common father. This father could not be Ahura Mazda, because their Holy Spirit was not the Prophet's Amesha Spenta but Ormuzd, whose name is a form of Ahura Mazda. Thus the original divine being and the begetter of the twin spirits, that is of both good and evil, became Zervan or 'Time'.

Zaehner explains that Ormuzd and Ahriman both had their own sphere, the first 'on high in endless light', the second 'below in endless darkness'. Having each their own allotted time and space, either of them was a finite deity. But of course the Zervanites needed an infinite god; this they found in Zervan, or Infinite Time [23]. In fact, believers venerate him as 'Zervan akarana', or 'boundless time'. They see him as fourfold, as the great regulator of the course of time, he also comprises the sun, the moon, and the zodiac [24]. The connection is that Infinite Time - infinite since it already existed before the universe was created - brought forth the finite time which dominates the run of the world and of history.

Zervan is only nominally the high god of Zervanism; the fact that those whom we - not themselves! - call 'Zervanites' are named after him must not mislead us. As Widengren says, Zervan is an abstract principle rather than a really living god. This scholar calls him a 'deus otiosus', an otiose divinity wo easily may be left out of account by the members of the sect. He is not the object of a cult; no sacrifices are offered to him. He is only there to explain why there are dual and opposed principles in the universe. These, Ormuzd and Ahriman, are the deities that really count for the Zervanites [25].

The version of the Zervanite myth, as given by Eznik, is, of course, of a fairly late date, and may, therefore, show some additions that are not to be found in the original tale. By a stroke of good luck we possess a short report by Eudemus of Rhodus who lived in the second half of the fourth century B.C. [26]. Eudemus categorically states that the Magians call the intelligible and unified whole partly time, partly space; from here the distinction between the good and the evil demon originates. This testimony is important because it dates from the latest Achaemenid period.

From the first century A.D. we have a report by Plutarch, in his 'On Isis and Osiris', which is valuable but must be handled with some circumspection. According to him, 'the great majority and the wisest of men' believe that there are two gods, who are rivals, one of them the maker of all that is good, and the other of all that is evil. Some call the better one a god, and the other a demon, "as did, for instance, Zoroaster, the Magian" [27]. Plutarch then goes on to relate what he himself calls 'fabulous stories' about these two gods. However, what Plutarch tells us looks more like Zervanism than like orthodox Zoroastrianism.

d. The Magians

The queer thing is that Plutarch dubs Zoroaster a 'Magian' which he was not. The Magians, or 'magi', were an Iranian priestly caste with which, as Zaehner, speaking for nearly all Zoroastrain scholars, categorically states, Zoroastrianism "originally had nothing to do" [28]. Plutarch is decidely wrong here. His Greek term for 'Magian' is 'magos' ('magus' in Latin) which is a rendering of the Persian word 'magu'. The etymology of this word is uncertain. In the Avesta it occurs only once in the form of 'mogu' but there, as Benveniste assures us, it has nothing in common with 'magus'. It denotes a member of a certain social or territorial group [29]. There also exists a form 'maga' occurring somewhat oftener in the Avesta, in particular in the older, authentically Zoroastrian part of it. In these passages it does not indicate a person but the doctrine. "Reward me because of my great maga" [30]. " 'Maga' is the Zoroastrian doctrine that must be spread, the spiritual content of the preaching" [31]. Enough to show that orthodox Zoroastrianism did not know 'magi', Magians, as its priests.

Very probably the original term 'mogu', or 'magu', underwent a slow development. From 'member of a group' it came to mean a priestly clan or tribe, one of the six Median tribes. This same idea of a sacerdotal tribe we find in Israel with the Levites. In a well-known passage Herodotus says that it was not lawful for the Persians to offer a sacrifice without a magus being present [32]. Although, being Medians, the Magi in some measure were considered a 'Fremdkörper' in Persian society, they often enough occupied high functions. A Magus called Parthizeites was Comptroller of the King's Household in which capacity he deposed King Cambyses when he was absent campaigning in Egypt, and in his place installed a pretender on the throne [33].

The Magi were noted for some customs that were peculiar to them solely. They did not bury corpses but laid them in the open so that jackals and vultures could eat the flesh away. In this way the body was protected from decomposition which would defile it. Later this indeed became the custom of the Zoroastrian community, but when Herodotus mentioned it, it still was the custom of the Magi alone; he says that the Persians buried their dead in the earth [34]. Another of their customs was that they married within degrees of consanguinity, very probably in order to solidify the coherence of the clan and to strengthen its closed character.

We know precious little of the body of doctrine that was peculiar to them. As professional priests - "all priests were Magi, but not all the Magi were priests", says Benveniste [35], which probably must be understood as 'not all of them really exercised their priestly function' - they were 'experts on worship', they knew about holy things, they interpreted dreams and foretold the future, they even had some knowledge of the occult. Perhaps it was this last circumstance that gave rise to the popular meaning of the word 'magician', that of conjurer, sorcerer, and even charlatan.

As Benveniste remarks, there is a 'western' history of the Magi [36] by which he doubtless means that the Greeks and the western peoples (like ours) saw and see them as we desire to see them. We may, for instance, view them as savants, the teachers of famous wise men like Pythagoras, Democritus, and even Plato, who travelled east to sit at their feet. Another tradition, far more popular and long-lived, is that they were occultists and astrologers; at this point they were lumped together with the so-called 'Chaldees' who in reality were something quite different from Magi, namely the priesthood of Babylon, hundreds of miles distant from Media. These Chaldees were renowned for their expertise in the arts of the occult, in magic, and in astrology. We hear an echo of this in the Gospel of Matthew where some 'magi from the east' arrive in Bethlehem to pay homage to 'the newborn King of the Jews'. Doubtless these were astrologers since they had seen 'his star' and probably came from Mesopotamia [37].

e. The role of the Magi in the history of Zoroastrianism

It will be clear by now that originally there was no connection between the Magi and Zoroastrianism. But both of them were significant groups exercising great influence and important elements in the fabric of the Persian Empire under the Achaemenids. It is self-evident that they could not stay apart from one another. Orthodox Zoroastrianism, pure and undiluted as it was in the beginning, underwent great changes in the fifth and fourth centuries B.C. Already in the sixth century B.C. elements from the old popular religion of Iran were picked up and inserted into Zoroastrian theology. Then came the turn of the Magi. An expert like Gherardo Gnoli states [38] that "the Magi were above all the means by which the Zoroastrian tradition and the corpus of the Avesta came down to us. He adds that this was 'their principal merit'.

I wonder whether the great Prophet would have found this as meritorious as this present-day scholar. In the course of time many adherents of the creed swerved widely from its orthodox moorings. Doubtless there must have been Magi who, in assuming the Zoroastrian heritage, transmitted it to posterity in its original form. Otherwise it would not have survived to this day. But other Magi must have been responsible for the conversion of authentic Zoroastrianism into Zervanism. Zervanism "seems to have been the special form that Zoroastrianism assumed for a good part of its history, from the rule of the Achaemenids to the Sassanid Empire" [39]. Gnoli, who writes this, adds that, since Zervanism became fairly general, it "cannot be defined as a heresy". Does a heresy grow less heretic by becoming wide-spread? Again, how would the Prophet himself have reacted to the fact that his great god Ahura Mazda was, as Ormuzd, relegated to a secondary place in creation and put on a par with an evil deity? However, to give Gnoli his due, he correctly states that the Zervanite dualism of Ormuzd and Ahriman (that we find in many Greek sources) differs from Zoroaster's own form of dualism in which, under the monistic aegis of Ahura Mazda, the Benevolent Spirit, Spenta Mainyu, and the Evil One, Angra (or Ahra) Mainyu are opposed [40].

Whether the Parthian kings were Zervanites is an open question. In general emperors of the Persian and Parthian Empires were loath to commit themselves definitely to one special form of religion; they had to consider the religious sentiments of too many subjects who professed other creeds. Nevertheless, the position of Zervanism at their court, in the priesthood, the aristocracy, and the leading circles probably was strong. Whether it really reached and conquered all other layers of society is quite another question [41].

f. Zervanism under the Sasanian Emperors

The Sasanian period was of the greatest importance for Zervanism. The emperors upheld the priesthood of this religion with all their might, so much so that the great King Shapur I was not only seen as a magus himself but even as the leader of the Magi [42]. On their succession

Sasanian emperors used to found a fire temple, with their personal fire; they themselves acted as fire priests and sacrificial priests [43]. The 'Chronicle of Arbela' relates that King Ardashir I erected many new fire temples; the Christian author of this report accuses him, not only of blasphemy, but still more of cruel intolerance since he forced adherents of other religions 'to bow down before the fire and the sun' [44].

Can it be correct what Widengren points out, that this makes clear that a fusion had taken place between Zervanite Magi and Zoroastrian fire priests [45]? After all, it was usual, both for orthodox and Zervanite Zoroastrians to pray with their face towards a fire or the sun. But also a scholar like Christensen contends that what is called Zoroastrianism in the Sasanian period is in reality Zervanism [46]. Some even speak of the Sasanian 'state church', hierarchically structured and strongly organized, with a powerful priestly caste that codified and canonized the tradition, and highly intolerant of other religions [47]. Gnoli says that "it (Zervanism) became a religion in the service of the ruling classes, the warrior aristocracy, and the clergy, as well as the crown" [48]. Thus it became a truly national religion, to such an extent that this dualistic Zervanism, called 'the good religion', grew more or less synonymous with Iran herself [49].

6. Mandaeism and Manichaeism

In my Volume IV I argued that Iran should not be made into the cradle of all and sundry kinds of dualism in world history. Nevertheless, Persia most surely was a hotbed of dualistic ideologies; many varieties sprang up here. It is indeed a curious fact that all religious movements in this country show a distinctly dualistic character. The later centuries of the Iranian Empire saw the spread of three separate denominations all of which meet our definition of dualism. They are Mandaeism, Manichaeism, and Mazdakism (for this last variety I refer the reader to the Appendix). Mithraism, although derived from the name of the old Iranian deity Mithra, is to all intents and purposes not an Iranian religion but a religion, rather, of the Roman Empire. Of Mandaeism and Manichaeism, however important they, and particularly the latter movement, may be, I shall give only a short description, mainly to make the religious picture of the Sasanian age more complete. Since both of them actually were Gnostic sects, and since Manichaeism became the most important form of the Gnosis in the later stages of Roman history, they must wait for a fuller treatment till we reach the Gnostic period in the west.

a. Mandaeism

Mandaeism originated in the Jordan valley in the centuries following the birth of Christ. Although it shows Jewish and Christian influences, Mandaeism was hostile to Judaism and Christianity. Mandaeans spoke an East-Aramaic language in which 'manda' means 'knowledge'; this already is sufficient proof of the connection of Mandaeism with the Gnosis = 'knowledge' (in Greek). For some reason or other its adherents left their home country; threatened by persecution they migrated always further eastward till they finally could settle safely in the Parthian Empire. They possess a holy scripture of their own called 'Ginza'. The Mandaean sect survived all vicissitudes and is still in existence in Iran and Iraq.

According to Mandaean mythology the universe, from its very first beginning, split apart into dualistically opposed entities like good and evil, light and darkness, and soul and matter. These constantly are struggling to gain control over the world and mankind. There is an upper realm, the Lightworld, and a nether one, the earth where mankind dwells. One of the Lightbeings, Ptahil, is responsible for the creation of the world, but he made a hopeless muddle of it. What man has to do is to free his soul (which comes from the Lightworld) from the body; at death, the soul of the good, of the good Mandaean that is, returns to the upper world where it came from, while the body is left behind in the tomb. As is to be expected, frequent purifications are necessary, the most important of which is baptism. A curious aspect of Mandaeism is that its adherents undergo baptism not once but frequently, for instance, at marriage, after childbirth, and, if possible, just before death [50].

b. Manichaeism

The religious movement that is called 'Manichaeism' is far better known than Mandaeism and became immensely more widespread. It moved from Iran westward through the Roman Empire, spreading through Asia Minor and the Balkans and along the coastal areas of North Africa - where in present-day Tunisia Saint Augustine was a Manichaean in his youth -, and finally appearing in Italy, Gaul, and Spain. In the contrary direction it spread through Turkestan to Central Asia and even China. Its founder, Mani, was adorned there with a Chinese name, Mo-mo-ni, derived from Mar Mani = Lord Mani. This prophet was born in 216 A.D. somewhere to the south-east of Ctesiphon on the banks of the Tigris; he was, however, an Iranian. He is the author of a considerable number of religious books, written not in Iranian but in Eastern Aramaic. As a missionary of his own religion he travelled far and wide, through Parthia and Persia, and still farther to what is now Pakistan. In his later life he met with increasing opposition by the Magi and was even condemned to death. He died, however, in 277 before the death sentence could be executed [51].

The Manichaeans kept themselves apart from Judaism, Christianity, and Zoroastrianism, and rejected every tradition not their own. What makes them truly Gnostic is that, with them, redemption is not effected by faith or dogma but by knowledge. What one has to know is that there are two radically opposed principles, the Father of Greatness, and the Prince of Darkness, the first being equated with spirit, the other with matter. The two constantly are warring with one another. At present we must steer clear of the very intricate Manichaean mythology. But it is important to know that the first human beings, Adam and Eve, were created by demoniac servants of the Prince of Darkness. They (Adam and Eve), and all their descendants, can obtain salvation by acquiring knowledge, or Gnosis. It is necessary to know that a great war is raging in the world between good and evil, and that evil is spreading itself by means of human procreation. In every new human being particles of light become imprisoned in the vile body which is no more than matter. By living the good religious life and by following the precepts of Manichaeism the soul (the light particles that is) will finally be freed and return to its luminous origin. At the end of time the two principles will separate for ever [52].

7. A mosaic of religions

It will be evident that, in the course of the centuries, Iran became a patchwork of religions. To assist the reader in finding his way through this tangle I shall finish this chapter with a short survey. He or she, however, should keep in mind that it never was my intention to present something like a history of religions in ancient Iran.

To begin with, we must not forget that in the outlying districts of Iran pagan tribes were to be found who professed a dualistic creed. But the leading religion of Iran was the Zoroastrian faith. It existed in two varieties. There still survived the original form of it that venerated Ahura Mazda as its true and only god; its adherents, however, formed a minority. The main branch was Zervanism; its position became more and more official, and, under the Sasanians, tended towards a state church. Zoroastrian clergy was, as Christensen states, intolerant. Inside the frontiers of Iran they strove for absolute mastery. In Mesopotamia large communities of Jews existed, most of them dating from the time of the Babylonian Captivity at the end of which by no means all of the deported returned to Palestine. Although the emperors did not view their presence with benevolence, they usually were left in peace since they constituted no threat to the state and its religion [53].

The wars with Rome were the cause that many Christians came to establish themselves in the Sasanian Empire. Numbers of them were prisoners of war who were settled in the empire; others arrived as part of whole communities who were forcefully transplanted from Syria. The Sasanians did not see them as a danger till the moment that the Roman emperor Constantine the Great became a Christian in 312. From then on Iranian Christians were seen as a kind of Roman 'fifth column'. They became the object of fierce persecutions; whole groups were deported, many thousands killed. Just as in the Roman Empire before Constantine, however, periods of relative peace alternated with times of harassment. In the fifth century, under Bahram V, many Christians sought a refuge in Byzantine territory. There were also internal divisions among the Christians. The Arians held that Jesus was not really the Son of God, the second person of the Holy Trinity. The Nestorians taught that the dogma that Jesus had two natures, a divine and a human one, implied that he also consisted of two persons entirely distinctive from each other - this in contrast to the Monophysite sect that held that Jesus' two natures became undistinguishably one in his one person. The orthodox Catholic point of view is that there are two separate natures in one indivisible person.

Furthermore, there were Gnostics. True enough, both Gnostics and Zoroastrians were dualists. Both acknowledged the existence of two different and opposed worlds. In Zoroastrian theology both worlds contain a spiritual as well as a material part. In Gnostic ideology, however, only the higher world is luminous and spiritual, while the lower world is dark and sinful. Far more than the Zoroastrians the Gnostics tended to downright pessimism and to asceticism [54]. I have already mentioned the two Gnostic sects operating in Iran, the Mandaeans and the Manichaeans. The intolerant Zoroastrian clergy also persecuted Manichaeism without succeeding in totally uprooting it. It subsisted as a secret movement. Finally, Mazdakism must be mentioned, a sect of mixed Zoroastrian-Gnostic origin.

To make the picture complete it must be pointed out that Buddhism penetrated into the eastern regions of the empire where many monasteries were erected.

APPENDIX TO CHAPTER IV

ON MAZDAKISM

It must immediately be stated that we know precious little about Mazdakism, and what we know comes from sources hostile to it. There is no doubt that the reports we possess are prejudiced and jaundiced. Some scholars see a reason in this not to speak about this movement at all. But the fact that the sources are biased does not mean that no Mazdakite religion ever existed. I, therefore, shall relate the tale assuming that the reader will take what I have to say with all due caution.

a. The prophet Mazdak

In contrast to Mandaeism and Manichaeism, Mazdakism is an offshoot of Zoroastrianism. Nevertheless, it is very likely that this movement too was influenced by later Gnostic tendencies [55]. Its founder Mazdak very probably was an Iranian who, like Mani, was born in Mesopotamia on the banks of the Tigris in the town of Madaraya. We do not know exactly when he was born but it must have been at the end of the fifth century. According to his teaching, the universe is presided over by the God of Light. This god, however, does not act as Providence and does not rule the world. For there is also a realm of darkness; light and darkness permanently fight one another, constantly mixing and separating again. The Gnostic element in this religion is that here too the way to redemption leads through knowledge. Particularly important in this system is the symbolism of letters and numbers. In order to be set free, one must interiorize the four, the seven, and the twelve - whatever this realization may mean [56].

b. Social revolution

It is stated that "blood and possessions were the two pillars of Iranian society" [57] which means that most of the possessions were in the hands of the (blue) blood. The distinction between commoners and nobles was so sharp that it may be called a case of social dualism. In every part of their behaviour, their demeanour, their clothing, their mansions, their gardens, the nobles showed that they were utterly different from everybody else and wanted to be different. The law, moreover, protected not only their possessions but also the purity of their blood [58].

Mazdak acted as a radical social reformer; Zaehner even calls him a 'communist' [59], although communists would not consider him one of them. He taught that the principle of darkness became apparent above all in a society where injustice, inequality, hate, and discord had the upper hand. In exhorting his adherents to fight injustice in the service of the divine forces of light, Mazdak surely was an authentic heir of Zoroaster. But in his revolutionary fervour he went much farther than the Prophet, who was essentially a man of peace. Mazdak is said to have told his followers that it was absolutely necessary to make very short work of all possible forms of inequality since all men are created equal and even the slightest trace of inequality made a deep inroad on man's original being. The sources impute a very radical remedy to Mazdak : all goods must become common property including women, whom he obviously regarded as goods. The general diet was to become vegetarian.

With regard to the following communication, the sources probably are at their most spurious. Mazdak is believed to have won over one of the later Sasanian rulers, King Kawad (488-531). This prince, the reports tell us, even changed the connubial laws - which were already rather lax - and introduced communal possession of women. It was to be expected that more traditional circles would strongly react; for a time - for this reason or for something else - Kawad was deprived of his throne. The whole country was seething with revolution; castles everywhere went up in flames. In their eagerness to denigrate the Mazdakite movement the sources contend that the populace divided the captured women among them; especially the royal harems should have proved a rich reservoir of beauties.

c. The end

Having succeeded in regaining his throne the king, utterly bewildered by what was happening, broke with Mazdakism and even initiated a fierce persecution of the Mazdakites. The final catastrophe took place at the end of 528 or at the beginning of 529. At the instigation of King Kawad a theological congress was convoked at which all the leading figures of Mazdakism were present. Soldiers surrounded the building in which the Mazdakites had assembled. At a given moment they burst in and massacred all those present. In this way all the chiefs perished. Then the rank and file were outlawed, butchered, and dispersed. Their properties were confiscated and their holy books burned [60]. From then on Mazdakism existed only as an underground movement; according to Christensen it even outlived the Sasanian Empire and manifested itself again in the time of Islam [61]. The final result of the uproar was the still firmer establishment of traditional Zoroastrianism as the official religion of Iran [62].

NOTES TO CHAPTER I

1) Ghirshman 212/213.
2) Ghirshman 214.
3) Ghirshman 214/215.
4) Ghirshman 240.
5) Ghirshman 241/242.
6) Ghirshman 244.
7) Ghirshman 251.
8) Christensen 79.
9) Ghirshman 281.
10) Christensen 82 who adds that this last trait is perhaps legendary.
11) Ghirshman 260/261.
12) Altheim 216.
13) Ghirshman 284/285.
14) Ghirshman 285; Christensen plate 14, 217.
15) Ghirshman 287.
16) Ammianus XVII 5.1-10. Christensen adds that Ammianus is giving a free rendering of the letters, but he must have had the originals under his eyes since he is giving Shapur's titles correctly, Christensen 232.

17) Ghirshman 289.
18) Christensen 501.
19) Christensen 501/502.
20) Boyce II 232.
21) Eznik II, Irrlehren, Buch 1. 83/84.
22) Yasna 30:3.
23) Zaehner 181/182.
24) Nyberg, Rel.Ir. 384.
25) Widengren, Rel.Ir. 292/293.
26) We have this on the authority of somebody who lived eight centuries later, Damascius (453-533), in his 'Dubitationes et solutiones' 125 bis, cited by Widengren, Rel.Ir. 149.
27) Plutarch, De Iside et Osiride 46. Moralia 369.
28) Zaehner 15.
29) Benveniste 11.
30) Yasna 29:11.
31) Benveniste 15.
32) Her. I 132.
33) Her. III 61.
34) Her. I 140.
35) Benveniste 18.
36) Benveniste 26.
37) Mt. 2:1-2. See for this passage Benveniste 26/27.
38) Gnoli, Magi 81.
39) Gnoli, Zurvanism 595.
40) Gnoli, Zurvanism 596.
41) Widengren, Rel.Ir. 215 and 388.
42) Widengren, Rel.Ir. 245.
43) Widengren, Rel.Ir. 239.
44) Cit. by Widengren, Rel.Ir. 244.
45) Widengren, Rel.Ir. 283.
46) Christensen 150-152.
47) Widengren, Rel.Ir. 243-245.
48) Gnoli, Zoroastrianism 589.
49) Gnoli, Zoroastrianism 589.
50) Buckley, Mand.Rel. 150-153.
51) Gnoli, Mani 158-161.
52) Gnoli, Manichaeism 161-171. I heroically withstand the seduction at this point to give this fascinating brand of dualism its full due. What is pleading for a treatment in this volume is its Iranian origin. Gnoli asserts that "the dominating imprint of Iranian dualism" must be recognized "since without a doubt the dualistic doctrine is central and pivotal to Mani's thought". According to this scholar it would be erroneous to "conclude that the principal inspiration for the Manichaean doctrine was Judeo-Christian gnosticism", Gnoli, Manichaeism 165. It seems to me that this author is the victim of several misunderstandings in stating this. The lesser one, with regard to our subject, is that Gnosticism is said to be 'Judeo-Christian'. On the contrary, it exists in its own right. More central to our theme is that, once again, dualism is obviously seen

as an exclusively Iranian phenomenon. Apart from the fact that it is to be found world-wide, one must never lose sight of the fact that the Gnosis is essentially dualistic. The Manichaean mythology is so typically dualistic that one must not see it, like Gnoli, as emanating from the Iranian religious tradition, that is to say, from Zoroastrianism, but rather as a flourishing branch of the Gnostic religion.

53) Christensen 261.
54) Christensen 37.
55) Nyberg, Rel.Ir. 421.
56) The significance of the numbers is well-known of course, but this interiorization of them is quite another matter.
57) Christensen 311.
58) Christensen 310-313.
59) Zaehner 188.
60) Christensen 354/355.
61) Christensen 357.
62) Widengren, Rel.Ir. 309/310; Gnoli, Mazdakism 302-303.

CHAPTER II

INDICA

1. India between particularism and the drive to unity

a. India from the inside and from the outside

Like Caesar's Gaul, ancient India was divided into three parts. The northern half, forming part of the Asian continent, consists of two river-basins. In the west the mighty Indus, with its numerous tributaries, is flowing southward from the Hindu Kush and the Himalaya Mountains till it debouches into the Arabian Sea. In the east, separated from the Indus basin by a wide and arid desert, the holy river Ganges, fed by the melting snows of the Himalayas, with its affluent streams flows imposingly south-eastward, through a large and fruitful plain till it finally empties itself into the Gulf of Bengal. The region of the two river systems with the interconnecting dry country all taken together is called Hindustan. To the south of this Hindustan and separated from it by the Vindhya Mountains, an enormous triangular peninsula juts out towards the Indian Ocean, with the island of Sri Lanka (Ceylon) at its southern tip. This peninsula, the larger part of which is called the Deccan, is mainly mountainous.

Life in the south, with traditions and civilizations of its own, was different from that in the north. Thus, from the earliest beginnings of Indian history, we detect a kind of partition between the two river-basins in the north and the peninsula in the south. Luciano Petech states that the history of India, when tending to unification, is characterized by attempts of the northern empires to annex the Deccan. But the subcontinent rarely was a unity; even to-day it accomodates three sovereign states, India, Pakistan, and Bangladesh, or four if we include Sri Lanka. The relations between these four states are not always friendly, to put it mildly. In periods of imperial decay it was always the peninsula that severed itself first from the north and fell back on its own regional existence [1].

India is separated from Central Asia by the Hindu Kush and the Himalaya mountain range stretching from Afghanistan in the west to Burma in the east. With the highest mountain tops in the world, it was and still is, although by no means unsurmountable, a formidable barrier. This does not mean that the Indian subcontinent was hermetically sealed off from the outside world. Far from it! The plains along the sea in the west and in the east, with the mouths of the great rivers, and the lower passes of the mountains form easy enough gateways to India. In the course of the centuries hordes of nomads freely made use of these accesses and penetrated into the country coming either from Persia or from China [2].

The result is that India presents the most curious mixture of races, nations, speeches, religions, and cultures. An ethnographic classification proposed by B.S. Guha and based on anthropological characteristics presents us with six main races ranging from the aboriginal proto-Australoids to the Oriental type [3]. Far over two hundred tongues may be heard here. But however easily the successively invading tribes may have spread over the great river plains in the northern half of the subcontinent, their way to the south was always blocked by the daunting, densely wooded Vindhya Range. Rapson says that these mountains "have in all ages formed the great dividing line between northern and southern India". Even at the present day, he goes on, "the two great regions which they separate continue to offer the most striking contrasts in racial character, in language, and in social institutions" [4]. At bottom, this contrast could constitute a dualistic opposition.

b. Prehistoric man and nature

In India no parts of the bones of the human beings who lived there during the Stone Age have been found [5]. This does not mean that man was not present then in India, for human artefacts, like handaxes and cleavers, have been found in regions that lie widely apart. The two river systems remained uninhabitable till about seven thousand years ago. It lasted countless centuries before the alluvial deposits, age after age ground off from the Himalayas, had created the enormous dry and fertile plains of the Indus and the Ganges [6].

For an extremely long period, beginning with the first appearance of man in India (about a hundred thousand years ago) to ca. 3500 B.C., all dates are entirely conjectural [7]. During the three stages of the Stone Age, the Early, the Middle, and the Late Stone Age, followed by the socalled Chalcolithic culture (when bronze was used along with stone), man slowly developed from a food gatherer and hunter living in small nomadic groups into a peasant who was at home in farming communities and in villages. Still later the townsman arose. This process entailed what Gordon Childe calls 'an aggressive attitude to his (man's) environment'. As long as human beings fed themselves on the fruits and roots they gathered, the virgin state of nature remained unimpaired. Hunting already meant an encroachment; animals freely roaming about were caught and killed. But the really deep inroads only began when man started farming; he then needed plots which he conquered from the jungle, more often then not by burning down the virginal forest. It would be fascinating to write a history of this human aggressiveness towards nature, the more so since, in our advanced age, it has turned into large-scale destruction [8]. In India the very first agricultural villages, still very small, appeared around 3000 B.C. along the ocean coast west of the Indus (in Baluchistan) and in the lower regions of this river (in Sind).

c. The Indus civilization

However interesting the long prehistoric period may be to the archaelogist and the historically orientated general reader, I do not believe that it yields data relating to my theme. During the third millennium B.C. the first great Indian civilization came into being. Its numerous sites are distributed over an area of enormous extent, mainly along the Indus

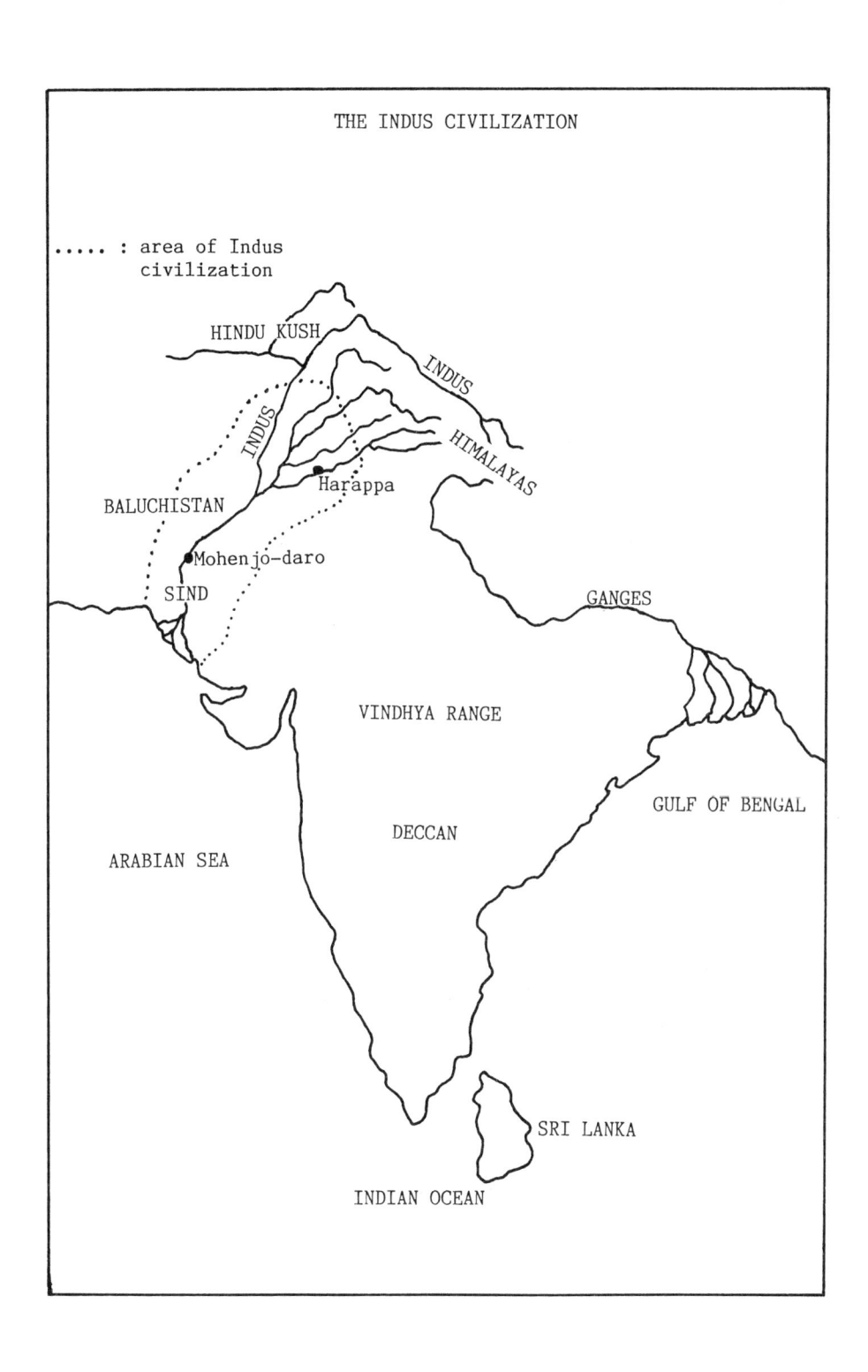

TIME TABLE OF INDIAN HISTORY
See also summary of religious history on pages 160-164

DATES	POLITICAL EVENTS	LITERARY EVENTS	RELIGIOUS EVENTS
B.C.			
ca. 3000	first agricultural villages		
2500-1500	Indus or Harappa civilization		
ca. 1500	Aryan invasions	The Rigveda	Vedism
1500-600	Aryanization of Indian subcontinent		
1500-600	The Vedic Period	The Vedas	Brahmanism
		The Brahmanas	8th cent.
		The Upanishads	Parshva
ca. 550	Rise of Magadhan power		
546-494	King Bimbisara		Vardhamana
494-462	King Ayatasutra		Gautama Buddha
414-362	King Sisunaga	The Theravada Canon	
362-334	King Mahapadma Nanda	ca. 400 B.C.-400 A.D. final version of the Mahabharata	spread of Jainism, Buddhism, and Hinduism
327-325	Macedonian invasion		
between 324-313	foundation of the Mauryan Empire		
324/313-302	King Chandragupta Maurya	Megasthenes at the Mauryan court	
305	invasion of Seleucus I		
302-269	King Bindusara		
269-232	Emperor Asoka		
200-170	Bactrian invasions		
after 165	nomad invasions, Scythians and Parthians in Indus valley		
A.D.			
60-ca. 300	Kushanite Empire in N.W. India		
300-335	beginning of Gupta dynasty		Yoga-sutras
320-335	Chandragupta I		
335-380	Samudragupta		Samkhya-Karika
376-415	Chandragupta II		Arthasastra
413-455	Kumaragupta II	The Puranas	
455-467	Skandagupta		Bhashya
fr. 500	later Guptas		
712	Islamic invasion		Spread of Islam

axis. The two most important centres are found at Harappa and Mohenjo-Daro; this culture is, therefore, called either the Harappa culture or the Indus civilization; it radiated far and wide. Nearly all its towns and villages were situated in the plain [9].

Although the main means of subsistence was agriculture, there is evidence of trade and commerce. The people of this civilization used a pictographic script that is found in inscriptions and on seals; however, it has not yet been deciphered. As is to be expected in an agricultural society, the veneration of the Mother Goddess, the great symbol of fertility, was the centre of religious life. Wheeler makes an interesting remark here. He dubs the Harappa religion 'a loosely knit complex of accumulated beliefs and observances'. In this complex a duality or multiplicity can be distinguished, namely one of higher and lower grades in which "the lower grades may in fact have had a greater hold upon the popular mentality than the higher". In his opinion the veneration of the Mother Goddess, represented by "numerous terra-cotta figurines of an almost nude female (is) more easily related to a household cult than to a state religion". At the other end, that is to say among the educated and well-to-do middle class of the towns, a male type of religion may have been predominant, with phallus-worship and with the figure of Shiva who was to become 'the great historic god of India' already pictured on seals [10]. The approximate dates of the Indus civilization are from 2500-2100 B.C. to 1600-1500 B.C.

The rise of this proto-historic culture was rapid; its culmination-point was soon enough reached. But then there followed a long period of stagnation; there was no longer any really new development. Petech says that we must imagine a petrified society dominated by a priestly caste, and with a business class that was content with its profits and averse to change [11]. The Indus civilization met with a sudden end. Very probably the Indus valley itself was conquered by invaders. Who, however, these invaders were is still somewhat of a problem. Some hold that the destruction was the work of tribes coming from the Ganges valley or from the north-west; others, among Wheeler in particular, defend the thesis that these invaders were the Aryans [12].

d. The coming of the Aryans

Whether or not the Aryans were directly responsible for the end of the Indus civilization, it is an historical fact that an Aryan invasion occurred in the centuries around 1500 B.C. Nazi ideology gave the word 'Aryan' ('arisch') its ugly meaning of a blonde master race destined to rule the world, and, because of its supposed physical and mental superiority, entitled to wipe other 'races' that were considered inferior. Originally, the word 'Aryan' had no racial implication whatseoever. It is a Sanskrit term signifying 'free born' or 'of noble character'; as such it is still current in many Indian languages. It first denoted members of the higher castes but later came to mean special tribes, ethnic groups that is. The ancient Persians knew this word too, for they used it to give their country its name, 'Iran' = land of the Aryans. Some scholars even say that the vernacular name for Ireland, 'Eire', is a derivation from 'Aryan' [13].

The important thing to keep in mind is that 'Aryan' first and foremost is used for a large group of cognate languages [14]. This same group of tongues is also called 'Indo-European' or, less correctly, 'Indo-Germanic'. It is, as Piggott writes, 'a relatively junior member of the old world linguistic family', the Sumerian and Semitic language groups being much older [15]. To the Aryan or Indo-European group nearly all European languanges belong, the Germanic branch (including English and Dutch), the Romance branch (French, Italian, etc., all derived from Latin), and the Slavonic languages (Russian, Polish, etc.). Although in Asia Minor and Mesopotamia mainly non-Aryan languages were spoken, we find, nevertheless, Hittite and Kassite. In Persia several older tongues were Aryan with the Avesta as their great literary monument.

That there also existed an Indian branch of this linguistic family remained wholly unknown till late in the eighteenth century. Then, in 1766 and 1786 respectively, the French missionary Coeurdoux and the British administrator Sir William Jones discovered that the ancient liturgical language of India, 'Sanskrit', possessed a grammatical structure and an etymology strikingly similar to that of, for instance, French and English. I remember that, as a sixteen-year old schoolboy, I amused myself, to the detriment of my home-work, with consulting numerous dictionaries and jotting down series of words that looked more or less identical in many languages, including Sanskrit; I did this for example with 'wine'. And indeed, a word like 'father' shows a great resemblance from one language to the other : vader (Dutch), Vater (German), père (French), patre (Italian), pater (Latin), patĕr (Greek), and pitar (Sanskrit) [16].

In India itself a great number of languages are derived from Sanskrit; among the older forms there is, for instance, Pali, and among the modern ones still in use Hindi, Punjabi, Bengali, Marathi, and still others. It is, however, important to realize that there also exist a great many non-Aryan tongues in India, among them the Dravidian group with Tamil, Telugu, Tulu, and others [17]. We should take due note of the fact that there is in India a difference between Aryan and non-Aryan languages that, at the same time, is a difference between north and south, the Aryan languages being found mainly in the north, and the non-Aryan ones in the south.

It is a hotly debated point where the ancient homeland of the Aryans is to be found. Nationalistic sentiments sometimes bedevilled this problem, for example when German scholars would have us believe that the cradle of the Indo-Europeans was the North-European plain (of which the northern half of Germany forms part); this was supposed to be the homestead of an blonde Nordic race [18]. However, it is common ground now that the original home of the Indo-Europeans are the steppes of South-Russia [19]. From there we see them migrate into the Balkans (the Greeks), Asia Minor (the Hittites), Mesopotamia (the Kassites), and Iran (the Medians and the Persians).

Another thorny question is whether the term 'Aryan' really indicates an ethnic group or only a linguistic family. Perhaps out of aversion to racial implications some linguists opted for the second solution. In Volume IV, Chapter IV, however, I cited a famous inscription of the Persian emperor Darius I in which he calls himself 'a Persian, an Aryan of Aryan descent'. There obviously is no difference here between 'Persian' and 'Aryan' both terms doubtless indicating an ethnic adherence.

Kosambi says that the Vedas, the oldest Indian documents, mention the Aryans as a people, namely those 'who venerate the gods worshipped in those Vedas' [20]. Remarkably enough there exists a treaty between the Hittite Empire and the Kingdom of Mitanni (in Mesopotamia) of ca. 1380 B.C. in which the Mitannian king takes the gods Mithra, Varuna, and Indra as his witnesses [21]. Now these gods are also the most important ones in the Indian pantheon; in Chapter IV of Volume IV we also met Mithra and Varuna in the Persian religion - enough to suggest a common origin.

Experts who compare the Avesta with the Vedas, in particular the most ancient parts of both, are struck with their great similarity, not only linguistically but also in mythology and mentality. There once must have been a common Indo-Iranian culture in South-Russia. Later both branches split apart, geographically when one group migrated to Iran and the other to India, but in many other respects too. Ghosh expresses this by saying that "the two peoples turned their backs upon each other as it were, and developed their distinctive civilizations apparently without the least mutual influence ... When later in history Iranians were forced to meet (i.e. with Indians - F.) as citizens of the same empire (that is under the Achaemenid emperors, Alexander, and the Seleucid kings - F.), they met as complete strangers, not as cousins of the same family" [22]. My account in Chapter I of the Parthian and Sasanian rulers proved that they too viewed the Indians as dangerous enemies.

Geographical circumstances may to a certain extent explain this antagonism. Perhaps the main reason for the incomptability of the two cultures is to be found in the religious sphere. Some scholars believe that the first seeds of discord were already sown when the Indo-Iranians still lived in their common Central Asian home. Their primitive religion knew nature-gods, divinities with a fairly concrete character, like the sky, the sun, the wind, all deities honoured by a fire-cult. Such divinities were called 'daivas' (found back in the Latin word 'deus' and its derivations like 'dieu' or 'dio'). But probably there was already felt a need for a higher form of religion, with more abstract deities, gods with an ethical character called 'asuras' [23]. Undoubtedly this theological difference has social roots. We may assume that the daiva-type was the favourite religion of the common people, of the peasants, the asura-type, on the other hand, that of the more cultured classes [24].

Aryan tribes entered India from the north and spread over the Indus valley in the second millennium B.C. Chronologically speaking this is discouragingly vague but there is much difference of opinion between scholars with regard to more exact dates. At any rate, the time of the invasions is nearer to 1000 than to 2000 B.C.; perhaps we may safely settle on a period around 1500, 1400 B.C. What we know of these long distant times is found in a large collection of hymns called the 'Rigveda'. It contains ten books with in all 1017 hymns. The main interest of those who composed this collection was not to write history but to keep intact the religious traditions. As a consequence, says Keith, "the light thrown by the hymns on social and politic India is disappointingly meagre" [25]. The hymns actually present an account of the Aryan invasions but not according to the rules of modern historical scholarship. The important fact, however, is that it is possible to date the Rigveda; it is usually situated around the middle of the second millennium B.C. [26].

2. The first power centre

a. The Vedic period

I shall now give an outline of Indian political history in these early times. Not all of it directly refers to our main subject. But since we all have a political bend of mind and tend to read history from a political angle, it will be difficult for the general reader who, I venture to assume, knows next to nothing of Indian history, to place religious, social, and literary elements in their historical context, when he or she cannot refer to a frame of political history.

Coming from the north as they did, the Aryans first settled in the northern part of the Indus plain, in the Punjab. From there they reached the Ganges valley and followed this river downstream; there was also a move southward from the Punjab along the Indus and towards

THE VEDIC PERIOD

- → : The Aryan invasions
- ///// : Early Vedic culture
- ≡ : Late Vedic culture

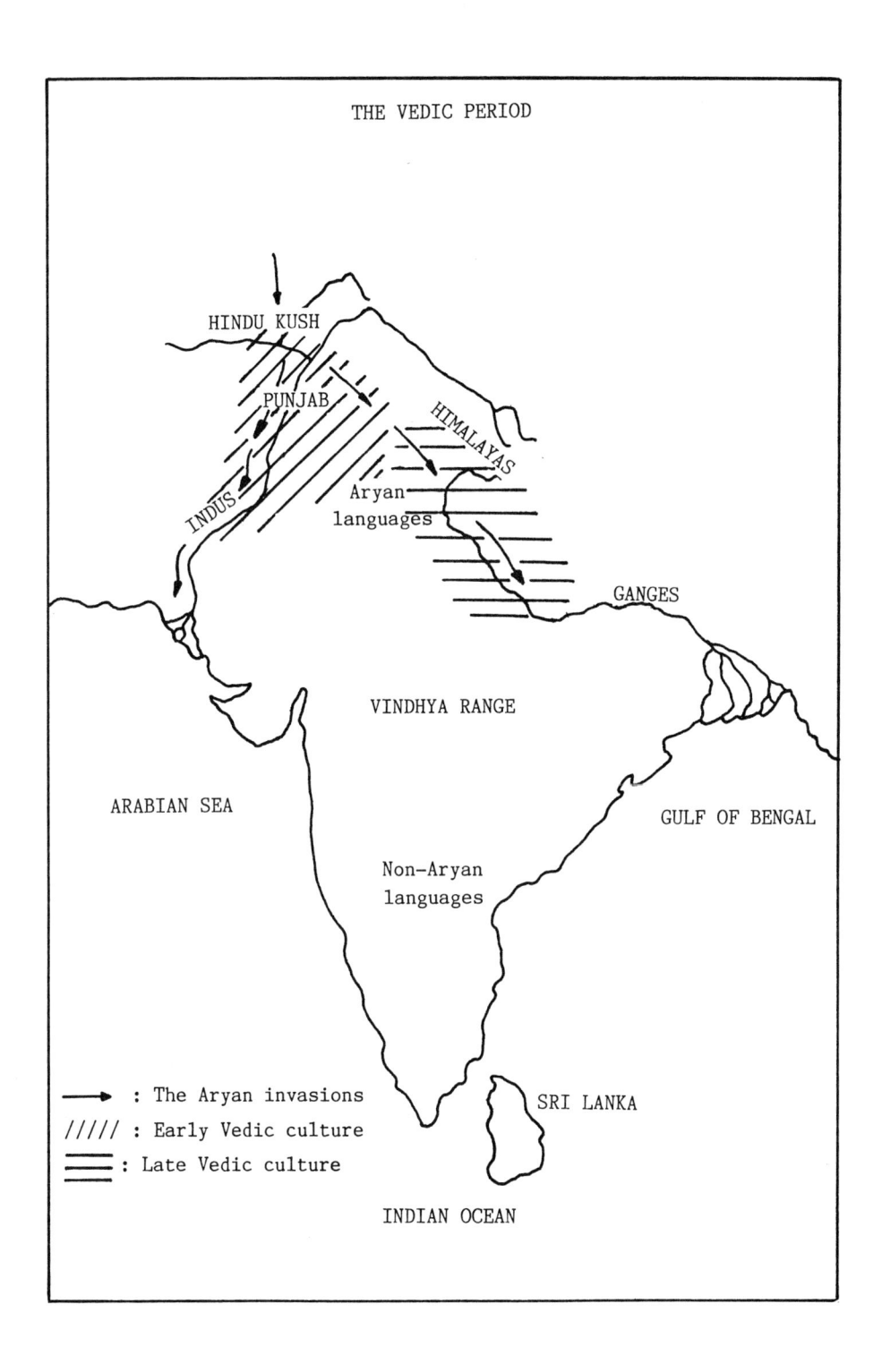

the Vindhya Range. This was a process that lasted many centuries. The conclusion is justified that about 300 B.C. the northern half of the subcontinent had been 'aryanized'; the peninsula, however, remained untouched. The usual course of events was that Aryan colonies were founded at ever greater distance; when the indigenous population was not willing to receive them, military force was used. The Aryans were a domineering race who prided themselves on their superiority to the neolithic aboriginals [27]. The nations and tribes they conquered were harshly subjected to Aryan rule; some of them fled before the conqueror but most of them were made slaves. As Petech states, the subjected populations were not so much relegated to a subordinate position but rather to one outside the Aryan sphere [28]. This doubtless is a dualistic element in Aryan India.

We know very little of the political history of the Vedic period. Tribes coalesced into new nations; kingdoms arose that fought for supremacy. The struggle for overlordship already then became, as Majumdar writes, a characteristic of political India. He adds that already "the ideal of universal empire loomed large on the political horizon" [29]. This author mentions an ancient Indian source referring to twelve kings who "were everywhere conquering the earth, up to its ends". Although we have no idea which historical situation may be meant, it is interesting to note that almost the same phrases are used that we found in the mouth of Mesopotamian kings [30].

Everyone will have heard of that great Indian epic, the Mahabharata. Very few, however, will have read what "probably (is) the longest single poem in world literature" [31], with its ninety-thousand stanzas each of them consisting (in English translation) of five lines. Like the Homeric epics, this great heroic tale was long in gestation; the definitive version dates from a period between 400 B.C. and 400 A.D. [32]. Although, again like the Iliad and the Odyssey, the Mahabharata is not an historical work but a product of literary fiction, some of the related events, and even some of the characters figuring in it, are concretely historical [33]. The time in which the action described takes place probably is 1000 B.C. or somewhat earlier. The paedagogic and literary impact is often compared with that of the Homeric poems; there exist translations of (parts of) it into Burmese, Chinese, and Javanese.

Indian legend has it that in mythical times there existed two royal races. The first claimed to have been descended from the moon; this was the 'lunar dynasty'. All the legendary kings of northern India, and even some later rulers like the Rajputs of the early Middle Ages, are said to have been the offspring of the moon. The other line is the 'solar dynasty' having the sun as its ancestor. The two dynasties are dualistically opposed since the lunar race was believed to be tumultuous and the solar race to be wise. This difference has its origin in the opposition of the sun and the moon, the first, represented by the god Mithra, behaving in a very regular way, the second, the celestial representation of the god Varuna, in contrast seen as fickle and unstable [34].

Speaking of the lunar dynasty the Mahabharata reports another dualistic conflict, that between the Pandus and the Kurus. The kernel of the story is the rise to power of a new and ambitious clan, the Pandus, or Pandavas. These allied themselves with kings in the neighbourhood; they then attacked the older dominating clan, the Kurus, whose seat of power was at Indarpat (near Delhi). Not every independent king, however, welcomed this; thus the Kurus too were able to win many a partisan. Hence two great coalitions came into being since all the kings of India took sides; even the rulers of the Greeks, the Bactrians, and the Chinese choose for one faction or the other. What this led to may be called a world war avant la lettre! The two armies, each of them enormously big, met in the Battle of Kurukshetra; in a slaughter that lasted eighteen days the Pandavas won.

b. Magadha's bid for power

What we know of Indian history in the period before 600 B.C. is too scanty to serve as a basis for sound scholarly conclusions. It is only after this date that the ground under our feet becomes somewhat more solid. We are, so to speak, passing from the dark to the dusk. We now reach the time referred to by legend as that of the 'nine Nandas'; these Nandas were kings in the Ganges region. We must, with Percival Spear,

THE EMPIRE OF MAGADHA

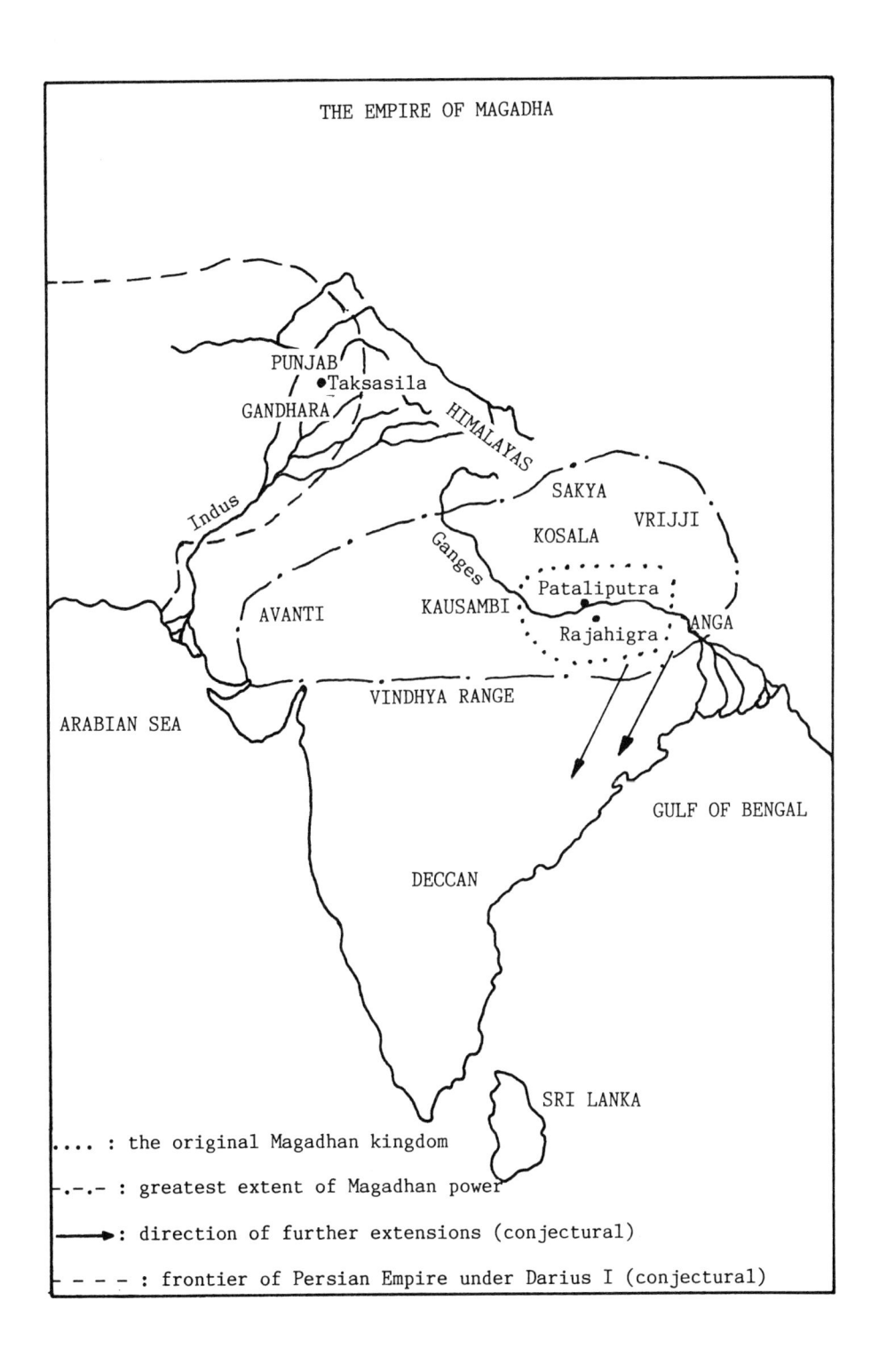

.... : the original Magadhan kingdom

-.-.- : greatest extent of Magadhan power

──▶ : direction of further extensions (conjectural)

- - - : frontier of Persian Empire under Darius I (conjectural)

admit that their "history has been falsified in some way and the chronology cannot be right ... The traditions about the Nandas ... are hopelessly discrepant in many respects" [35]. But one thing we may assume as historically certain. In the Ganges basin the first Indian power centre came into being. Its rulers tried to extend their sway far beyond their original borders. Even a region as far away as Orissa was probably at some time one of the Nanda domains, while it is also possible that there was Nanda influence in the Deccan too. However, it is necessary to caution the reader that not every event related in the next paragraphs may be considered the ultimate historical truth about the Nanda era. We still are only halfway between myth and real historical evidence.

The Aryan part of India at this time consisted of a great number of sovereign states. Four kingdoms were the more important of these; they often fought each other in order to attain the supremacy, all of them seeing an easy prey in the smaller states [36]. It was the kingdom of Magadha that finally emerged from the interminable internecine struggle as the leading power. Magadha is situated in present-day Bihar on the lower courses of the Ganges. Even to-day the inhabitants call this region Maga [37]. The Indian historian Raychaudhuri compares the role Magadha played in the history of India to that of Wessex in English history, or of Prussia in Germany, that is to say, the role of a founder of a unified empire [38].

The founder of the historic Magadhan dynasty was King Bimsibara (ca. 546-494). He is said to have had a meeting with Gautama Buddha but not to have understood the significance of this great man [39]. He is surnamed 'Seniya' which means 'with an army'. Now earlier kings had had armies too, but this epithet is supposed to point to the fact that Bimbisara was the first to possess a regular army [40]. This already is a sign that he was not without ambitions; this impression is strengthened by the fact that he built an enormous new capital, Rajahigra, the rough walls of which had a circumference of twenty-three miles [41]. It was this king who inaugurated the policy of conquest, for he invaded the neighbouring kingdom of Anga lower down the Ganges. Unfortunately for him, his son Ajatasatru was still more ambitious than he was himself

: he dethroned his father and threw him into prison where he died of hunger [42].

This ferocious Ajatasatru was king of Magadha from 494 to 462. This means that he was a contemporary of Xerxes I of Persia. It is far from impossible that Persian imperialism was the source of inspiration for Bimbisara and his successors. It is well-known that the realm of Darius I reached well beyond the Indus. Basham suggests that the kings of Magadha cannot have remained ignorant of what happened in the north-west of India. Bimbisara sent his sons for purposes of education to Taksasila - the Taxila of the Greeks - that stood near the Indus where western influence was strong [43]. Very probably the kings of Gandhara of which country Taxila was the capital were vassals of Darius I. If this supposition is correct, it leads to the interesting conclusion that from the line of imperial ambition stretching over thousands of years from the early kings of Sumer to the emperors of Persia a side-line branches off to north-eastern India.

Ajasatru struck out westward, and helped by an overflow of the Ganges that destroyed the greater part of the opposing army, he annexed the kingdom of Kosala, higher up the river. The country of the Vrijji followed, north of Magadha, between the Ganges and the Himalayas. By using, for the first time in Indian history, catapults and heavy chariots, the forerunners of modern India's armoured forces, the Magadhan king succeeded in beating down the obdurate resistance of these tribes. When this king died, according to some sources murdered by his own son, just as he had killed his father, the greater part of the Ganges plain was now solidly in the hands of the Magadhan kings.

It is not an incident of paramount historical importance but, nevertheless interesting to note, that the new prince annexed the small kingdom of the Sakyas in the foothills of the Himalayas, for Gautama Buddha was a member of this tribe. The tribesmen were virtually annihilated in the process. Basham supposes that the deadly sin of the Sakya kings was that they too fostered 'ambitions of empire' [44]. We know that imperialistic rulers are dualistically minded and are impatient of all forms of competition. In consequence the Magadhan ruler showed no clemency to this tribe even although it did not look like a serious rival to his power.

To the south-east of the Indus and to the south-west of the Ganges, north of the Vindhya Range, that is to say in the southern half of continental India, we find in this period another great state, Avanti. It became the first great centre of Buddhism but the history of this new religion will occupy us later. The kings of Avanti had embarked on a career just as ambitious as that of the Magadhan princes; in the course of the time Avanti had absorbed all the neighbouring kingdoms. Their most important gain seems to have been the annexation of the kingdom of Kausambi, to their north-east, between their own territory and the Ganges. If this is correct - for the great question always is how reliable the sources are -, Avanti and Magadha became neighbours in this way 45).

A conflict between this ambitious and expanding powers seemed unavoidable. It actually broke out and lasted for a whole century, for the first hostilities already took place in the reign of Ajatasatru. It was King Sisunaga (ca. 414-396) who finally overcame Avanti. From their new capital Pataliputra (now Patna) the Magadhan kings of the fourth century B.C. ruled the greater part of India north of the Vindhya Mountains; this means that the whole of the peninsula fell outside their scope. Nor did they possess any foothold in the Indus valley and in the Punjab. This part of the country was divided between a number of weak kingdoms that proved unable to withstand the pressure of the Persians and later the onrush of Alexander.

3. Persians and Greeks in India

a. Persian influence

The Persian conquerors reached India around 516 B.C. under Darius I. When this king summed up his dependencies, he also mentioned 'Hidu', pronounced 'Hindu'; this is the Indus region called 'Sindh' by the Indians themselves. Via the Greeks who in their writings spoke of the Indos and the Indioi, these terms came down to us. Later 'India' became a geographical term designating more and more of the country till it finally indicated the whole of the subcontinent [46]. Darius was able to organize an Indus-satrapy, the twentieth and the most easterly of his possessions. How far it extended beyond the east bank of the river is unkown; it may have comprised Gandhara. Very probably the direct political rule of Persia disappeared early in the fifth century B.C., but Persian cultural influence subsisted in the Indus region for another two centuries and radiated eastward. Petech says that the two main political maxims of the Persians exercised an influence on Indian rulers. The first was that an empire should be well-organized and closely knit, rather than a loose confederacy of vassal states; the second maintained that monarchical power should be based on on ethical principles rather than on sheer political pragmatism [47].

b. Alexander beyond the Indus

From ca. 362 to 334 Mahapadma Nanda was Emperor of Magadha. He was the first of a new dynasty, the Nandas. The reign of this ambitious king saw expansion from the mouth of the Ganges southward along the coast in the Kalinga region, now the modern Indian states of Orissa and the northern half of Andhra Pradesh on the east coast of the peninsula. This means that he was the first northern king to penetrate into the Deccan [48]. His successor saw the invasion of the Macedonian army in the period from May 327 to October 325. This is, indeed, a period that has received considerable emphasis in Greek and western historiography. The Greeks in exotic India, what a romantic idea! But from the Indian point of view it was no more than a ripple on the broad surface of their history. True enough, cultural contacts were established, but from a political standpoint there was no lasting impact.

Alexander did not proceed very far beyond the Indus. He soon had to return because of the unwillingness of his soldiers to march further on, according to Greek historiographers. But there may have been yet another consideration. If Alexander had pushed on eastward, he would soon have had to confront the Nanda emperors of Magadha.

These would have been opponents of another calibre than that famous king Porus who, in spite of his daunting elephants, was defeated by Alexander at the Jhelum river. For this courageous man of whom so much has been made and who was admired by Alexander himself, was, after all, no more than the ruler of a petty Indian frontier state. Is it wholly unthinkable that the Macedonian turned back also out of fear for the power of the Magadhan emperor [49]?

It is not realized in the west but Alexander left a bad reputation behind him in India. His troops committed many cruelties against Indian cities in some of which the whole population was mercilessly put to the sword. Many people were sold as slaves [50]. Nevertheless, all this did not result in a fierce antagonism between the Greek and Indian worlds. In my opinion, they were, geographically, too far apart for a dualistic relationship. True enough, in the days of Alexander, they touched upon each other. But the empire of the Macedonian conqueror was short-lived. Within five years after his death the Macedonian strongholds east of the Indus were all of them recaptured by the Indians.

However, although from a political point of view little or nothing remained of the Graeco-Macedonian invasion on Indian soil, reciprocal interest was greatly strengthened by these events. The first acquaintance of the Greeks with the Indians had been when they saw Indian lancers, as auxiliaries in the Persian army, marching through their own towns in the beginning of the fifth century B.C. After Alexander's campaigns Greek authors described the wonders of the Indian world to a fascinated Hellenic public. Some of the farthest Greek colonies founded by Alexander remained in existence as centres of Greek culture in the Indian borderland. According to some modern Indian authors, another effect of the Macedonian conquest was a strenghtening of Magadhan imperialism [51].

4. The Mauryan Empire

a. The foundation of the empire

The years immediately following Alexander's retreat saw the irresistible rise to power of an hitherto utterly unknown young man called Chandragupta. He is surnamed 'Maurya' and became the founder of the Mauryan Empire. This is a very significant event in Indian history since, in the words of Spear, "the advent of the Mauryan dynasty marks the passage from darkness to light for the historian" [52]. According to some modern authors 'Maurya' signifies 'son of Mura' - Mura being a low-born concubine of a Nanda king of Magadha [53]; another possibility is a derivation from 'mayuru' ('mora') = peacock, 'maurya' then meaning something like 'peacock clan'. Anxious, perhaps, to provide him with a more dignified origin other sources say that the Mauryas formed part of a famous clan, the Kshatriyas, the caste 'of the solar race', to which, possibly, the Buddha belonged [54]. In his earlier years Chandragupta seems to have been a fortune-seeker trying to advance where the going was good. Very probably he began by taking the side of the Macedonians. Plutarch mentions a certain Sandrocottos - who is nobody else than our Chandragupta - who acted as Alexander's adviser; he wanted him to attack the Magadha empire [55]. Is it really over-suspicious to assume that this advice was given in his own interest too? But later the king and the young man fell apart; Justinus reports that Chandragupta was even condemned to death for speaking too boldly to the king [56]. Perhaps we may, with Basham, surmise that Alexander remained a source of inspiration for the young upstart (who escaped with his life) [57].

In the period after the Macedonian withdrawal two events happened, the order of which is uncertain; they took place between 324 and 316. Chandragupta filled the power vacuum left in the Punjab through the retreat of the Macedonian army by recapturing the Greek garrison towns. He also dethroned the last Nanda ruler of Magadha and became emperor in his stead. It is not certain whether he was able to drive out the Greeks because he made himself king, or whether the fame he had acquired by his military exploits enabled him to usurp the royal power. Although the centre of his power was Pataliputra, the capital of Magadha on the middle course of the Ganges, he succeeded in extending his sway as far as Sindh (the lower region of the Indus), Gujarat (the territory east of this region), Kathiawar (the peninsula to the south

THE MAURYAN EMPIRE UNDER ASOKA

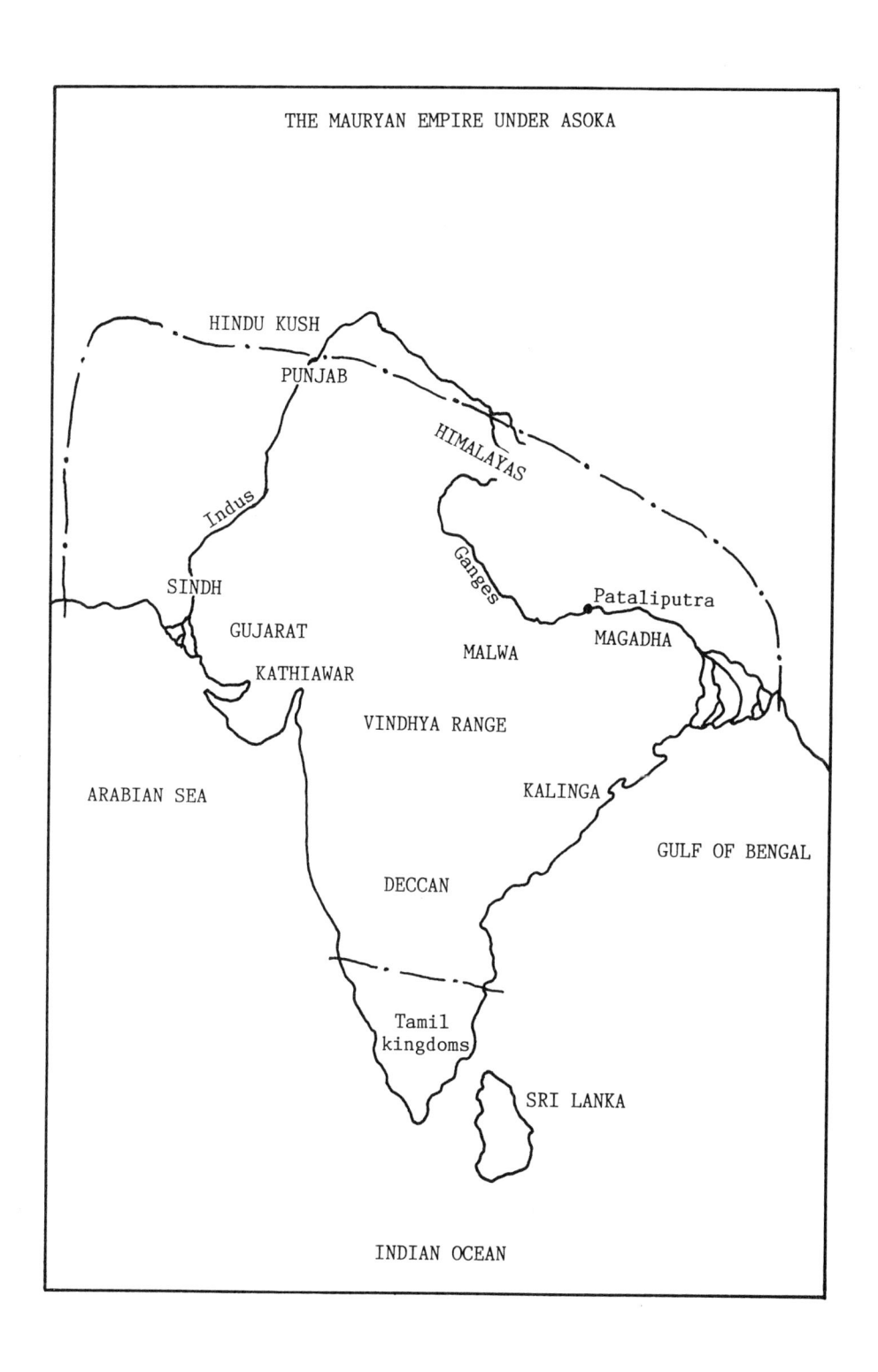

of Gujarat), and Malwa (the region just north of the Vindhya Range) [58]. This means that the whole of Hindustan - the Indus and the Ganges valleys, and the territories in between, north of the Vindhya Mountains - was firmly in the hands of the new emperor. It is, however, not impossible that he did not rule this large realm directly but by means of feudal princes and viceroys [59].

b. Chandragupta's power test

The great test of Chandragupta's power came when Seleucus I, king of Syria, in 305 B.C. marched down on him in an attempt to re-establish the Hellenic dominion along and beyond the Indus. East and west met again, in the same unfriendly manner as twenty years earlier. We remember Seleucus as the ambitious successor of Alexander, as the man who finally won the overlordship over the largest part of the Macedonian conquests, virtually the whole of the former Persian Empire, with the exception of Egypt. He too wanted to extend his rule far beyond the Indus. However, since the death of Alexander a major shift in the balance of power had occurred, for, in contrast to his predecessor, Chandragupta was 'a great military genius' and 'a far-sighted politician'[60].

Alas, next to nothing is known of the course of the Graeco-Indian war, but it is certain that Seleucus had the worst of the fighting. The Syrian had to cede to his opponent the districts of Kabul, Herat, and Kandahar, and the Gedrosia (Baluchistan) region, that is, in modern terms, (parts of) Afghanistan and Pakistan. So the result of this renewed east-west clash was that, instead of the Greeks conquering Indian territory east of the Indus, the Indians were able to extend their rule far to the west of this river. All that Seleucus got out of it was that his rival sent him five hundred elephants. After the conclusion of the peace treaty, Chandragupta married a daughter of Seleucus so that the Mauryan dynasty is partly Macedonian in origin [61].

There is a tradition, or a legend, that Chandragupta Maurya 'abdicated his throne and became a Jaina monk' (we shall have to discuss Jainism later); it is said that he fasted so severely in the main Jaina temple that he died. His reign lasted twenty-four years [62]. This Jaina legend, however, is contradicted by Greek sources [63]. He was succeeded by his son Bindusara who reigned from approximately 302 to 269. The main merit of this king was that he kept his father's empire intact and even began to extend it southward into the Deccan.

c. Asoka

We must now rivet our attention on Bindusara's son and successor, King Asoka, who ruled the Mauryan Empire for thirty-six or thirty-seven years (269-232). Historians vie with one another in calling him 'great' and 'noble' - 'the greatest and noblest ruler India has known, and indeed one of the great kings of the world' [64], 'one of the greatest names in the history of the world' [65]. Bindusara possessed a great harem and had many, many sons with his numerous concubines. Buddhist sources have it that Asoka was a usurper and ascended the throne after having killed his ninety-eight brothers. Now the Buddhist tradition presents Asoka as a paragon of this faith; he later underwent a conversion. In order to stress the importance and radicality of this change of heart, these sources possibly try to depict his former life in as black a manner as possible. This induces Majumdar to dismiss the story that Asoka "waded to the throne through the blood of his ninety-eight brothers" as "pure fiction" [66].

It was, however, not uncommon in Antiquity (and later) for claimants to the throne to eliminate their rivals, in particular when these had a better position in the line of succession. The number of ninety-eight brothers is very probably a mythical exaggeration nor need we suppose that all Asoka's relatives were killed by him. One of his rock inscriptions mentions brothers living thirteen years after his accession. But there is every reason to believe that the new king had to fight his way to the throne and that one or more of his brothers paid with their lives for their better claims. In another Rock Edict the repentant Asoka accuses himself of 'unseemly behaviour to relatives' [67].

When Asoka had reigned eight years he fought a bloody war to conquer the Kalinga territory which is situated on the north-eastern shores of the peninsula. With this country firmly in his hands he was master of an empire larger than Indian history had ever seen. It stretched from Afghanistan and Baluchistan (Pakistan) in the west over the whole width of continental India to Bengal (Bangladesh), and from the Hindu Kush and the Himalayas in the north to a line far south of the Vindhya Range. All the regions on the peninsula north of a line running westward from Nellore (on the east coast) formed part of the Mauryan Empire. Only the Tamil kingdoms of the southern half of the peninsula stayed out of it" [68].

The Kalinga war was a bloody and cruel affair fought with all the cruelty that is the consequence of dualistic imperialism. Asoka himself gives the extent of the losses in human life suffered by the Kalinga population; they show that no regard was paid to the right of existence of the country and its inhabitants. "A hundred and fifty thousand people were taken captive, a hundred thousand were killed, and many more died" [69]. But then something happened that we have not yet encountered in the history of political dualism : the conqueror repented of what he had done. Calling himself 'the Beloved of the Gods', he states that he "began to follow Dharma" which is probably best, although inadequately, translated by 'Righteousness' [70]. "The Beloved of the Gods considers that the greatest of all victories is the victory of Righteousness". From now on the converted ruler strove after 'safety, self-control, justice and happiness for all beings' [71].

It is a difficult problem to determine exactly the religion to which the Beloved of the Gods was converted. 'Dharma' is a term used by Buddhists, and in all probability he became an adherent of Buddhism. But it is a moot point how much of a Budhhist he became. Some say that, somewhat later, he entered a Buddhist order of monks, the 'Sangha', and that he "made a deep study of Buddhist scripture" [72]. Others argue that Asoka, although doubtless a Buddhist, had 'no easily definable religion' [73]. Like Darius in his relation to Zoroastrianism, Asoka had no eye for the finer metaphysical points of Buddhism; for instance, he never speaks of another typically Buddhist concept, 'Nirvana' [74]. Perhaps he was conscious of the fact that he must not stress his Buddhism too much, since there existed other religions in his realm. Basham even says that "the Dharma officially propagated by Asoka was not Buddhism at all, but a system of morals consistent with the moral tenets of most of the sects of the Empire" [75]. However, authorities agree that Asoka's reign was a turning-point in the history of Buddhism since it became a world religion in this period. This means that the emperor exchanged his former political imperialism for a religious one. He claims 'victories' won in Syria, Egypt, Macedonia, in the Tamil countries, and in Sri Lanka. We shall have to return to this.

We may describe Asoka, after his conversion, as an 'enlightened despot'; like his namesakes of the eighteenth century he governed his peoples with a strong hand, according to broad humanitarian principles. But just as he did not wholly relinquish his imperialist policies and still wanted to make 'conquests', he also remained a despot. Sometimes he showed himself intolerant; he even says as much of himself : "If anyone does him (the king) wrong, it will be forgiven as far as it can be forgiven" [76]. Forgiving he might be but he also remained a political realist reserving to himself the right to punish severely. Even the killer occasionally showed himself up. "But the Beloved of the Gods is not only compassionate, he is also powerful, and he tells them to repent, lest they be slain" [77]. These menacing words were addressed to the wild forest tribes that were not eager to lose their freedom to the Mauryan Empire. Confronted with their fierce resistance the emperor threatened to resort again to his policy of extermination. The verb 'to repent' lets it transpire that, in his eyes, it was even a kind of religious offence not to submit to Mauryan power.

d. The Bactrian menace

The kings who followed Asoka were not of his calibre; there were seven of them in half a century. Disintegration soon set in; the area south of the Vindhya Range, always difficult to keep under control, was soon lost. Hindustan remained a Mauryan domain until about 183 B.C. Then the last Mauryan king was deposed by one of his generals.

Magadha, the kingdom from which Mauryan imperialism had originated, once again became one of the many states of northern India, for the dependencies in the Ganges and Indus valleys and in the hill country in between all threw off the Mauryan yoke.

True enough, Toynbee speaks of the urge to eternity, to existing forever, that is found in the 'universal states' that great empires are. But, at the same time, this urge is entirely frustrated by what Thomas Wolfe calls 'devastating impermanence' [78]. Often, indeed, empires, even at the time of their greatest extension and their strongest coherence, lead a precarious existence crumbling to pieces at the first puff of wind. Even the mightiest realm is to some extent a house of cards.

The downfall of the Mauryan Empire occurred precisely at that moment when the Indian states should have acted as a unity. For the third time in succession east and west met, and once again the encounter was not friendly. As I already related in Chapter I, large chips soon fell off the Seleucid block. In the far east of this empire two provinces made themselves independent, Parthia and Bactria. This happened about 250 B.C. For half a century the Seleucid rulers tried to re-establish their sovereignty over these outlying regions, but gave up all further attempts about 208 B.C. Now while Parthia - we saw this too - got a national dynasty, the kings of Bactria were Greeks. Their kingdom comprised the north-eastern provinces of modern Iran, some of the southern Soviet-republics of the present day, and the western part of Afghanistan. The range of the Hindu Kush separated Bactria from the Mauryan Empire. These mountains, however, are not too formidable; its passes can easily be crossed. The Bactrians, being the nearest neighbours of the Indians, were not unknown to them; they called these Greeks 'Yavanas' which is derived from the Persian 'Iauna', and this in its turn from the Greek name for 'Ionians' [79].

About 200 B.C. King Euthydemos of Bactria pushed beyond the Hindu Kush conquering some strongholds eastward of these mountains. His son, King Demetrius, succeeded in occupying south and east Afghanistan, and a large part of the Indus valley and of the Punjab.

Several cities called 'Demetria' and 'Euthydemia' were founded. Heaven knows what this powerful and aggressive ruler would have done to the weakened Mauryan Empire had he not been pushed aside by a usurper called Eucratides in 175 B.C. This man extended Graeco-Bactrian rule in north-west India still further. After him came a king whose name was Menander and who, according to the Greek geographer Strabo, "conquered more nations than Alexander" [80]. He is reported to have crossed the river Beas (the Hyphasis of the ancients) that was the farthest limit of the Macedonian's conquests and to have pressed on eastward to the Ganges valley which he actually reached; it is possible that he (or one of his successors) even was in the old Mauryan capital Pataliputra (Patna). This does not mean that these conquests became permanent Bactrian possessions; they rather were successful raids which, extending so far eastward, prove the great weakness of the Indian states at this juncture. Anyhow, King Menander lives on in Indian literature as 'Milinda' (the only Graeco-Bactrian ruler to be mentioned by ancient Indian authors).

In the second half of the second century B.C. the Bactrian motherland was conquered by the Scythians. Graeco-Bactrian kings, however, continued to rule in Afghanistan and in the Indus valley. The Bactrian dominion there soon feel apart into two, or even more, kingdoms. Later nomads from the north occupied much of the Indo-Bactrian territories. About 150 B.C. there still existed some Greek rulers with small kingdoms in the Indus valley; the very last of them was a certain Hermaeus who, about 40 B.C., was swept away by the Kushanites [81].

5. Nomad incursions

There is no need for us to retrace the history of ancient India in any detail; for the present more than a broad outline would fall beyond our scope. In the era we are speaking of invaders came and went making India a prey to their ambitions and rapacity. Important migrations were going on all the time in Central Asia. About 165 B.C. the always restless tribe of the Huns, when trying to invade China, shrunk back with bloody foreheads from the Great Wall. They then hit upon a people called the Yüeh-Chi that lived in the modern Chinese province of Kansu and drove them on. The Yüeh-Chi migrated to the west, being between half a million and a million souls strong [82], reached Turkestan, and there chased before them hordes of other tribes.

Among them were the Scythians - the 'Sakas' of the Persians - who moved southward and made an end of Greek rule in Bactria. Large parts of western India too fell into their hands; we find them far to the south in Gujarat and Malwa where they set up independent kingdoms. Greek geographers of the centuries around the birth of Christ used to call the whole region simply 'Scythia'. Later, in the first century A.D., Parthian, or Pahlava, invaders joined them or took over from them (it is very difficult to distinguish the Scythians from the Parthians in India). It is interesting to note that the Indo-Scythian kings even usurped the old and proud title of 'King of Kings' (or 'Great King'), although they, at least in name, recognized the Parthian emperor as their suzerain. Coins of Indo-Scythian kings are found with dates as late as 388 A.D. [83].

In Chapter I I mentioned the Kushanites who became the founders of the Kushan Empire. The Kushanites, or Kushanas, formed part of the nomad tribe of the Yüeh-Chi. With the Huns on their heels they moved on, took Bactria from the Scythians, and became a settled nation there. Originally Bactria was divided among the five tribes of the Yüeh-Chi, but at some time between 25 and 81 A.D. the chief of the Kushana tribe succeeded in making Bactria into a united kingdom now called 'Kushan'. "Thus" - as Rapson has it - "once more Bactria became the nursery of a great power which was destined to dominate N.W. India" [84]. The preceding centuries had successively seen the attempts of the Greeks, the Scythians, and the Parthians, to make continental India their own; now it was the turn of the Kushanas, but like all their predecessors they finally failed. The Mongols of the sixteenth and seventeenth centuries came very near to complete unification but even the great Akbar (1565-1605) was unable to conquer the southern Deccan. Until the 'British Raj' no foreign invaders succeeded in uniting the Indian subcontinent under their rule.

Soon the Kushanite kings penetrated into the lands beyond the Hindu Kush occupying southern Afghanistan. From there, about 60 A.D., northwest India was reached. New conquests were made farther east; perhaps even Benares, on the middle course of the Ganges, temporarily was in Kushanite hands. The Pahlava-Saka (Parthian-Scythian) kings had to submit to them; these kinglets became satraps or viceroys of the Kushan emperor. During the reign of King Kanishka who ascended the throne in 78 A.D., the Kushan Empire comprised many countries on both sides of the Hindu Kush, in India proper including Kashmir, the Indus valley, the western part of the Ganges valley, and the territories south of these rivers down to the Vindhya Range. Not for nothing the Kushan ruler styled himself the 'Son of Heaven'; possibly this term was borrowed from the Chinese. Until deep in the fourth century the Son of Heaven managed to keep his empire mainly intact but then he had to bow before the might of an authentically Indian dynasty, the Guptas [85].

6. Particularism or unity?

Neither titles like 'King of Kings' or 'Great King', especially when they were worn by petty Pahlava or Saka rulers, nor even such lofty claims as 'Son of Heaven', that suggested the near kinship of the far mightier Kushan emperor with the celestial beings themselves, were powerful enough to fill the political vacuum that was continental India at that time. The history of this country as we have studied it so far has taught us that there continually existed two impulses to unite India - one foreign and coming from abroad, the other springing from the Indian soil itself. The first urge, that of the aliens, always originated in Bactria; it was from there that successively Alexander, the Seleucids, the Graeco-Bactrian kings, the Scythians and the Parthians, and finally the Kushanites, came to the Indian plains. All these invaders descended the slopes of the Hindu Kush, penetrated into the Indus valley, and marched on, or attempted to do this, to the Ganges and the Deccan.

But none of them saw the treacherous waters of the Gulf of Bengal, at the mouth of the great holy river; none of them succeeded in crossing the Vindhya Range. Their sway over continental India was always like an exotic tree alien to India's climate and short-lived like Jona's ivy-plant that withered away in one morning's time. Did the indigenous dynasties fare so much better, we may ask? True enough, the Mauryan Empire reached a far larger extent than any other empire of earlier or later days. But it did not comprise all India, while its hold on some of its dependencies was rather weak. Even the great Moghul Empire of the centuries after 1500 did not surpass its Mauryan predecessor in extent.

Once again, in the age of the discoveries, foreign invaders appeared, the Dutch, the French, the English, this time not coming from Bactria but from over the seas. The British became the first power able to unite all India, for finally the British Raj included the whole subcontinent, together with Kashmir and Jammu, Baluchistan, Sri Lanka, and Bengal, while further east Burma too fell into the orbit of the British Empire. But when all is said and done, seen from an historical perspective even the British Raj was of short duration : the British disappeared almost overnight in 1947 leaving an explosive heritage to their nationalist successors. The modern rulers of the Indian subcontinent by no means are of one accord as is proved by the fact that the British Raj finally became divided into four sovereign states, Pakistan, India, Bangladesh, and Sri Lanka.

What is persistent during the whole course of subcontinental history is a dualistic, obviously unbridgeable opposition between particularity and the urge towards unity, and it seems that particularity suits the natural trends of Indian existence more comfortably than unity. The subcontinent presents such a mosaic of the most different races, languages, civilizations, and religions, that every attempt to establish unity is felt as doing violence to the Indian temper. We saw all the empires give up, we saw the British, more powerful than all the others, resign too. Their departure in 1947 was hastened by the outbreak of bloody strife between Hindus and Moslims resulting in the creation of two separate republics, India and Pakistan, that keep up a permanent quarrel over Kashmir and Jammu.

The British were only able to govern the subcontinent by granting a fair amount of autonomy to the old principalities. Their successors adopted this system too; India in fact is a federation, the Indian Union, consisting of a considerable number of autonomous provinces each with its own government (but no longer ruled by princes). Nevertheless, central rule from New Delhi is often felt to be oppressive; there is, for instance, a running conflict between the All-India government and the proud Sikhs. Bloody incidents, like the storming of the Golden Temple at Amritsar, and the subsequent assassination of the then premier, Mrs. Indira Gandhi, prove that the dualistic opposition between particularity and unity is as fierce as ever. Let us now return to the past and see whether the gifted monarchs of the Gupta dynasty managed this inveterate problem with more luck.

7. The Gupta dynasty

As was already related in Chapter I, the rise of Sasanian power in Iran led to a gradual but irreversible decline of the Kushan Empire. It disintegrated into several separate kingdoms which, perhaps, formed a very loose federation under the supremacy of the Kushan ruler. For some time the Son of Heaven continued to rule in much diminished glory over an obscure corner of the Indian borderland where he soon came to feel the irresistible might of the Gupta arms.

After a century, the third A.D., during which no claimant to imperial overlordship presented himself, something began to stir in Magadha again. Shortly after 300 A.D. Sri-Gupta, or Gupta for short, was a petty ruler there. His son was not greater than his father but his grandson was made of sterner stuff. His name was Chandragupta; we must not confuse him with the Mauryan Chandragupta of several centuries earlier. He came to the throne as Chandragupta I in about 320 (dates are still far from certain in this period). His original position was considerably strengthened by a lucky match with a Licchavi princess, the heiress of great power and prestige in northern Bihar (between the Ganges and the Himalayas) and perhaps even in Nepal [86]. Soon Chandragupta began to extend the frontiers of his own small domain; soon his possessions included Allahabad and the region of Oudh much farther westward up the Ganges river [87].

Consequently he felt himself important enough to adopt a title more grandiose than any we have encountered before in all imperial history : he called himself 'Maharajadhiraja' a title which is an inflation of the well-known 'Maharaja' = 'Great King'; the longer title signifies 'Supreme King of Great Kings' which sounds considerably more lofty than the Persian 'King of Kings' [88].

From about 335 to ca. 376 or 380 his son Samudragupta governed the Gupta realm. "His whole reign was a vast military campaign", says Majumdar [89]. Left and right, near and far, kingdoms fell like blades of straw before the onslaught of his arms. First of all, he made himself master of the whole of the Ganges valley. The ancient Mauryan seat of power, Pataliputra, had perhaps already surrendered to his father but it was without doubt in the hands of the son; anyhow, it was he who took up residence there. Farther to the east and north, he penetrated into Bengal, Assam, and Nepal, and made many princes his vassals there. To the west, in the region between the Ganges and Indus river systems, nine independent states were defeated and annexed by Samudra. He seems to have left intact the Saka dominions that still existed there (in all probability they were dependent on the Kushan empire). To quote Basham, "he did not measure swords with them, or if he did, he was unsuccessful" [90].

Quite another problem was that of the independent states in the Deccan. Very probably Samudra was desirous to subdue them in order to equal or even to surpass the range of the Mauryan sway. He conducted a long military raid along the east coast of the peninsula that brought him as far as Kancheepuram or Conjeeveram, at some distance south-west of Madras. Claims made by some Indian historians that he even reached the southern tip of the peninsula at Cape Comorin are not in accordance with the facts (although it must be admitted that the copper plates on the Allahabad pillar, and other sources which record the events of this reign, are difficult to read). It is true that Samudra defeated more than twenty Deccan kings and took them prisoner, but the fact that he re-instated them as his vassals proves that he was none too sure of his possibilities with regard to these southern regions. Actually he seems to have remained content with a nominal acknowledgment of his suzerainty. Pataliputra really was too far from the Deccan, and the lines of communication still were too slender and insecure to enable the exercise of direct, or even indirect, political rule south of the Vindhya Range. Basham supposes that the southern vassals "probably heard little more of their titular overlord" 91).

The reckoning with the last vestiges of Saka or Kushana power came under Samudra's son, Chandragupta II (376 or 380-413 or 415). We do not know much of this emperor's campaign in Malwa, Gujarat, and Kathiawar, but the result is well attested. Saka rule was brought to an end there and these territories were annexed by the Gupta state that now bordered on the Arabian Sea. The attentive reader, however, will have remarked that the Indus valley is not mentioned; this region remained out of the scope of Gupta conquests. This means that in the event the Gupta Empire was not as large as the Mauryan one. This nothwithstanding, Chandragupta II was considered great enough to perform the famous horse-sacrifice, the so-called 'digvijaga', the 'conquest of the quarters', that is of the whole world, the typical imperial claim. This ritual is mentioned in the old Vedic books; in later times it was reserved for great conquerors.

Then came his son Kumara Gupta I (413 or 415-454 or 455). He too was entitled to perform the horse-sacrifice, although he was no conqueror. On the whole, his reign was peaceful; he kept the vast Gupta inheritance intact, except in the last years of his reign which saw a great invasion by the Hunas or Huns. Although some historians believe these to be Iranians rather than Mongolians, most scholars assume that they were a branch of the Turco-Mongolian tribes that

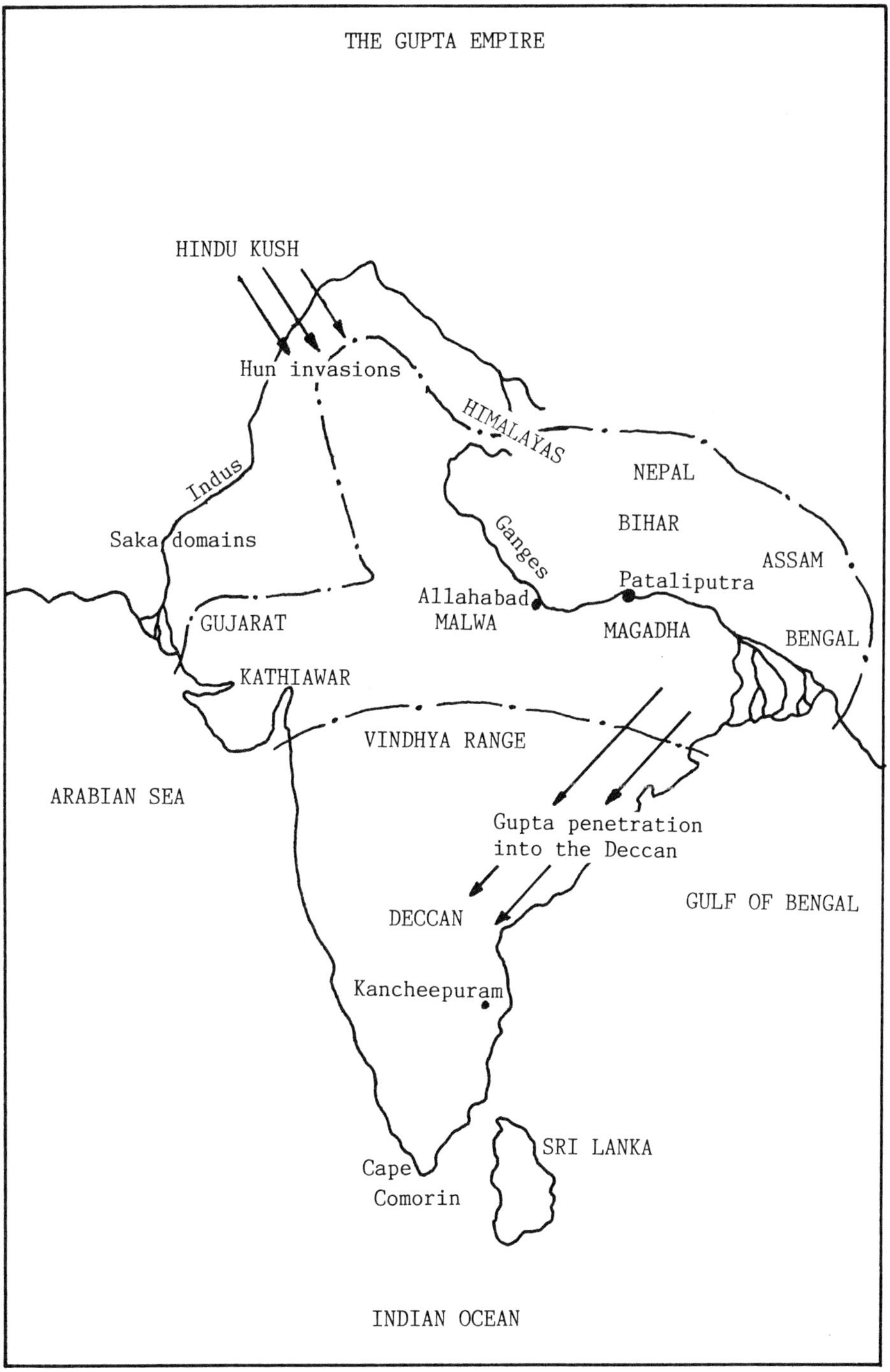
THE GUPTA EMPIRE
HINDU KUSH
Hun invasions
HIMALAYAS
Indus
NEPAL
BIHAR
Saka domains
Ganges
ASSAM
Pataliputra
Allahabad
MALWA
GUJARAT
MAGADHA
BENGAL
KATHIAWAR
VINDHYA RANGE
ARABIAN SEA
Gupta penetration
into the Deccan
GULF OF BENGAL
DECCAN
Kancheepuram
SRI LANKA
Cape
Comorin
INDIAN OCEAN

go by the ill-famed name of Huns. Having established themselves in Bactria they attempted to penetrate into India by following the usual routes. A capable prince, a younger son of the reigning emperor, succeeded in warding off these devastating inroads. Having become king as Skanda Gupta (545/455-467), he had to continue the fight with the Huns and other invaders and upstarts. Succesful though he was, the constant exertions seem to have tapped the resources of the empire too much.

After his death Gupta power began to wane. There were territorial losses in the west, but on the whole imperial unity was maintained until 500 B.C. From then on the empire disintegrated into several more or less independent provinces. Probably two or even more branches of the Gupta dynasty existed side by side then. These kings are known as the 'Later Guptas'; some of them were fairly succesful in maintaining themselves and in extending their domains. The last vestiges of Gupta power disappeared as late as the eighth century. It was in these latter days that Islam made its first appearance in India. As early as 637 an Arab army landed on the coast near Bombay. The main way of approach, however, was through southern Afghanistan and Baluchistan. In 712 the Arabs gained a foothold in the Indus valley. We shall make this arrival of Islam in India the limit of our treatment of Indian political history in this volume.

8. The Harappa culture

We shall now proceed with an exposition of dualistic tendencies in Indian social life. First of all we must, for a short moment, turn our attention to the ancient Harappa or Indus civilization.

Excavations of Stone Age civilizations yield useful information on the way people then lived and how they buried their dead. They tell us much less about social life and about political organization. It is only after 3000 B.C. that the general picture becomes somewhat clearer. It was the period of the so-called 'Harappa culture' or 'Indus civilization' that, as I have already mentioned, existed in the Indus valley.

Something that resembled developments in the Nile and the Euphrates and Tigris valleys took place here too : a well-organized system of irrigation using the waters of the Indus was needed to ensure the regular growth of crops. These crops were abundant enough to feed a non-agricultural population living in cities some of which, like Harappa and Mohenjo-Dara, were fairly large. Now large cities call for a highly organized form of government in contrast to small peasant communities. Furthermore, the elaborate irrigation system needed regular and expert supervision. These two fundamental traits of Harappa social life led to ' a strong system of centralized government' that, in the words of Piggott, was 'controlling production and distribution and levying a system of tolls and customs in the territory under its rule' [92]. This does not mean that one great Harappa kingdom existed in the Punjab and the Indus valley. By no means! But we may safely assume that, already at that time, there was a sharp distinction between the rulers and those who obeyed, paid, and did the actual work.

We must not think of a professional political class yet, deriving its power from some written or unwritten consititution. It still had a predominantly technical or practical character; this leads Malik to speak of a 'central agency for the coordination and distribution of products'. The expertise needed for this managerial work very probably led not only to the emergence of an 'elite class' but also to making this kind of function hereditary in order to pass on expert knowledge as intact and complete as possible. Thus this knowledge became continuous and, at the same time, somewhat 'secret'. It will not surprise us that some authors identify this 'elite' class with the 'priestly' class. "Thus", Malik concludes, "the 'central agency' of Harappa culture must have served many different functions, such as the social, political and economic ones, in addition to the religious one" [93]. Kosambi assures us that each city's rulers "may on general probability have had priestly attributes" but "were essentially secular in outlook" [94].

The great problem, of course, is that, in consequence of the total absence of written texts, we know precious little of the spiritual attitudes of the people of the Indus civilization. Probably Kosambi means that the Indians at that time had not yet developed a (mythological) 'ideology of kingship' of the type that already existed in Egypt [95].

9. The Aryans, their kings, and the conquered peoples

Then the Aryans came. We know that they came as nomads who, from 1500 or 1400 B.C. onward, flooded the Indus and the Ganges valleys finally subjecting the whole of continental India north of the Vindhya Range. The newcomers were organized in tribes each with its own king or 'rajan'. He was chosen by the assembly of the nobles and came from the ranks of the leading classes. We must not see these tribal kings as absolute monarchs. Their power was hemmed in by the popular assembly and the royal council, the last being called the 'sabha', although the word may perhaps have designated the council's seat [96]. The word lived on in Indian politics, for even to-day one of the two chambers of Indian parliament is called the 'Lok Sabha', the People's Chamber. Furthermore there was the influence of the priestly class.

As we may expect in a period of conquests, the main task of the king was to conduct the army. He sat on horseback, or in a chariot drawn by horses, surrounded by his mounted nobles; the common people fought on foot [97]. In the course of time the status of the king grew more and more exalted. Slowly but certainly the election by the nobles became a mere formality; to all intents and purposes kingship became hereditary. The difficult conditions of the conquest also strengthened the position of the ruler.

There are many indications that the indigenous inhabitants did not exactly welcome the arrival of the Aryans. We have no records of how they reacted to the invasions but we know something of the way the conquerors saw them. The Aryans simply loathed the autochthonous populations; in their eyes these were subhuman. The hostile non-Aryan tribes were called 'Dasa' or 'Dasyu', a term that later significantly came to mean 'slave' or 'helot'. The victors did not like the way the Dasyu looked : in contrast to the Aryans themselves they were dark-skinned and flat-nosed. To their conquerors this meant that they had no nose at all, that they were 'anasa'. On top of this, their speech was an unintelligible mumble. Worst of all, they did not venerate the great Aryan god Indra but, instead, the phallus. To the Aryans this meant that they had simply no gods at all [98].

The relationship between victors and vanquished was, as I stated earlier, of a purely dualistic kind. Conquerors despise those whom they subjugate; their defeat justifies their own right to conquer. In this case we can also note the difference between the warlike and horse-riding nomads who venerated male gods, and the agricultural populations that adored fertility and female divinities. We must, however, never forget that a dualistic attitude always conceals fear. Or perhaps we should say that it is prompted by fear. Not for nothing is the opposite pole despised and belittled as inferior, and even threatened with extinction. Having once conquered such an enormous extent of land, the Aryans found themselves in the midst of peoples richer, more highly organized, and more civilized than themselves. True enough, in the course of the centuries India, at least north of the Vindhya Range, became thoroughly 'aryanized', while, by the same token, the conquerors, to a certain extent, were 'indianized', with the result that the two poles neared each other, so that a more homogeneous society came into being. But, at this early stage, the opposition between the two kinds of population was still very fierce. It made the Aryans rely on strong leadership, since they feared the aboriginals.

However practical the duties of an Aryan king were even in the tribal and nomad stages, there was a connection of the prince with the powers above. After all, one of his principal tasks was to offer sacrifices [99]. The nature of these sacrifices shows that a mythological dimension was already present in the idea of kingship. The main sacrificial animals were male, like the bull and the stallion; even male human beings might be offered. The most important sacrifice was the already mentioned 'horse-sacrifice' that later became the privilege of great conquerors. The chosen animal was a white stallion; after its ritual consecration it got another lease of life for a year during which it freely roamed about. Then a chariot race was held, and finally the animal was killed to ensure the king's success in war and peace. As soon as the animal was dead, the chief queen pantomimed copulation with it in what was very probably a fertility rite [100].

10. The emperors

The conquest of the northern half of India by the Aryans meant the end of their nomadic wanderings. They too became settled, tilled the ground, and founded and inhabited cities. Kingdoms and principalities with more or less fixed frontiers arose everywhere; political organization became more elaborate than it had been in former, far simpler days. The function of the king acquired a more theological, or mythological, character. If it is true that Indian rulers borrowed the idea of empire from the Persians, then they also adopted from their western neighbours the idea that the emperor was more than human - he was, indeed, divine. In India too we find the typical Persian conception of the king as a man with an (ethical) mission, who first and foremost has to look after the moral and material well-being of his subjects [101]. Considerations such as these raised Indian kingship to an ever loftier status, the more so when some kings succeeded in spreading their wings far and wide by founding an empire.

I am, of course, thinking now of the Nanda, Mauryan, and Gupta emperors of Magadha. For the first time we are confronted here with absolute monarchies. The older idea that a king was hardly more than a leader in battle was gradually supplanted by a totally different one. One of the Upanishads, from perhaps the seventh century B.C., relates how gods and demons were at war. The gods, being hard pressed, prayed to the highest god who sent his son Indra who led them to victory [102]. This gave kingship a divine sanction "since the king of the immortals (Indra), who was the prototype of all earthly kings, held his office by appointment of the Most High" [103]. The elaborate ceremony of consecration not only served to make the king holy but also to divinize him. "Of mighty power", prayed the officiating priest, "is he who has been consecrated; now he has become one of yours (the gods); you must protect him"[104]. The power of the king was felt to be mythical rather than political or military. The consecration ceremony imbued him with magical powers.

So far it may seem very simple. But there is another theory of kingship that is of Buddhist origin[105]; it is said to have been proclaimed by the Buddha himself. It is based on the myth of the cosmic cycle according to which mankind originally lived in a kind of paradise. But when things began to deteriorate and strife and murder appeared on the scene people felt it necessary to bring about some measure of order. Therefore they defined their mutual relations by means of a 'social contract'; one man was appointed to superintend the implementation of this contract; in exchange the others provided him with food[106]. Now it was not the case that one or other of these two theories was adhered to, either the mythical or the juridical. As Drekmeier states, "in Hindu political thought, social contract and divine origin meet in a shadowy union ... often rather incongruously combined"[107]. Yet Basham believes that, as we might expect, "it was the mystical theory of kingship which carried most weight with succeeding generations"[108].

The king, therefore, was a being of an higher order, different from all other beings. Although he himself was not considered a god, his function was divine and had its origin with the gods. Of course, this conception radiated back upon the king as an individual person; it made him godlike and quasi-divine[109]. Since there were no intermediary stages between king and subject, no gradual transition from one plane to the other, we may dub this relationship as dualistic. This does, however, not mean that the king necessarily was a cruel tyrant, acting according to his own whims. On the contrary! I have already mentioned the ethical nature of Indian kingship. The king was subject to 'dharma', the general rule of the universe ruling everything on earth. Since the king had first and foremost to promote his people's welfare, "the Hindu state was, thus, a civil rather than a military polity"[110]. Utterly practical as the king's task of creating and maintaining order may appear, this too strengthened the mythical side of kingship since this order was supernaturally decreed [111]. It will be self-evident that not all kings lived up to the sublime precepts of their office. Subjects sometimes rose in revolt, kings were occasionally dethroned by rivals or even murdered. Their quasi-divine status did not protect them in such emergences.

11. Empire and unity

Now a word must be said about the significance of the concept of empire with regard to all-Indian unity. In the foregoing sections it was shown that many invaders and many Indian-born rulers tried to lay their hands on the whole of the subcontinent. For what I am going to say it is of no importance that none of them succeeded in this design. For instance, the northern Deccan hardly ever came into the orbit of these conquests, and the southern half never at all. What was the real aim of the great emperors? To unite all India under their sceptre? Putting it like this we would not go wrong of course. Their ambition is borne out by the titles they wore : 'Maharaja' = Great King, 'Paramesvara' = Supreme Lord, 'Paramabhattaraka' = the Most Worshipful one, 'Maharajadhiraja' = Supreme King of the Maharajas, and the most lofty of them all, 'Maharajadhiraja Paramabhattaraka' = Supreme King of the Maharajas, Most Worshipful Lord. The inflation of these terms was so great that the title 'maharaja' was used for petty rulers only [112]. Accordingly the term lost much of its intrinsic power. For as Beni Prasad formulates it, "every real (Indian) kingdom is an empire. An empire or a kingdom is largely a feudal organization (that is to say, it always consisted of a number of more or less autonomous provinces ruled by feudatories - F.). As the internal autonomy of the various regions is respected, it partakes of the nature of a confederation" [113].

This brings us to the point I want to stress and that I have mentioned before, that of the innate strength of Indian particularism. There existed no organic concept of political or national unity in India; there was no national or historical consciousness in our sense, no historiography with a national character, or rather no historiography at all. India did not possess a corporate national personality. However, we must never lose sight of the fact that there existed, at least till the Moslims came, general agreement on some important spiritual tenets to which I shall return later. There was always tension between the sentiment of belonging to one big spiritual family and particularism. When ambitious emperors conducted an imperial policy (which, in practice, meant that they made conquests), they did not do so because 'manifest destiny' commissioned them to bring about organic unity as the deepest desire of the Indian soul. This gave their enterprises a dualistic tinge since there was nothing in Indian existence to justify them. All the conquerors ran counter to the inherent tendencies of Indian history. After every bout of imperialism, therefore, the continent returned to its particularist habits.

Up to the treshold of the present age there was no Indian nation. It is a debatable point whether the developments of the last hundred years have led to the birth of one coherent Indian nation. When in 1885 the Indian National Congress was founded, it proclaimed as its first and foremost aim 'the fusion of all the different and conflicting elements that form the population of India into a national unity'. The Indian state of to-day is officially called 'the Indian Union' since it consists of a number of autonomous political and national elements. However, the absence of nationhood does not mean that there was and is no coherence. Long before India began to grope her way towards a common nationality, she formed a society, or perhaps rather a community.

12. The three great Indian concepts

In his fine and penetrating essay that is simply called 'India' Herbert Härtel explains that this community was based on and held together by three great concepts, dharma, samsara, and karman. These ideas are fundamental in pre-Buddhistic thought and were subsequently adopted as their own by all great Indian religions. All three have always exercised and still do exercise such a deep influence on Indian mentality that they may be considered the constitutive elements not only of the Indians' mode of thought but also of their way of life [114].

a. Dharma

Let us begin with the concept of 'dharma'. Mahony says that 'dharma' is the nearest equivalent of our word 'religion' [115]. It is a Sanskrit word derived from the root 'dhr' that signifies 'to sustain, support, uphold'. Every Indian religion uses it to describe its creed and practices [116]. But even our word 'religion' does not full justice to it, and still less do terms as 'order, rule, custom, law, norm, or duty' [117]. It rather "designates the universal order, the natural law, or the uniform norm according to which the whole world runs its course (samsara)" [118]. Centuries before Buddhism we find it ca. 1200 B.C. for the first time in the Rigveda (as 'dharman') signifying there 'cosmic ordinance'. In a work by the Brahman Kanada, the 'Vaisheshika-Sutra' (the date of which is unknown) dharma is defined in the following words : "(It) is that what generates happiness (on earth as in the transitory heavenly world) and the supreme good (which is the freedom from suffering)" [119].

That dharma is described here as a productive principle means that we must not give in to our western idiosyncrasy of seeing such ideas as pure abstractions. On the contrary, "dharman characterizes those personal actions than engender or maintain cosmic order" [120]. To Europeans and Americans it may seem unthinkable that one's moral (or immoral) behaviour would have consequences for the universe, but to Indian thought it is simply self-evident that the stability of the universal order depends on the strict observance of all rules and prescripts that are derived from dharma [121]. There is a very close connection between the cosmos and personal action, or, philosophically spoken, between being and (human) existence. Improper action is untrue, unreal, it makes the universe less real and condemns it to non-being. In later centuries the term 'adharma' = without dharma, was coined. Mahony writes that "in classical Vedic literatures dharma carries ontological weight : being arises out of proper activity while improper action leads to non-being" [122]. We detect a dualistic opposition here, that between two modes of life leading to two totally opposed ontological positions.

b. Samsara

The second concept of fundamental importance is 'samsara'. This too is a Sanskrit term meaning 'passing through a series of states or conditions' [123]. Samsara is the cyclical course of all that exists. Very probably we would prefer to translate it with 'rebirth' or 're-incarnation'. There is nothing against this as long as we realize that not only rebirth but also birth and death are implicated in it, and that everything that lives - gods, demons, animals, human beings - is subjected to it. Samsara also refers to the universe, or rather, it is the universe in its state of change and impermanence. Here again a dualistic distinction presents itself, for there is also an unconditional and eternal state of the universe which is known as 'moksa', or to use a term more familiar to us, as 'nirvana'.

Indian cosmic theology does not explain how, or when, everything came into being. Indians are not so concerned with this question as we are. What is more important to them is the problem why there exist such differences in the world. For when dharma is the law, or the ideal, of universal harmony, how must we explain the fact that there is such general diversity in nature and among mankind. It is the idea of samsara, in combination with that of 'karman', that provides an answer to this question. All Indian religions, each with its variations, agree that samsara is a condition of impermanence, and, therefore, one of suffering and sorrow. The cause of this is that people unintentionally or knowingly act against dharma since they are ignorant of the true nature of reality. As a consequence, they and their lives are in an imperfected state and have to be re-incarnated. One may be reborn as a human being or as an animal, in heaven or in hell, according to some traditions even as a plant or an inanimate object, for instance a rock. There can be countless reincarnations [124].

c. Karman

The third concept, that of 'karman', is closely connected with the idea of samsara. Karman is Sanskrit too; its root 'kr' signifies 'to act, do, bring about' [125]. We might describe it more or less adequately as 'a deed with its (moral) consequences'; it is 'any correct activity in general'. Acting produces karman which is something like the sum total of our activities. This 'product' is seen as a potency with a very subtle material nature; it clings to the soul, to the 'atman', or indestructible part of the human personality. When a person dies, the body disintegrates but the atman remains. The value of the atman is conditioned by the karman. Is this negative, then one must stay some time in hell; is it positive, then in heaven. In accordance with a human being's final condition at the moment of death, he or she is reborn as an heavenly being, a demon, or an animal (or worse). Ever again one is submerged in the stream of samsara [126].

The great question is whether it is possible to force one's way out of samsara, whether one can finally jump off the 'wheel of rebirth'. It is possible indeed, but to explain this something more must be said on the nature of karman. In recent decades, what with the growing interest in eastern mystical religions, this term has found its way to the west as 'karma' (a grammatical form of karman). I have the impression that it is often profoundly misunderstood, for to the westerner it seems to mean a mysterious spiritual force that propels the believer upwards to the heights of deeper insight. This is exactly what it is not. In Indian religious thought karman denotes the fruit of all that a person did or thought in all his former lives together. With this end-product he or she begins a new life the nature of which is determined by his or her karman - one may be (re)born as a king, a slave, or a dog. The new lease of life again adds to the karman and conditions one's next life that may be better or worse than the present or foregoing ones.

Since a person's life never will be ethically perfect, it is almost impossible to free oneself of samsara. One's atman is, so to speak, always at grips with it; the soul feels that it wants something far better, an unchangeable and utterly healthy condition, but it is unable to attain this. "Gift giving, acts of devotion, and other methods of merit making are designed not to obtain release from the cycle of rebirth but rather to achieve a better position within it" [127]. To escape from the bondage of samsara the atman needs something special, a form of higher knowledge that obviously is not given to everyone. To this idea that is common to the three great Indian religions, Hinduism, Buddhism, and Jainism we shall have to return. For the moment we must content ourselves with the important conclusion that India, in spite of all dividing trends, basically forms a spiritual community holding the same tenets.

This short exposition makes it perfectly clear that, at bottom, India was a non-dualistic community. The three great spiritual concepts that I described go a long way towards explaining many of the personal and communal attitudes of Indians to their existence. Their life in common, one knows now, has a uniform background. But we also know - I brought this forward in the chapter on Israel in Volume IV - that even homogeneous societies are not without rifts and fissures. And when it comes to this, ancient India, notwithstanding her common spiritual basis, was not really a homogeneous society. In fact, the spiritual heritage itself contains some elements that play into the hands of dualism.

13. Slavery as a divisive element

a. A Greek observer

Slavery is such a divisive element : at one side the free, however poor, at the other the slaves who cannot dispose of themselves. From my perusal of scholarly literature on ancient India I did not get the impression that authors are highly interested in this subject. Perhaps it hits a blind spot [128]. No blind spot was more impervious to the light than that in the eye of Megasthenes, a Greek who was ambassador of the Seleucid king to the Mauryan court around 302 B.C. In his elaborate account of the Mauryan court and administration he left behind, he categorically declared that no slavery existed in the Mauryan Empire. Several authors believe that he overlooked the phenomenon since slaves in India were far more mildly treated than was the custom in Greek society [129]. But a slave, even when mildly treated, remains a slave, just like a prisoner in comfortable conditions remains a prisoner. The treatment is not the basic fact; what is central is that both categories of people have lost their freedom. Even in ancient India a slave was no more than a marketable commodity. When Megasthenes divided the population of India into seven classes, he did not so much as mention the slaves. In his eyes they doubtless formed a non-class and were a non-people. This was in accordance with his Greek upbringing. And it is also possible that "Indian slavery must have looked so different to a Greek observer from slavery at home that he did not recognise it for what is was" [130].

b. Who became slaves

It is beyond any doubt that in ancient India slavery really existed. It is as Rhys-Davis states : "The distinct and unanimous testimony of all the Indian evidence is decisive that the status of slavery was then an actual factor in Indian life, though not a very important one" [131]. Indian economy and the upkeep of daily life were not so dependent on slavery as their Greek counterparts, nor were slaves so numerous as in Greece. As I already related, the word for slave was 'dasa' which is homonymous with the name of the people the Aryans subjected, the Dasas or Dasyus. Some authors believe that the main body of the slave population (though not all of it) was descended from this defeated nation [132]. Others, on the contrary, consider this a misconception. They say that "the process of amalgamation of the invaders with the conquered aborigines took the form of intermarriage" [133]. Some ancient texts, however, seem to lend force to the first hypothesis; the Arthasastra, a political handbook of the fourth century A.D., declares that servitude is not in the nature of the Aryan [134]. Although without any doubt there were Aryan slaves, a text like this one proves that the Aryans felt that the aboriginals were predestined for slavery by their inborn nature.

Perhaps the notion that the conquered Dasyus became slaves has also something to do with the fact that prisoners of war, unless ransomed, were reduced to slavery. In Antiquity this was the custom everywhere; India was no different in this respect. The Mahabharata categorically states that "it is a law of war that the vanquished should be the victor's slave"[135]. As in Greece wars were constant providers of slaves. However valiantly a soldier might have fought, the fact that he was brought down proved that he was an inferior being, so that his obvious place was among the serfs. Those who were born from a sexual union between slaves became slaves themselves. People who were unable to pay their debts might sell themselves, their wives, and children into slavery.

c. Utterly different

True enough, slaves usually were not harshly treated. The free day-labourer or hireling often was worse off [136]. This attitude was not so much dictated by pure human feeling but rather by practical sense. "A man may go short himself or stint his wife and children, but never his slave who does the dirty work for him"[137]. Slaves could be set free by their masters; those who became slaves on account of their debts were free again once the debt was paid. Freed slaves could rise to high positions, even become counsellors of kings.

All this is true enough. But the basic fact remains that a slave always remained an inferior being utterly different from the free. He was a possession himself, an object that could be bought and sold and even mortgaged [138]. Slave-girls were given away as presents; the most beautiful ones could be bestowed on kings to win their favour. A slave could not become a monk whereas a priest could under no condition be reduced to slavery. In fact, there was no sharper opposition than that between priest and slave, the slaves being referred to as 'the blacks' whereas the priests were white. The horde of campfollowers and helpers that accompanied an army was called 'the black mass' since it was mainly composed of slaves [139]. When, on the basis of the Abolition (in the British Empire) of Slavery Act of 1833, the British-Indian government abolished slavery in 1834, there were still millions of slaves in India [140]. But even to-day the Indian government itself estimates the number of slaves in the country at some 236.000.

14. Women as the lesser sort

a. Harappan matriarchate?

In the religion of the Indus or Harappa civilization, the Mother Goddess occupied a place of prime importance. Everywhere little statuettes of girls and women are found, whereas those of males are much more rare. This makes scholars conclude that society then was more favourably inclined towards women than towards men. Thomas even speaks of a matriarchate [141].

b. The 'macho' Aryans

The invasion of the Aryans meant the arrival of a 'macho' race of warriors and conquerors; we may expect that other norms would prevail henceforward. For the Vedic period we must glean our knowledge from the Vedas of that period and from the great Indian epics - works, however, that were not composed in order to give us detailed sociological and anthropological information. They are books with a sacred, although fictional, character; we shall never know how much of what is told represents the actual facts of everyday life. Among the early Indo-Aryans marriage seems to have been a mainly juridical contract. It was based on the idea of property the wife being to a certain extent and her children wholly the property of her husband. It also seems that monogamy was the rule still; the later custom of child marriage did not as yet exist [142].

There are indications that (married) women enjoyed a considerable freedom then, in sexual matters too. The husband was supposed not to be jealous. In the Mahabharata King Pandu relates how "in the olden days ... (women) were not dependent on their husbands and male relatives. They went about freely enjoying themselves". In another passage a certain Swetaketu observes how his mother is being led to her bed-chamber by a guest. He complains but his father tells him that his mother is not to be blamed since this is the time-honoured custom of their clan. The young man, however, continues to judge this custom unworthy. The practice that guests were honoured in this way by the wife or daughters of their host lived on for a long time in distant corners of India (and was by no means confined to this country alone) [143].

c. The greater importance of the sons

But if it is true that the position of women in early Vedic days in some respects was enviable [144], a decline soon set in. Thomas describes this process in the following words : "The story of the Indo-Aryan women is a tragic tale of gradual subjection beginning from the legendary age of free love and ending up in the Middle Ages when they had lost all individuality and were even made to mount the funeral pyres of their husbands" [145]. In the early days with regard to religion there existed no difference between men and women. They prayed and sacrificed conjointly as is testified by this incantation : "Gods! May the husband and wife who, with one mind, offer oblations and purify themselves, propitiate you with the soma (= the sacral potion) mixed with milk" [146].

We are now entering the age of Brahmanism of which more will be said later. Although the idea of metempsychosis (the migration of souls) had not yet taken shape, there was 'a firm belief in survival after death'. The arrival of a soul in the regions beyond death was seen as a second birth; this means that a reborn soul was at first young and feeble and had to be nourished. Nourishment was provided for it by means of oblations of food and drink. It will be obvious that these oblations had to be offered by the relatives of the dead. The development of the doctrine of metempsychosis brought no change in this respect. The corpses were no longer buried but burnt; the soul of the departed was supposed to be clad by a new body that, as a body, however subtle this was thought to be, needs nourishment. When the relations neglected their task, the deceased would be consigned to hell or be reborn in a most deplorable condition [147].

It was the son who was charged with the regular offering of the oblations. It will be self-evident that the son had to be the officiant, since the daughter was married into another family. Because she was no longer an integral part of the family, it was the son who continued the line. In itself this was not yet a deprecation of women but it is evident that it could easily lead to a serious deterioration of their position within the family. This decline actually set in and was probably speeded up by the fact that, already in the early and more idyllic Vedic age, there was a darker side to the medal. We saw that, in a juridical sense, women were 'property' then. The Aryans especially honoured the fighter, the warrior, who was a male. In the oldest of the Vedas, the Rigveda, we find some unfriendly utterances regarding women. Although this collection in general pictures the idyllic age, it is stated that "the mind of women brooks no discipline, her intellect has little weight" [148]. Downright hostile is the statement that "with women there can be no lasting friendship; the hearts of women are the hearts of hyenas" [149]. It is no rejected lover who is saying this in his chagrin; no, it is a woman, even a celestial woman who came down from heaven and married King Pururava [150].

The new ritual obligations gave the son an overriding importance in the family and caused a corresponding lowering of the status of daughters. What would the father be in the hereafter without his son! He would be utterly lost! A husband, therefore, always feared that he would beget only girls and prayed the gods for sons, the more the better, to exclude all risks. "O Prajapati, Anumati, Sinivali, put a daughter elsewhere, but here a son" [151]. "O Pinga, defend thou (the child) in the process of birth; let not the evil ones turn it into females" [152]. Here the fact that a child is born female is seen as a nasty trick by the fiend! Later Vedic sources see the foetus as 'essentially male' [153]. But if the evil forces were capable of changing the male embryo into a female one, the good forces could be marshalled to prevent this calamity. The Indian author Shastri aptly remarks that this is somewhat incongruous since "without a woman the race might become extinct". There was a special ritual for avoiding the birth of a daughter. A 'mantra' (= a ritual formula) was repeated, prayers were uttered, a ceremony with Kusa grass was performed [154].

But, in spite of everything, girls were born of course. They were, as may be expected, far from welcome. A girl could not fight, she could not work as hard as her brother, and, worst of all, she had to be given away in marriage which often meant giving costly gifts to the bridegroom. Therefore, "the daughter is known for a misfortune" [155]; "the daughter is the bitterest woe", whereas in particular the eldest son was as good as his father [156]. From the hour of her birth the father was harassed by the question who would marry his daughter (and what it would cost him). "To be the father of a daughter is an affliction for him that seeks after honour, and no one knows who will (or shall) take a maiden to his house; thus it is, o daughter. The mother's kindred, the father's, and they to whom she goes in marriage - three families are brought into danger by a daughter" [157]. We must, however, not lose sight of the fact that utterances such as these are plucked from literary fiction and may, in consequence, have a somewhat conventional ring to them. Natural feelings must often have triumphed over doctrine and convention; many a father must have cherished a warm paternal sentiment for his nice little girls.

d. Polygamy

However true this may be, the fact remains that, in every respect, a son was of far greater value to a man than a daughter. It goes without saying that this attitude had unfavourable consequences for other categories of women, in particular for a man's own wife. She was primarily expected to give birth to a number of sons. But sometimes only girls were born, or she was sterile. There were many remedies for overcoming unfruitfulness : magic spells against barrenness, sacrifices and fasting, mantras, the wearing of luck-bringing objects [158]. But finally every means might fail. In that case a man could take an additional wife, or even more than one. For though monogamy was the general rule, polygyny was not forbidden. Prof. Indra, who is an Indian woman, admits with an audible sigh that "the practice of polygamy ... was much in vogue in the Vedic and post-Vedic ages" [159].

This freedom of having more partners than one remained restricted to the males; although polyandry seems to have existed in India in very early days [160], now a woman had to be content with one husband. "No blame is laid on the men that marry many wives, but very great blame is laid on women, if they offend their husbands (= by a new marriage)" [161]. The only exception is when the husband was impotent; in that case he might ask a near relative, preferably his brother, to produce children for him with his (the sterile man's) wife [162]. Monogamy remained the ideal, but polygamy seems to have been fairly wide-spread. Kings possessed large harems with numerous concubines. High officials followed suit, and many others as far as they were able to bear the costs of such big families [163]. When a woman proved barren, it even was a religious duty for a husband to take a second wife.

All this proves that man and woman no longer were on the same footing and no longer shared the same rights. In this new situation the woman was inevitably the loser. Instead of being her husband's lifelong loving companion, her main task now was to produce (male) children. An old Hindu law says : "Women have been created for the sake of propagation - the wife being the field and the husband the giver of seed. The field must be given to him who has the seed" [164]. So this was what was expected of her; when she did not fulfil this obligation, she practically lost her significance and her value. She was not divorced then (for divorce did not exist) but she had to bear with the presence of another woman in her home, and often even more than one, who, in all probability, were younger and healthier than she. For a polygamous man it is impossible to love all his women in the same way, to care for all of them equally, and to see all of them as his equals and companions. It is of course he who is the lord and master; his women are hardly more than his servants. A great loss in valuable human relationships is the result.

The law prescribed that a man should treat all his wives alike, but, as Basham states, "this was a rule which could hardly be enforced by law and was usually a psychological impossibility" [165]. Across the centuries we hear the bitter complaints of women who see a rival arrive under their roof : "Grief of a childless woman, and of him who feels the breath of a tiger at his back; grief of the wife whose husband has married another woman, and of one convicted by witnesses in court - these griefs are all alike" [166]. Jealousy between the concubines is a regularly recurring theme in ancient fiction. True enough, as Basham also writes, a first wife might reconcile herself to the new situation, "with the knowledge that she was the chief wife, the mistress of the household, entitled to the first place beside the husband at the family rites" [167]. What this author overlooks is that the hierarchy of personal relationship was extended still further : first, on top, the husband, then the chief wife, and finally, still further down, the concubines.

e. The sad fate of the widow

In pre-Vedic days widows were free to remarry. But as time went on remarriage of such women was looked at more and more unfavourably by law and society alike. In the later stages of the long period we are treating here remarriage had virtually become an impossibility, especially on the higher layers of society, even for those women who were widowed when still very young [168]. In contrast to Jewish and Christian practice the marriage bond was seen as so unbreakable that it persisted even after the death of the husband. "Only a wanton woman can marry another husband. A virtuous one can never even dream of remarriage" [169]. A remarried widow was scorned at by many. The same taboo did not apply to the husband who had lost his wife : "Having given at the funeral pyre the sacred fire to his wife who dies before him, he may marry again and again kindle the (nuptial) fire" [170].

The fate of a widow was far from enviable, even in the case she was left behind well provided for. The only thing she could hope for was to be remarried with her husband in the next life - one of the reasons why she could not remarry. To achieve this end she had to live an ascetic life till the end of her days, eating only a meal a day, sleeping on the ground, constantly wearing her widow's weeds without any ornaments. She had to spend her life in praying and fasting; neglect of these duties could endanger her husband in the afterlife. Because of being so conspicuoulsy associated with death she was shunned by all others (with the exception of her own children) and was not allowed to take part in the family rites [171]. In the hierarchy of women we thus find the widow still below all those who had a male partner.

We know that it was an Indian custom that widows mounted the funeral pyres of their husbands to die in the flames that consumed his corpse. And we wonder what could have induced a living being to commit such an act of self-immolation. For we must not forget that this was a voluntary act. This practice was forbidden by the British long ago but still occurs here and there. First of all, a widow's lot was so sad, she must have felt so despised, so lonely, so utterly superfluous that anything seemed better than this kind of life [172]. Then the result of her voluntary death would be that she became reunited to her husband and might be reborn with him as a respected woman. This made the prospect of death less appalling to her than it is to us. Although cremation together with the husband was voluntary, social pressure and age-old custom made it an almost inescapable obligation. "His (the hero's) wife, loyal and loving, beloved and fair, followed close behind him into the flames" [173]. This implies that a husband was not loyal and loving when she did not follow her husband into death.

The earliest mention of this custom we have dates from the time of Alexander's incursion into India; the great epics give only a few instances [174]. The custom of widow-burning only slowly became widespread; not before the centuries after the birth of Christ it became fairly general [175]. Prof. Indra says in as many words that self-immolation was a practical means of getting rid of widows since these unhappy beings formed an unnecessary burden on society [176]. And because these women died of their own free will, society could wash its hands of them.

f. Child marriages

The continuing debasement of women is also pictured by the constant lowering of the marriage age. In the society that is mirrored by the Rigveda the bride had to be a full-grown girl [177]. She had to be fully mature since she was expected to take over the reins of the household from her parents-in-law; Altekar believes that she was at least from sixteen to eighteen years old [178]. Till about 400 B.C. sixteen remained an acceptable marriage age for girls, at least in cultured circles [179]. Then, in the period from 400 B.C. to 100 A.D., this age was gradually lowered till girls of twelve years old were seen as nubile. When a girl had reached puberty, that is to say when the first menses had come through, she could be given away in marriage - which does not mean that the marriage was already consumated at this tender age [180]. Still later, after 100 or 200 A.D., pre-puberty marriages became the order of the day. We then hear of girls of seven or eight being given away in wedlock. One of the reasons for this habit may have been that the sooner a girl was married the lesser the chance that she would lose her chastity - absolute chastity having become an unconditional prerequisite for a bride although not for a bridegroom.

It will be obvious that in this way there was no moment in a girl's life in which she was able to dispose of herself. After the conclusion of the marriage the still very young maiden went to live with her husband's family which she must come to know as early as possible in order to become perfectly adjusted to it. The custom of child marriages is dying only very slowly. When the British came to India, eight or nine was still the normal age for girls. As late as 1929 it was computed that ca. 39 % of the girls were married before they were ten years old. Then the Sarda Act of 1929 prohibited the marriage of girls younger than fourteen. But in spite of this in 1951 the percentage of girls married before that age was 14 [181].

The gradual introduction of child marriage spelled a serious deterioration of the position of women. In older times they doubtless had a say in the choice of their marriage partner. Man and wife were seen as 'the complements of each other' [182]; the husband should treat his wife 'as his dearest friend' [183]. As Altekar says, the aim of the Hindu marriage is to foster the growth and development of husband and wife and to promote the preservation and progress of society by enjoining upon the couple the procreation of children and their proper education [184]. Child marriages, as will be obvious, made the fulfilment of this ideal far more difficult, if not downright impossible. To begin with, girls of a very tender age were incapable of choosing their husbands themselves. The father did this in the name of his daughter; because he found it an unbearable burden to have a marriageable girl in his home he tried to dispose of her as soon as possible [185].

Since the girl was placed in her future's husband's home, there remained very little opportunity for her education. Whereas in former times a well-educated, even a learned woman had been highly estimated, now the illiteracy of married women became the rule. For a long time girls had been admitted to Vedic studies on the same footing as boys; that both sexes took part in the initial ceremony, the so-called Upanayana, and followed the same course of sacred studies, was then considered 'very essential to secure a suitable match' [186]. But from about the beginning of the Christian era the Upanayana was seen as the privilege solely of the boys; to be married was now considered the real Upanayana of the bride. Her husband became her teacher - a preceptor who even had a certain right to punish his young wife physically in case of mistakes and offences on her part [187]. Altekar concludes that "owing to the growing helplessness of women on account of their illiteracy and ignorance, they became an easier prey to ill-treatment and tyranny". The view that the husband had the supremacy over his wife became 'quite popular' [188].

g. The dualistic relationship of men and women

Our conclusion from the foregoing must be that slowly but certainly the distance between marriage partners became dualistically great; for an husband it grew increasingly difficult to see in his spouse a person of the same worth and value as he himself. More or less condemned to stay at home, mentally undernourished and illiterate, having had their children at too early an age and looking worn out and old before their time, more often than not wives must have been boring and unattractive companions to their husbands. Thomas says that "this was in no small measure responsible for the extraordinary high position prostitutes gained in later India and the hold they obtained even in temples and places of pilgrimage" [189].

The spread of prostitution was only a corollary of the deterioration of the status of married women. Another one is that ancient Hindu texts speak very ill of women. True enough, one could easily quote passages that show a very high regard for them, in particular in older literature. Such words full of praise are still in accord with the original Vedic ideology that considered male and female as equals. But texts of the subsequent period mirror the gradual subjugation of women and the contempt they are held in [190]. Scolding women is a habit that set in very early; even the Mahabharata is not sparing of it. This famous epic categorically states that "there is nothing more sinful than woman. Verily women are the roots of evil". Fierce hatred is expressed in the following words : "The destroyer, the god of the wind, death, the nether regions, the equine mouth that roves through the ocean, vomiting ceaseless flames of fire - all these exist in a state of union in women" [191].

This one comes from another source : "Women are like the leech; but while the leech draws your blood only, the woman draws your riches, your property, your flesh, your vitality and your strength" [192]. It is especially their erotic radiation that inspires fear, their 'impure desire'. "It is the nature of women to seduce men in this world ...; women are able to lead astray in this world even a learned man" [193].

They are infidelity personified. "They betake themselves to all men; just as creepers growing in a thick forest (they) lean themselves on any tree" [194]; "they are never satisfied with one person of the opposite sex". Women are even incapable of real love : "They have none whom they love or like" [195]. And then in a paroxysm born from fear : "There is none whom a woman sincerely loves. She, for serving her purpose, does not hesitate to kill even her husband, children or brothers" [196].

So males beware! The Mahabharata says : "Men should not love them, nor should they cherish any jealousy on account of them. Only for the sake of virtue, men should enjoy their society, not with enthusiasm or attachment, but with unwillingness or absence of attachment. By acting otherwise a man is sure to meet with disaster" [197]. To avoid this disaster men should refrain from consorting with women as much as possible [198].

h. Buddhist attitudes towards the female sex

The question now is whether Buddhism did anything to ameliorate the position of women. Modern westerners are quick to believe this since this religion is seen as a very civilized one with lofty ideals. What is easily lost from sight is that Buddhism essentially is an ascetic religion that does not devote 'much attention to the ideals and duties of lay women' [199]. Not even a nun is the equal of a monk in Buddhist eyes. It is said that the Buddha himself was reluctant to accept nuns in his monasteries and that he did this only on the entreaties of his foster-mother.

The discipline for nuns was more severe than for monks. A new nun was only accepted after having been 'voted by ballot' in which the monks too took part, whereas a new monk needed only the permission of his male colleagues. Monks preached to nuns, a nun never to monks. As Altekar says, rules like these "betray a lack of confidence in the character and judgment of women" [200]. Monks were instructed to shun female company as much as they could. This was difficult enough : since monasteries were dependent on alms the monks had to visit houses to collect gifts; in doing so they frequently came into contact with the housewives who were the principal almsgivers. Diana Paul thinks that this economic dependence on women reinforced the monks' feeling of contempt for them. Their attitude to women was antagonistic [201].

The Buddha himself - Prince Siddharta, to give him his personal name - was a married man. Probably at the age of sixteen he married a girl of the same age or somewhat younger, Yasodhara. He had a son with her, but later he turned his back on the marital home and his family, and henceforward lived a celibate life. He did not believe that a man, for religious reasons, needed a son nor that he was not complete without a wife. On the contrary, he thought that it was very difficult for married people to get off the wheel of rebirth. In his eyes celibacy was the real norm of higher life; marriage was no more than a concession to ordinary mortals [202].

The Buddha did not think highly of women. When his foster-mother had persuaded him to admit women to his monastic order, he dejectedly said to his favourite disciple Ananda that the consequence would be that his religion would not outlast five centuries - a prophecy that was not fulfilled [203]. "Do not see women", he said to Ananda. "But if we see them ...?" "Abstain from speech." "But if they speak to us ...?" "Keep wide awake" [204]. Nevertheless, the rise of Buddhism initially had a wholesome effect on the situation of women. The Buddhists were averse to the Brahmanic idea that marriage was something like a sacrament. In consequence, they allowed widows to remarry and forbade child-marriages. "Buddhism recognised the individuality and independence of women" [205].

On the whole, however, this religion saw women as inferior to men. It inherited, after all, the main ideas of Indian mythology about the female sex, with its hovering between glorification of motherhood and defilement of the sensual female. Buddhist literature is not free from misogynist tendencies either. As Prof. Paul states, "symbolically, woman represented the profane word, samsara. Perhaps more detrimentally, women were potential obstacles in actual life to man's spiritual growth" [206]. The ferocity of anti-female utterances varied with the several sects. An early Buddhist sect like the Theravada would have liked to eradicate root and branch the whole female world, closely connected as it was 'with bondage, suffering, and desire, which led to cycles of rebirth' [207]. Here too the relationship between male and female became dualistic.

15. The caste system and the lesser breeds

What do western people know of India? Many associate it with ancient wisdom, with holy men called 'gurus' - Mahatma Gandhi obviously being one of them. But at the same time they think of it as a country were widows are burned, and where the streets are full of beggars, to say nothing of the holy cows that freely obstruct the traffic; a country, furthermore, dedicated to neutrality and non-violence, that however, in spite of all its peaceful maxims, was involved in an astonishing number of wars since its Independence Day. It is also the cradle of Buddhism, a religion that became popular with disgruntled western Christians and agnostics, although at the present day no more than 0.75 % of the Indian population professes this religion. And finally, there is its incomprehensible caste system, with its 'untouchables', its 'pariahs'.

One of the books I consulted on this subject says in its preface that more than five thousand publications have appeared describing this social system [208]. Of course, I consulted only a few of them. Had I studied each of my subjects in all bibliographical width and depth, not one of these volumes and chapters would ever have seen the light of the day. The view that the caste system is a typical and unique Indian institution is correct. In other parts of the world there have existed, or still exist, social systems that bear a certain resemblance to the Indian one, but a full-blown caste system has never developed anywhere else [209].

a. The word 'caste'

The word 'caste' is somewhat deceptive since it is not an Indian word at all. The authentic Hindi word is 'jati'. It seems that it was the Spaniards who first used a word 'casta', but the Portuguese were the first to apply it to the typically Indian social stratigraphy when they came to know it in the middle of the fifteenth century. It is a derivation from the Latin 'castus' = pure, but in Spanish and Portuguese it means 'lineage' or 'race'. Other nations spelled it as 'cast'. Our modern spelling 'caste' or 'kaste' (Dutch, German) dates from after 1800. In this form it superseded not only the older spelling but also the original Spanish meaning of the word, viz. 'a mixed breed'. The Portuguese who did not really understand the caste system thought that it served to preserve purity of blood [210].

b. The origin of the caste system

Just like the origin of slavery in India - did the slaves descend from the aboriginal population or did they not? -, the beginnings of the caste system are a hotly debated point. Theories abound. The traditional one is culled from ancient Hindu literature. It says that the caste system owes its origin to the four 'varnas' ('varna' means 'colour'). These four groups are the Brahmans, the Kshatriyas, the Vaishyas, and the Shudras. They present a remarkable stratification : at the top the Brahmans, the privileged class, and at the bottom the Shudras, the underlings.

Since the Brahmans were so obviously favoured by this system, eighteenth-century European authors believed that the whole idea was an astute invention of the Brahmans themselves. As the Age of Rationalism, the 'enlightened' eighteenth century had a strong penchant for 'inventions', one of them being religion, with its inevitable corollary of 'priestcraft'. Later, in the nineteenth century, a social point of view gained pride of place, for then some authors thought that the caste system comes from the division of society into clergy, nobility, and bourgeoisie, and that it was not the varnas but the many subdivsions of this stratification that were responsible for the rise of this system.

The mistake these authors made was that they thought that this purely European notion could be applied to societies the world over. Twentieth-century conceptions often base themselves on conceptions of race and colour [211].

c. What is a caste?

In order to get the picture as clear as possible we should not confuse the notions of 'class' and 'caste', like some authors with a Marxist bend of mind. According to them the Brahmans were the oppressors who used their privileged position to relegate the others, as Anant says, 'to the lower orders' [212]. However, a caste is not a class in the general European or more narrow Marxist sense. Difficult as it is to define the concept of 'class', we all know that social classes have no fixed frontiers. A person may climb the social ladder and end far higher than where he or she started, or the reverse. And those whom we call 'a-social' are not be compared with 'pariahs', for we believe that a-socials, with good care and proper education, may become 'social'.

It is safe to state that the caste system has the closest ties with marriage customs. One must marry outside the family but within the caste, c.q. subcaste, of the family. Contracting a marriage outside the (sub)caste is not permitted. This means that a caste is primarily an endogamous group. However, we should pay attention to what Dumont states, that Hindu people are by no means free to marry unrestrictedly within their own caste; they often marry within a certain, for instance territorial, fraction of the caste [213]. We shall not go far wrong if we quote the somewhat arid definition given by the Indian Census Report of 1911 : "A caste may be defined ... as an endogamous group or collection of such groups bearing a common name and having the same traditional occupation, who (i.e. the families - F.) are so linked together by these (i.e. marriage) and other ties, such as the tradition of a common origin and the possession of the same tutelary deity, and the same social status, observances, and family priests, that they regard themselves, and are regarded by others, as forming a single homogeneous unity" [214]. A caste, therefore, has historical, social, juridical, ritual, mythical, professional, as well as psychological characteristics.

d. The castes and the varnas

There is not much in India that is not considered to have a divine origin; the caste system makes no exception to this rule and is, in consequence, seen as having existed from all eternity. However, the oldest Vedic book, the Rigveda, does not mention castes; it only speaks of the four varnas that I already described. We may safely assume that early Vedism did not know the elaborate caste system of later times. In fact, the caste system originated in Brahmanism; it gained such a strong hold on Indian society that none of the other religions was able to steer clear of it. Buddhists, Jainists, Sikhs, they all saw the emergence of castes within their own ranks. Even religions that, on principle, are caste-less, had to submit to this all-pervading influence so that Islamites and native Christians too were to develop a kind of caste-system of their own. Rapson even explains the gradual disappearance of Buddhism from Indian soil as due to the fact that this religion "has been gradually absorbed into the Brahman caste system" [215]. This influence of Brahmanism in the course of the centuries slowly spread from the Ganges valley till it finally permeated all India. This means that the caste system did not appear in all regions of India simultaneously.

It is a very moot point whether or not the caste system was derived from or originated in the four varnas. Many scholars believed or still believe that the castes came into being by a process of intermarriage between members of different varnas. This process is supposed to have been responsible for the steady growth of castes and subcastes of which there finally were some three thousand. But an expert like Basham sighs that "it is impossible to show its (the caste system's) origin conclusively ... since early literature paid scant attention to it" [216]. What pleads for this view is that, in ancient literature, varna is always mentioned as different from 'jati' (caste). Whereas the concept of jati underwent a slow development - for instance, it originally was by no means so rigid as it has become later, - the varnas remained essentially the same, with the same order of precedence until this day [217]. That the word 'varna' means 'colour' must make us aware that it has something to do with ethnic differences. Weren't the Aryans light-skinned and the aboriginal Dasas dark of colour?

The problem, however, is not of prime importance for my subject. The decisive factor is that, from the beginning, divisive lines were running through Indian society. A first, such frontiers were not impassible, for there were intermarriages. But in the course of time, the castes became increasingly exclusive with regard to each other, especially as the result of the prohibition to marry a member of another clan.

All this means that a Hindu is a member of a varna as well as of a jati. With the exception perhaps of the highest orders, he or she is more affected by belonging to a caste than to a varna. A caste may be based mainly on a region or a nation or a tribe or a profession or a religion. Personal life was and often still is entirely lived within the framework of the caste which provides its members with their cultural and social identity. Customs, folklore, ritual, ceremonies, professions, crafts, mythology, rules, laws, and most of all the sentiment of belonging, all these factors are typical of caste life. Basham says that the caste "received much of the loyalty elsewhere felt towards king, nation, and city" [218]. In cases of distress a person had to appeal first to his family but, after that, the caste would come to his or her help. The social security that is now provided by the state, and in medieval Europe by the Church and the guilds, was in India offered by the castes.

e. Outcastes and pariahs

There was no greater catastrophe, no worse fate than to be without a caste, to be 'casteless', an 'outcaste'. It was possible, indeed, to be expelled from one's caste, in case of grave and repeated offences. Such a person henceforward could only consort with the dregs of society and lost his whole meaning as a human being. Nobody would help him, nobody would stay with him; unless his wife followed him, he remained utterly alone.

In the west those casteless people are often confused with 'pariahs' or 'untouchables'. This is a profound misunderstanding, for 'untouchables' (the term is now forbidden) were not casteless but belonged to a caste, a very low and despised one, as will be obvious by their generic name. The Indian word for 'untouchable' is 'pariah' - a word that found a place in the languages of the west. It seems that it is derived from a Tamil word 'paraiyar', or 'drummer'. There existed a Dravidian tribe, the Paraiyar, who were great drummers and provided the necessary professionals for religious festivals. This drumming was not seen an occupation of very high standing; the social status of these people was correspondingly low. The term 'pariah' gradually came to include all people of low status, like labourers and servants, in general all those who were engaged in 'unclean' work. These included those who killed animals, like hunters and fishermen, those who disposed of dead cattle or worked with their hides, like shoemakers, those who came into contact with dirt or with the excretions of human bodies, like streetcleaners, barbers, or washerwomen, and finally those who fed themselves on the flesh of cattle, pigs, or poultry. In particular the hill-tribes fall into the last category; from the dawn of Indian history they were considered wild and uncontrollable.

The Untouchables were subjected to a system of 'apartheid' that was downright dualistic. The ordinary Hindu shunned every contact with them for fear of becoming defiled himself. Even their touch was felt as polluting; in that case a long and elaborate ritual was needed to become clean again. The rules excluding pariahs from normal social intercourse were not identical everywhere in India; they were more severe in southern India than in the north. Often pariahs were grouped together in separate locations. Very few temples and very few schools admitted them. In the peninsula even their being sighted by a member of a higher caste was thought to be defiling, which meant that the Untouchables were condemned to a nocturnal existence. True enough, untouchability is now banned by a law of 1955, but this does not mean that the former pariahs were and are welcomed with open arms by Indian society; centuries of the deepest contempt are still exerting their influence.

f. Mutual exclusivity

The social position of the Untouchables is only the most telling and radical example of the way castes saw and treated each other. Before the caste system was officially dissolved in India in 1950 and in Pakistan in 1953, and discrimination on account of caste was penalized, all castes saw each other as mutually exclusive. This is not only because they found each other's social status inacceptable. There has, in fact, never existed a fixed hierarchy of castes; (sub)castes could grow and diminish in social significance. It is far more important that a caste was a moral and still more a natural entity. Belonging to a caste meant accepting a way of life, with its special kind of behaviour, its code of rules and norms, even its costume and manner of speech. At a still deeper level we find that the caste is, so to speak, primarily a biological community; its peculiarities are proper to this caste alone and alien to others. They are passed on to posterity by means of marriage and procreation as a biological heritage. This is the main reason why a caste member must marry within his or her own caste, for all members of the caste share the same natural inheritance.

People did not believe that there was any advantage to be gained by breaking away from their caste. On the contrary, sticking to one's caste, however low, was the consequence of karma. A change for the better, that is, acquiring the membership of a higher caste, could only be effected in a later life, and could only be attained by adhering strictly to the dharma of the present caste.

g. The Shudras

Finally, we must pay some attention to the fourth varna, the class of the Shudras, that of the servants and labourers who were at the beck and call of the three other varnas. The question 'who were the Shudras?' was raised emphatically by the late Dr. B.R. Ambedkar, who was a Shudra himself and became the great champion of all those who stood on the lowest rung of the Indian social ladder [219]. With regard to the origin of the fourth varna several theories exist; the problem is, of course, closely connected with the fate of the Dasas or Dasyus, the remnants of the pre-Aryan population in northern India. Some theories suggest that the Shudras really were Aryans. One theory says that they formed an earlier wave of the invasions and that they were subjugated by later arrivals. Other scholars think that they were rather late in coming, only arriving towards the close of the second millennium B.C., and that they had to be content with a subordinate place in the already existing Vedic society [220]. Next, there is the possibility that they belonged to a higher order, the Kshatriyas, but had the worst of a long conflict with the Brahmans, and ended at the bottom of the social pyramid [221]. The etymology of the word 'shudra' does not help us at all; nobody knows what was the origin of this term [222].

Dr. Sharma's conclusion seems very sensible to me, viz. that the Shudras were neither wholly Aryan nor wholly pre-Aryan. The period of the conquest of northern India by the Aryan tribes was one of great upheavals and terrible clashes, mainly about land and cattle. There were not only fights between the invaders and the autochthonous population, but also, for the booty, between the conquerors themselves [223]. So it is no wonder that a large underclass came into being consisting of those who were robbed of their possessions as well as of those who fell short of the prizes [224]. This does not mean that the Shudras and the Dasyus (on the assumption that these were the descendants of the pre-Aryan population) really were identical. In all probablity they were not, although the difference in social status was not great. Petech believes that "presumably the most reliable elements of the Dasyus were absorbed by the fourth class" [225]. The advantage hereby gained by these Dasyus was that they henceforward belonged to a definite social order, whereas the rest of the serfs formed a non-class.

Whatever the origin of the Shudras may have been, all scholars agree on this point that their social status was very humble; they were subjected to a harsh regime. Again we are in the presence of a dualistic opposition, that between the three higher varnas and the Shudras who were despised, exploited and maltreated. In the beginning the condition of a Shudra may not have been so miserable as it became later. Ambedkar even believes that originally 'upanayana' (= admittance to the study of the sacred Vedic lore) was permitted to them - a right they later lost [226]. In the later Vedic period - 1000-600 B.C. - the Shudras to all intents and purposes constituted the labouring class. They were the carpenters, chariot-makers, potters, fishermen, farmers, and so on [227]. Does this mean that they were now slaves? Very probably not. But, says Sharma, "just as the community exercised some sort of general control over land, so also it exercised similar control over the labouring population" [228]. I suppose that this means that the farmer was not free to leave his land and try his luck elsewhere. We see that the Shudras were not yet wholly excluded from participation in politics and ritual. On the other hand, we can observe a tendency to push them out of communal life altogether.

In the post-Vedic era (600-300 B.C.) what Sharma calls 'disabilities' were imposed on the Shudras. In that period the great majority of them were agricultural labourers, usually landless themselves. The pitiful condition of their lives had reduced many of them to slavery. They were poorly clad and their diet was meagre. They no longer occupied a place in the political organization. The law discriminated against them; in many cases they were punished for the same offences more severely than members of other orders. They were excluded from the fulfilment of all offices, even the minor ones. Slowly but certainly the idea gained ground that contact with a Shudra meant defilement, especially for Brahmans.

Shudra men and women could not marry persons who belonged to a higher class, but men from these orders could take a Shudra concubine. Special purification rites had to be performed by a husband who had such concubines. A very telling point is that the study of the holy books was no longer open to a Shudra. A consequence of this exclusion was that he or she could not take part in ceremonies and rituals, for to perform them one had to know the sacred texts. It will become clear that some of the most despised sections of the Shudra population were identical with the Untouchables [229]. Matters did not improve for the Shudras in the Mauryan period (300-200 B.C.). The Mauryan Empire was a strong state exercising control over the labouring population. It was only in the Gupta period (200-500) that the Shudras experienced some amelioration of their condition. They then regained some of their civil and religious rights. But for the Untouchables there was still no hope.

h. Conclusion

Thus ancient India showed - and to some extent modern India still does show - many divisive lines such as, for instance, between the several castes, with the Untouchables firmly stowed away into a watertight compartment. The future will prove whether India, in principle an egalitarian and democratic state, will be able to triumph over the dualistic attitudes that have been constitutive elements of the Indian collective mentality since the dawn of history.

16. Dualistic tendencies in Indian philosophy

I am now going to speak of ancient Indian philosophy, and after that, of Indian religion. It will be necessary again to give more information than my subject strictly requires, in order to prevent confusion or uncertainty in the mind of those readers who are not fully at home in this field.

Early Brahmans reflected on the nature of existence; they were lovers of wisdom, and, therefore, we may dub them 'philosophers'. Since India was, and still is, a deeply religious country, philosophy which is a spiritual occupation can easily blossom there. Indians by and large are not much given to abstractions; their philosophizing is never far from daily life, not even from myth and popular belief. As the great Indian scholar Radhakrishnan said : "To those who realise the true kinship between theory and life, philosophy becomes a way of life, an approach to spiritual realisation", and then, "every doctrine is turned into a passionate conviction, stirring the heart of man and quickening his breath" [230]. More than in the west, philosophy always remained intertwined with religion. A philosophical system is called 'darshana', something like 'viewpoint', but a generic term for philosophy does not exist [231].

a. The Indian conception of existence

There exist many resemblances between Indian and western philosophy but also great differences. To Indian thought the natural world, the created world, is, by the same token, a moral world; everything that is done, or spoken, or thought, necessarily will be requited, perhaps already in this life but most surely in a following life. As Glasenapp says, every action has a visible as well as an invisible effect. This is what he calls 'moral causality' which works just as effectively and systematically as physical causality. This, he continues, means that all Indian thinkers (with the exception of sceptics and materialists) base themselves on the same metaphysico-ethical ground [232]. This moral world is not the consequence of the will of an omnipotent God; it is autonomous and not dependent on anybody or anything else (we already encountered it as karma).

Indians see the world, subjected as it is to karma and to the inexorable law of rebirth, as utterly unhistorical; everything is bound to return. All that happens is only temporal (as different from 'historical'); everything is fleeting, without any other than strictly personal moral significance for the future. Therefore, existence is without any value whatsoever; there is no idea of redemption or final fulfilment. An Indian also sees no ideal in being continually reborn. On the contrary, it is a sad fate. What is really important is freedom from the wheel of rebirth and attaining the blissful situation in which all individuality is dissolved, losing all consciousness and sinking away in a sleeplike being-without-oneself - the situation that is known to us as 'nirvana' [233].

The conception an Indian has of existence shows him as being, at least morally or intellectually, at war with it or with himself. This does not mean that he is incapable of living without murmuring or rebellion. But far easier than a westerner he is able to accept his fate, since karma orders him to do so; he knows that rebellion is senseless because he is aware that this existence is not the real one, and that, in order to be, he must cease existing. So there is a (dualistic) divergence between being and existing in Indian thought.

b. Unity and diversity

As in ancient Greece, the oldest philosophical speculations in India attempt to answer the question of how everything originated - the problems of theogony and cosmogony -, and, closely connected with this, the relationship of the One and the Many. In a famous hymn of the Rigveda [234] we find the earliest speculations on this point. "In the beginning there were neither nought nor aught", it begins. In western philosophical terms there was as yet neither being nor non-being. Then follows the obvious question : "What then enshrouded all this teeming universe?" (the initial chaos is meant). The answer is that nothing specific had been defined or created; "only the Existent One breathed calmly, self-contained". This 'Existent One' (the accent must be placed on 'One') is the 'Ekam', the One that sovereignly exists amidst Nothingness [235].

To put this into more technical terms, this hymn presents a monistic point of view. Monism, says Petech, has always been dear to the Indian mind [236]. But whereas Indian philosophy has known its absolute monists who, like Parmenides, virtually deny or are utterly uninterested in pluriformity, the hymn I am quoting from immediately tackles the question why then there is so much diversity in the cosmos. The answer is this. The Ekam, out of itself, developed a 'force of inner fervour and intense abstraction'. This force is 'tapas', here to be translated as 'heating' but later meaning 'ascetic meditation' [237]. By radiating heat the Ekam generates 'Kama' = love, the 'productive germ'. Here, thus the hymn ends, the Wise detects the bond between Entity and Nullity, between Being and Non-Being. By stating that the Ekam generates Kama the hymn is suggesting that the originally monistic principle is responsible for the existence of pluriformity in the universe. But finally the poet admits that he has no idea how individual beings, be they gods, men, or animals, came into being. Even the gods, since they have been generated themselves, cannot tell us. This means that not only the question how we came to be remains unanswered but also why we are here.

This way of thought is, to some extent, based on or resulting from what the Aryan myths had to report. Heaven is the father, the earth is the mother, and between them they beget all that is. But to Brahmanic thought this was not really satisfying; its tries to probe deeper, it posits the Ultimate One, the Ekam, which is prior to the male-female duality, but proves incapable of solving the riddle of the universe. However, it will be evident that this Rigveda hymn, with its Brahmanic background, has no room for gods, most of all not for a creator god. In Brahmanic eyes the gods originally were not immortal but they become so by receiving sacrifices. In this way they became dependent on the Brahmans who guaranteed the permanency of the sacrifical rites [238].

c. Male and Female

There is no saying which of these two notions, unity and duality, had the strongest impact on the Hindu mind. 'Ekam', the One, is a very abstract principle, highly philosophical, and, therefore, not highly attractive to the average mind. But in Brahmanic speculation the Ekam originally divides itself into a duality. The One has a dual aspect; the duality is unified in the One. This makes it possible to venerate the duality without utterly neglecting the One. We must not forget that the duality mentioned is a very obvious and highly alluring proposition since it is the duality of masculinity and femininity. Its needs no explanation that, put in this way, duality had an easy appeal to everyone.

The Rigveda says ; "What you describe to me as Male are in reality also Female" [239]. "Whatever dualities there are in the world may be traced to the source in the Ardhanarisvara cell ('Ardhanarisvara' is the androgynous figure of Shiva - F.) or the fertilised ovum from which the bodies of living beings are developed" [240]. The great Hindu god Shiva is, indeed, often represented as half male, half female. Some of his images show one side of his body as male, the other as female, as an androgynous being therefore [241]. As Monier Williams wrote, this "symbolizes both the duality and unity of the generative act" [242]. It indicates that Shiva "combines in his own body maternal as well as paternal qualities". He adds that "the ordinary Hindu finds no difficulty in accepting the theory of a universe proceeding from a divine father and mother", other ideas being too 'mystical' for him [243]. This means that, to some extent, the notion of a general and original duality in the popular mind supersedes that of an equally all-compassing primeval One.

d. Matter and Spirit

Transported back to the philosophical plane the male-female duality proves to have close ties with another duality, that of Spirit and Matter, or Spirit and Nature. For the Indians it is impossible to think of purely inorganic matter, I mean of matter without any form of life. There is life in everything. But although all manifestations of Nature, including the human person, are imbued with Life, with a 'spiritual monad', living existence is only possible as long as this monad, this parcel of Spirit, does not leave the material form. The majority of Indian philosophers hold that "empirical living beings consist of two totally different elements, of Matter and Spirit". According to Glasenapp whom I am quoting here, this is a dualistic theory, and one that has been dominant in Indian philosophy for the last two thousand five hundred years [244].

At first sight this flatly contradicts what Petech has to say of the Indian predilection for monism. But apart from the fact that it is really the western scholars that love monism - so much that they detect it everywhere -, we have already seen that, paradoxical as it may sound, unity is basically dual to the Indian mind. Dualism is never far away then. Glasenapp dubs the Spirit-Matter opposition dualistic because Matter can only gain significance in a living entity. And such an entity is only brought to life and kept living as long as there is Spirit in it. In the Spirit-Matter combination Spirit is prior and superior; it is the decisive factor in creating a living being. It will be clear that the human person does not escape from this dualistic notion of being composed of different and opposed elements, body and soul.

17. Dualistic tendencies in Indian mythology

a. Vedic devas

Vedic supernatural powers, be they gods or demons, represent in one form or another the forces, favourable or pernicious, with which a human being is confronted during the course of his life; we may call them symbols or hypostases that incorporate the sum total of all that happens and of all that is thought and felt in the human sphere as well as in the universe. As a consequence these powers cannot be considered moral models since they do not embody ethical principles. This, however, does not mean that mortals cannot sin. On the contrary! They do, and the gods punish them for it [245].

We may hold one thing for certain : there are powers from above and powers from beneath that are hostile to each other and try to thwart one another. In other words, we are in the presence of a dualistic opposition. The first category is that of the high gods who are, almost without exception, benevolent; they are worthy of worship which they abundantly receive. Without actually being personified forces of nature they hold sway over such forces as the sun, the wind, and the thunder. Mankind too has to bow before their ordinances; the gods determine everybody's span of life and decide on the fulfilment of human wishes. Apart from the high gods, the devas, there exist lesser divinities, genii loci, and those beings whom we meet in fairy tales, like elves. Great heroes of the past are also deified; they have their abode with the gods.

Let us now mention a few of the most important devas. The most dominant of them are the so-called 'Adityas' whose numer varies from six to (in the Brahmanas) twelve. They are all of them sons of the goddess Aditi, that is 'boundlessness'; she is often called 'the wide one'. Though she is the mother of high gods, Aditi must not be considered a Magna Mater or Mother Goddess. There is no real feminine principle in the Rigveda; goddesses occupy no conspicuous place in it [246]. The Vedic religion is, when all is said and done, a masculine one. Aditi is not so much an object of veneration but rather the ground of all being, the womb of all that is, of heaven and earth, of the gods and humanity. She is the great protrectress of the world order; in her rests all "that is born and will yet be born"; in her womb 'being and non-being lie' [247].

Her most powerful son is Varuna whose name we also encountered in the old Iranian religion (Vol. IV, Ch. IV). He is the god of heaven (but not to be identified with heaven); he commands all the phenomena of heaven and under it, the sun, the moon, the stars, the clouds, the rain, and the wind, the course of the rivers and the fertility of the earth. This means that he is the great upholder of the cosmic order. Mithra, who much later rose to great fame as a Persian sun-god, is a solar deity in the Rigveda too, 'the personification of the sun's beneficent power' who is closely associated with Varuna [248]. In passing I mention Vishnu, another solar deity who, in Vedic times, was not yet a first-rank divinity but who came to occupy a very prominent place in Hinduism. Then there is Agni, the fire-god to whom one-fifth of all the Rigveda hymns is devoted. This is because fire, the sacrificial fire, is such an important element in Vedic ritual.

One of the gods was more popular, more widely venerated, more 'national', says Gonda, than all the others : Indra. One quarter of all the Rigveda hymns are devoted to him. He is represented as more anthropomorphic than other divinities, which means that he has a more easily recognizable form; his hair and beard are red. He is big and strong; armed with lightning he rides a golden chariot. He is equally great in eating, drinking and love. He can be very irascible but, at the same time, he is generous and true to his friends. Is not this a portrait that shows a very good likeness to the (ideal) Aryan warrior? No wonder then that he was the favourite god of this warlike people, in particular of its fighting class, the Kshatriyas. But Indra is more than a war-god alone; he is also the god of powerful natural forces, of thunder and rain, of vitality and fertility [249].

b. Rifts and fissures in the Vedic pantheon

A superficial survey of the Vedic pantheon might reveal it to us as a homogeneous group, many of the gods exhibiting properties and fulfilling functions that are identical with those of others. But on a closer inspection, deep differences appear. For instance, when Varuna is a civilized being, Indra is a rough fellow [250]. It is not unthinkable that both belong to different historical layers of Vedism, in which case Indra would represent the period of the conquests and Varuna that of agricultural settlement. This difference is also accentuated by the fact that Indra seems to have a different origin since he is not unequivocally an Aditya, a son of Aditi [251].

Varuna and Indra lived in marked opposition; especially in later Vedic times they are seen as rivals, even as enemies; the Rigveda says that Indra robbed Varuna of his virility [252]. In the running conflict between the two gods Varuna steadily had the worst of it; in the course of time he sank back to a relatively subordinate position. I venture to guess that this conflict, with its dualistic character, represents the quarrel between two conceptions of existence : on the one hand the ideal of civilized life, of peace, order, regularity, normality, and, in general, 'the static aspects of life under sovereignty' [253]; on the other, the never-satisfied, deep seated, primeval and uncouth urge to conquer, to subdue, to expand, and to build empires [254].

But we must look still deeper into this matter. In the old Iranian religion we met the 'ahura'. This word, meaning 'Great God' or 'Sovereign Lord' (a 'Hochgott' in German), has a Vedic equivalent in the form 'asura'. It is said that this form is derived from 'asu' = vital force, spirit of life. Anyhow, an 'asura' has power and does things; he is active and causes effects in nature. Now it is highly important to realize that this working is ethically indifferent : it may be beneficent but also disastrous. Hail can destroy whole crops, lightning sets houses afire, a snake may dart forward from the grass, a tiger be hiding for you in the bush. Therefore, there is a dark side to Varuna. He is opposed not only to Indra but also to the other devas, or heavenly gods. It is he who causes earthquakes. Illness and lack of success must be laid at his door; sometimes his name is 'Death'. He can be very angry and malicious, in particular when sacrifices are not made in the correct way. As Gonda writes, the ambivalence of this deity is obvious since, to quote an ancient text, as "the god who tied his belt (i.e. of misery) around our waists, (he) will (also) try to bring about the end of our difficulties; he will redeem us" [255].

c. Demons

Because Varuna shows both a bright and a sinister side, being beneficent and malicious at the same time, he is an asura as well as a deva. Now the meaning of the word 'asura' suffered a continous decline. From signifying, as in old Iranian, a 'Hochgott', it came to mean a being hostile to the gods. Brahmanic authors use to tell us that "gods and asuras fight for the possession of the world". The final victory fell to the gods, but initially "the all was in the power of the asuras; the gods had only the word". Yet, on account of an inspiration, it was the 'word' that ensured their final victory over the asuras [256].

When we transform this utterance into modern parlance, one might say that, in the long run, reason proved more powerful than sheer force. This is a typically post-Vedic, Brahmanic insight. Anyhow, it will be evident that, of old, there exist two utterly opposed divine groups in the universe. The asuras represent the higher class of the hostile gods, the demons the lower order. The asuras (who are equally demoniacal) are thought to be the offspring of the goddess Diti who, of course, is the counterpart of Aditi, the mother of most of the devas [257]. Thus asuras and devas were, to a great extent, members of two dualistically opposed divine families.

It is remarkable that demons in Vedic and Brahmanic writings are often referred to as dasas or dasyus, exactly the same word that was used for the aboriginal population and later for the slaves. It will not surprise us that they were seen as the unrelenting enemies of the Aryan war-god Indra [258]. A peculiar group of demons, the Raksasas, made it their work to plague human beings. They made wives and cows barren; they were even capable of insinuating themselves into human beings, causing illness and insanity. As mortal enemies of the gods they tried to disturb the sacrificial rites. At night they hovered around the houses, rode through the air, or posted themselves at the crossroads. Sometimes they assumed the shape of an animal or even of a man or a woman; then they were difficult to recognize. Another time their aspect was horrifying; they had three heads or yellow eyes or hands without fingers [259].

18. The Brahmanic religion

a. The difference between Vedism and Brahmanism

First of all, it is necessary to make a distinction between Vedism and Brahmanism, although the two really do not stand far apart. Vedism is the oldest form of the mythology of the Aryan invaders of the Indus valley. They accepted the Vedas as their holy writ containing, as I have already indicated, the hymns, formulas, ritual prescriptions, and philosophical explanations they needed. 'Veda' means 'knowledge', and what it presents is 'sruti' = revealed truth. Brahmanism is a somewhat later development of the time when the Aryans penetrated into the Ganges valley and further south. The Brahman sects too accept the Veda as revealed truth, but add law books, the great epics, and other, even non-Vedic myths to it as sources of inspiration. This means that Brahmanism presents a wider array of religious notions than Vedism. The Brahmans called the non-Vedic texts 'smrti' = remembered truth' [260].

Obviously the fact that the Brahmans were in the possession of the truth, both in its revealed (or divine) and in its remembered (human or interpreted) form, secured them a privileged position - the more so since this knowledge was not directly open to everyone (the Shudras, for instance, and later the women, were excluded from it). Hence, according to Gonda, the extent to which the ancient Indian population partook of these philosophico-religious conceptions which, after all, are refined literary products of an upper class culture, remains an open question. Perhaps people used them in eclectic way; that is to say, everybody took from them what suited them best [261]. The popular religion that finally grew out of Vedism and Brahmanism is called Hinduism.

Another difference of Vedism and Brahmanism is this. We must not expect to find in Vedism, in particular not in the Rigveda, 'a consistent mythology or a clearly structured pantheon' [262]. Heesterman explains that we must not ascribe its indeterminancy to 'the fluidity of archaic thought' or to the authors' problems with verbal expression. It rather is 'a matter of principle' since this deliberate vagueness is used 'to enhance and exploit the power of the deity' [263]. Brahmanic theology is more systematic, more philosophical; it tries to harmonize the inconsistencies of Vedic mythology.

b. Brahma, Brahmanas, and Brahmans

The concept from which the term 'Brahmanism' (a modern construction, of course) is derived, is 'Brahma(n)'. What this word means depends on where the accent is placed. Is it 'bráhman', then it is the neuter for 'godhead' [264], or 'cosmic principle or power'. When pronounced as 'brahmán', it denotes a member of the Brahman varna, more often than not a priest or a scholar. The connection between the two spellings is that 'bráhman' as a divine cosmic principle is contained in inspired words; the brahmán, or priest, pronounces these words [265].

Another term connected with the two former is 'Brahma', the non-neuter proper name of the creator god. Then again we have 'brahmana'. A brahmana is a statement regarding the cosmic principle 'bráhman' and all that is based on this principle, viz. the Vedic-Brahmanic sacrificial ritual. Taken together the brahmanas or statements constitute the 'Brahmana' which, written with a capital, should be considered to include all these statements. The brahmana texts are very old, in fact the oldest Sanskrit prose texts we know; their dates, however, are extremely uncertain, perhaps 1200 B.C. or later. They contain the ritual texts and prescripts for the sacrificial rites, and the 'mantras', or formulas that have to be spoken on these occasions. These books, therefore, are didactic in character [266].

With regard to the Brahmans (or Brahmins), as we use to call them in the west, we have already met them as members of the first and highest order, or varna, of the four that had their origin in the early Vedic period. From 'brahmán' the word 'Brahmanism' is derived; this is a purely western term unknown in the languages of India. The great question is whether a word like Brahmanism fits anything that exists in India. Anyhow, it must not be seen as the common religion of all those Indians who are not Buddhists, Moslims, or Christians, for the simple reason that Brahma, as a divinity, even before the advent of Buddhism was never universally adored; he is neither the most important nor the most conspicuous Indian godhead [267]. But since there exist several Brahmanical sects and forms of religion, we may group them together and apply the generic term 'Brahmanism' to them, as long as we realize that it can only be used very loosely.

c. Brahma(n) as the highest principle

The deepest cause of all that exists may be taken in an impersonal way as 'Brahma(n)'. Perhaps in olden days Brahma was seen as a personal god, but in fully developed Brahmanism thinkers made him (or it) into something impersonal [268]. Glasenapp, therefore, calls him 'the impersonal Absolute'. Now, in questions of dualism 'absolute' is a keyword since it means 'excluding' or 'putting basically apart from'. As soon as the term 'absolute' is used we may expect the proximity of dualism. Brahma is 'sat' = being, the essence of all and everything. He is infinite, incomprehensible, unborn, unfathomable, immeasurable. It is impossible to define him, to describe him in human words. He is ineffable. "Word and thought went out looking for Brahma but returned without having found him" [269]. This quotation proves that we are not dealing with the Judaeo-Christian God. Although Jahve-God and man are by no means identical, they are, as I explained in Chapter II of Volume IV, analogous. But there is not the slightest analogy between Brahma and created beings [270].

Another consequence of Brahma's absoluteness is that it makes it very difficult to accept the actual world and human life as they really are, and not consider them as inferior and worthless. True enough, the texts see the world as real and not as a phantom-world or a pure illusion - though some Hindu thinkers come very near to this notion [271]. "The Upanishads nowhere say that the infinite excludes the finite" [272]. Radhakrishnan takes great pains to prove that the Brahmanic philosophical system is not dualistic. I agree with him that there is no question of absolute dualism, in the sense of Being (Brahma) and Non-Being (the actual world). But there is certainly dualism in the idea that a truly philosophical person (who, in Indian thought, is not different from a religious person) should leave the world behind him in order to become united with Brahma.

d. The Brahmanic idea of unity in the cosmos

If we want to understand the Brahmanic notions about the cosmos and its unity, we must compare them with what Vedic mythology has to tell us. The first part of the Vedic tale does not essentially differ from other ancient cosmogonies. As in the Book of Genesis, at first there was nothing but water. But these waters already contained the germ of life. Then a clod of earth appeared drifting on the surface; this grew into a mountain that later became our planet. Kuiper speaks of 'undifferentiated unity' here [273], but I would rather modify this as 'a unity only insofar as a state of undifferentiatedness may be called a unity'. Exactly because of being undifferentiated it may develop along different lines. Kuiper adds that this is no creation myth since there is no creator. "Things were considered to exist, somehow, in their own right".

Now, outside this still unformed whole, a god originated, Indra. How this happened is not explained. Anyhow, he started working on the cosmos as it then existed. What he did was to transform unformed matter into individualized forms and beings. And what is crucial, he gave this world of concrete objects a dual, not to say, a dualistic character. First of all, he divided the cosmos into an upper and a nether world, and the supernatural beings into the devas of the upper world and the asuras and demons of the nether one. Further, it is important to note that Indra did not use all of the primeval matter. Hence the ordered world is surrounded by chaos. To Indian philosophers, "the world was a precarious balance between the powers of cosmos and chaos" [274]. When in winter time the earth lay barren and yielded no crop, it was clear that chaos was intruding upon nature. And the fact that man, although a thinking being, is blotted out by sleep for one-third of every twenty-four hours, means that chaos is near to him too [275]. Finally, the dual(istic) nature of Indra's cosmos manifested itself also in "the all-prevailing contrast between man and woman, male and female" [276].

If it is true, as Kuiper asserts, that the key to Vedic religion is that "every decisive moment in life was considered a repetition of the primeval process, (and that), therefore, the myth was not simply a tale of things that happened long ago" [277], then the conclusion is inescapable that Vedic philosophy, in spite of an apparent tendency to monism, basically took a dualistic view of life.

To most people, however, the notion of a dualistically split up world that is not fundamentally one seems uncomfortable. So it will not surprise us that, at a later stage, the learned Brahmans were searching for a principle of unity in the cosmos. We find their ideas in the already mentioned Brahmanas, and in the 'Upanishads', a collection of about one hundred and eight works, dating from the sixth to the fourth centuries B.C. [278]. The word 'upanishad' means 'confidential communication' or 'esoteric lesson'; these books were not intended to become widely popular. They constitute a search for the ultimate reality. Everything on earth is fleeting, changing, and temporal; even human life is finite. We cannot feel ourselves at ease with this kind of things; "only the infinite gives us durable happiness" [279].

We have seen that already in the Rigveda there occurs a monistic principle, the Ekam. Many later Indian philosophers hold that, while there are many divinities ('devata'), there is, nevertheless, only one eternal 'Lord of the world' ('ishvara'). He has brought about the world and will also destroy it; he is morally perfect and the ground and origin of all natural and ethical laws. Philosophical texts do not state with which one of the gods this 'ishvara' must be identified, with the result that sects of Hinduism equate him now with Vishnu and now with Shiva. This betrays a tendency to transform ishvara from a kind of principle into a personal god. Probably this was a reaction to Brahmanism, for to the Brahmans the impersonal Brahma was the ultimate reality, the principle on which the unity of the cosmos was based.

e. Theism or pantheism

There has been much discussion whether Brahmanic religion, seen from this angle, is theistic or pantheistic. Part of the problem, I believe, is due to the fact that scholarly terms current in western thought cannot be applied to Indian thinking without reservation. Radhakrishnan somewhat indignantly states that "the Upanishads are not pantheistic in the bad sense of the term. Things are not thrown into a heap called God, without unity, purpose or distinction of values ... It is pantheism, if it is pantheism to say that God is the fundamental reality in our lives". And he adds that God is 'transcendent as well as immanent' [280].

Put in this way the Brahmanic idea of God seems very close to that of Christian orthodoxy. However, there is a problem. Like most mythologies, the Brahmanic creed, and the Hindu creed in general, does not see God as Providence. Not only matter but souls also exist along with him from eternity, and are, therefore, to some extent independent of him. The Lord of the world is often believed to restrict his working to the upkeep of the cosmic fabric and its laws. This is in accordance with the impersonal character of Brahma too. In this view he (or it) is certainly far less theistic than the Judaeo-Christian God, and more like a principle, more 'deistic', that is [281]. This also means that there is not only a difference but also an obvious distance between the godhead and the actual world including humanity.

In passing we may note that Hindu materialists and sceptics try to resolve this duality of god and world, the one by denying that anything extra-material exists, and by considering matter the real monistic principle, the other by calling all transcendental ideas in question so fundamentally that there is no room left for a divine world.

f. The importance of ritual

Sacrificial ritual served the double end of propitiating the gods and warding of the demons. This makes us understand why the ritual of Vedic and especially of Brahmanic times was so elaborate. Sacrifices have a highly intricate texture, are often repeated and usually last a long time. The 'Agnistoma', for instance, with the sacred potion, the 'soma', as its central feature, is a whole series of sacrifices lasting five days. The famous horse-sacrifice, that I have mentioned more than once already, lasted three days. Then there is a considerable amount of domestic ritual too, for example the marriage ceremony. What is important to our theme is that, in the great dualistic contest between gods and demons, human people, by means of their ritual, try to side with the gods.

Believers want to secure the goodwill of the gods by praying to them, by praising their goodness and greatness, and by offering them the food they like, grain, milk, butter, ghee (Indian fat), the flesh of goats and sheep. There is not much personal devotion in this; most of the time the gods are addressed as a group and ritually treated as such. They are invited to attend the service, seats are reserved for them, and they see the fire consume what people offer them. The ritual has a strongly utilitarian character, with a conspicuous technical side; the issue is whether dangerous powers may be laid off and benevolent one put in motion [282].

What the Brahmans did was to systematize the already elaborate Vedic ritual in the most thorough way. Being intellectuals they performed their work in such a scholarly manner that modern authors feel entitled to speak of 'pre-scientific science' (a contradictio in terminis, I should say), of a 'doctrine', and of a 'science of ritual' [283]. The almost inevitable result is that the ritual began leading a life of its own; ritual development led to ritualism. This does not only mean that an overriding impulse was felt to perform every detail of the ritual to the highest perfection. Far more important is that the gods slowly but certainly recede into the background. A new and curious opposition arises, that between the ritual and those for whom it is designed; in this conflict the gods have the worst of it. The ritual becomes a 'rule-governed activity per se' [284].

The word 'magic' will not be far from our minds now. Magical rites doubtless play a great role in Vedic ritual. Magic may be described here as an attempt to make the ritual so powerful that the gods are compelled to obey, or rather, that the ritual becomes effective without the cooperation of the gods. Especially in daily life we find innumerable magic acts. Do you want to win the favour of a woman? Then take two chips of wood, cut from a tree and from the liana that winds itself around this tree (a symbol of the inseparable unity of a man and a woman), rub them down together with an arrow-head, an unguent, liquorice, and other ingredients, and touch your beloved with this mixture. And you unhappy teacher pestered by unruly pupils, there is hope for you too! Take wood from a ficus plant and straw from the homes of the pupils, and burn these materials. Then collect earth that has been excreted by ants, make a heap of it, and sacrifice ghee, honey, grain, and other ingredients in it. Finally make your pupils swallow grains of corn mixed with sesam seed. After this calm will reign in your classroom. I admit that for a townsdweller it will be difficult to collect this ants' earth in sufficient quantities, and, still more, to force this corn-sesam mixture down the pupils' throats, but the result is worth the trouble [285]. And so on, ad infinitum.

What Brahmanism intends to do is, in my opinion, to connect the upper world of the gods and the human world in such a way that the nether demoniacal world becomes incapable of doing any harm. In other words, the Brahmans attempted to dissolve the dualistic opposition by making the inimical forces powerless to intervene. They did this by relating the macrocosmos to the microcosmos up to the point of identification. Thereby, as Heesterman states, "the ritual system as such is given in the Brahmanas as a perfectly ordered mechanism to dominate and regulate the cosmic processes, both as regards the individual's life and the universe at large ... The ritual is identical with the cosmic order. When set in motion and correctly executed the ritual automatically controls the universe. Thus, for instance, it is said that the sun would not rise if the morning libation of the Agnihotra were not offered in the fire". In this conception the gods are the great losers; they never possessed much personal identity but now they are no more than impersonal cosmic forces [286].

This shows how difficult it is to get rid of an old dualistic tenet. The attempt to do so may easily result in the origination of a new one. The gods, being now virtually at the sacrificer's beck and call, are practically excluded from the ritual, and, in this way, from religious life; they have degenerated into forces that can be controlled by the rites.

19. The superiority of the Brahmans

a. The Brahmans as sacrificial experts

It would be far from correct to see in Brahmanism a religion pur et simple, and to consider all Brahmans professional priests. We must take to heart a remark made more than a century ago by Monier Williams that "Brahmanism was rather a philosophy than a religion, and its fundamental doctrine was spiritual Pantheism" [287]. It is safest to see Brahmans as a social class, the highest and the most important of the four varnas, whose members had diversified functions, not only priestly ones. Nevertheless, it is certainly true that the priestly office was the original function that made the Brahman class into what it was to become later. The hub of the Brahman's life and work was the 'yajna', the performing of sacrifices; he brought sacrifices himself and was present as priest at the sacrifices of other persons [288].

The principal element of a sacrifice was fire - the fire that totally consumed the sacrificial offerings. Originally sacrifices were mainly meant as thank-offerings, but the foodstuffs that were burned served also to nourish the gods. The gods had to be healthy and vigorous since it were they who kept nature going. "Every man throughout his whole life rested his whole hopes on continually offering oblations of some kind to the gods in fire, and the burning of his body at death was held to be the last offering of himself in fire" [289]. The efficaciousness of every sacrifice came more and more to depend on its elaborateness and its precise execution. It was accompanied by the singing of hymns, by praying and preaching, and by reciting and repeating sacred texts. This development had some important consequences. First, as I explained earlier, it gave rise to ritualism, to putting the accent more on the 'technical' side of the sacrifice than on the sacred act itself. Second, it enormously strengthened the hands of the Brahmans, the experts who became absolutely indispensable in every act of worship that was not wholly private [290].

In the long run the expert knowledge of these Brahmanic 'engineers of ritual' got severed from the actual rites themselves in such a way that it was considered perfectly possible to perform them in the spirit alone, that is, without doing anything at all. Deep meditation was sufficient. It will be clear that expert knowledge of the intricate ritual, together with mastery of the difficult technique of meditation (especially of controlling one's breath) assured the Brahman of an elated position in the eyes of his fellow-men. He obviously was able to transcend the banality of everyday life.

The true Brahman is 'der Welt abhanden gekommen'; he has renounced the world. He is no longer willing to accumulate wealth; he looks down on sensual pleasures; he is not even interested in the normal religious duties of the father of the house. In this way he sets himself apart from human society and even over against it. He considers his own soul, his atman, identical with the world soul, the Brāhman. Thus we may discern "two opposed and incompatible spheres : the transcendent sphere of the renouncer's individualistic rejection of society as against the social world and its requirements" [291]. What the Brahmān aims at is release from samsara and attaining a state of 'moksa', or 'nirvana', which is an absolute state, painless, emotionless, motionless.

b. The purohita

Mention must also be made of a special type of religious Brahman, the 'purohita', the house priest or family priest "who performed the many rites and ceremonies ... for a family or group of families, and has survived in this sense to the present day" [292]. Subcastes too could have their own purohitas. It will be evident that this function gave its occupant a considerable influence since everything was, in one way or another, connected with religion and ritual; it was, therefore, a much coveted position.

The highest office to which a Brahman could aspire was to become the purohita of a king. It was he who announced to the people that a new king had ascended the throne. He was never far away from the side of his royal master. A king had to perform a great many religious duties; in all ritual matters the purohita was his regular adviser taking part in the long and elaborate sacrificial services, some of them extending over a period of more than a year. It was a highly important part of his task to stand by the royal chariot in battle, warding off all dangers by pronouncing prayers and magic spells. It will not surprise us that the purohita advised his master in political matters too; in those days there was no real distinction of 'Church and State'. From the priestly adviser a straight line leads to the later Brahmanic statesmen who, in several periods, were fairly influential. The purohita was richly rewarded for his services by his royal lord; large donations, especially of landed property, came his way [293].

c. Brahmanic wealth

The social pre-eminence of the Brahmans was much heightened by the fact that it was considered a meritorious act to present gifts to them. There were even days for such almsgiving which, as more propitious than others, were determined by means of astrology - for instance, the two equinoctial days, the eclipses of sun and moon, and the new and full moon [294]. An eclipse is an important disturbance of the natural course of events which asked for propitiating acts [295]. The donations consisted not only of money but also of cows, land, gold, and so on; the recipients were either individual Brahmans or groups of them [296]. Kings could be very liberal on special occasions, like their coronation or great victories [297]. They sometimes gave whole villages away.

Ordinary people presented gifts when a child was born or when the child became able to eat rice [298].

Of course, the original aim of giving and receiving such gifts was to free the Brahmans from the care for their livelihood; landgrants were destined for Brahman settlements where the inhabitants could sacrifice and study and teach in all tranquillity of mind [299]. At the same time it will be evident that the Brahman class grew very rich in this way; they became large landowners, in many districts the largest. This transformed them into a sort of landed gentry with vested interests and made them act as semi-feudal lords. All this signifies that the Brahmans in the course of time became a major socio-economic power. Strange as it may sound, this influence did not grow less because the Brahmans, next to receiving, were obliged to give. Ideally a Brahman must distribute his property to others and keep for himself only what he really needed. But, as Gupta sighs, "the number of ideal Brahmans was certainly few".

What often happened is that the Brahmans bestowed gifts - of land, for instance - on other people, or on institutions such as temples, but retained shares so that they could profit from these endowments. Other Brahman proprietors settled landless Brahman families on their own land, which made these people dependent on their benefactors [300]. Land-owning Brahmans so arranged it that their estates were farmed either by hired hands or serfs, or by free peasants who paid their taxes to the Brahmans (and not to the king) [301]. Thus, in one way or the other, many people became wholly dependent on Brahmans who, as a consequence, were not unreservedly popular.

The original Vedic religion knew no temples; the fire-sacrifices were performed in the open air. No temples from before the Gupta age (third century A.D.) have been preserved, although there may have existed religious buildings since the third century B.C. [302]. The erection of temples is closely connected with the waning of the people's interest in the extremely long and elaborate Brahmanic services. When temples, with their whole retinue of priests, musicians, dancing-girls, and prostitutes came in vogue, many Brahmans became temple-priests, finding in the liberality of the visitors a new source of wealth [303]. As Gupta writes : "The temples refrained from being mere religious institutions. They became sources of dynamic socio-economic activities" [304].

Returning now to a much earlier period, we must state that many Brahmans were great scholars; they were the intellectuals who founded schools and colleges and taught many students. The sacred study of the Vedas was entrusted to them. However, there were far too many Brahmans to find for all of them a priestly or a scholarly function. Brahmans might be farmers or craftsmen. Gupta tells us that there were also 'degraded' Brahmans, with a correspondingly low social status [305].

d. A highly privileged class

All things taken together, the Brahmans constituted a highly privileged class of society utterly different from the three others. The Brahman varna had its heyday in pre-Buddhistic days (since the rise of Buddhism dealt a heavy blow to the priestly class and must partly be seen as a reaction against Brahmanism). It was a kind of super-class; its members were seen as more than human, or, in many cases, as invested with more than human powers. They were 'twice-born', or 'dvija'; the first birth, of course, was the natural one, the second the Upanayana, the initiation ceremony which entitled an Aryan to study the Vedas and made him a full member of society. The initiated dvijas received the 'sacred thread', a cord hanging obliquely over the breast from the left shoulder to under the right arm; from then on it belonged to their normal outfit. It is still worn by orthodox Hindus.

True enough, in the olden days Kshatriyas and Vaishyas too were entitled to the ceremony of the second birth, whereas the Shudras were excluded from it. Thus there were three classses on one side of the dividing line and one on the other. But even so there was a difference between the three privileged classes. The ideal age for the initiation was eight for a Brahman, eleven for a Kshatriya, and twelve for a Vaisya. Now the Upanayana meant the start of a long study of the Vedas, under the tutorship of a Brahman guru. It is doubtful whether many Vaishya boys, whose fathers, naturally enough, wanted them to take their share in the family work, would have embarked on such exacting studies. The same applies to the Kshatriyas, the warrior class; professional soldiers nowhere show a great aptitude for abstract studies. So the dividing-line between once-born and twice-born steadily shrank back, and more and more people failed to occupy the rank of more than mortal. Finally the twice-born became mainly synonymous with being a Brahman. Basham reports that even to-day orthodox Brahman families celebrate the Upanayana ceremony [306].

The law favoured the Brahmans in many respects; confiscation of property and banishment were possible but corporal punishment was not inflicted on them. There were even Brahmans who believed they were above the law [307]. The power of the Brahmans did not lie in their organization - for there was no Brahman Church nor a Brahman pope - but in their hold on the supernatural. Village Brahmans acted as fortune-tellers and magicians; the more educated not only knew everything about natural phenomena but also how to handle them. As I have already pointed out, it was believed that the sun could not rise before a Brahman priest ordered it to climb above the horizon. If the purohitas refrained from assisting the king and his army with their prayers and spells, the whole host could be destroyed. No wonder that a Brahman expected precedence always and everywhere, and honour from all and sundry. Understandably their pride and their privileges elicited jealousy and satire [308].

20. Dualistic tendencies in Hinduism

a. Vishnu and Krishna

Most people, Indians not excluded, do not possess a philosophical mind. To the average Indian Brahma seemed a god who was too far off, and no more than an abstraction that it is impossible to venerate. When, after Vedism and Brahmanism, the third stage of the authentically Indian religions, Hinduism, still the main popular religion of present-day India, began to develop, other more interesting and colourful deities were seen as the ishvara. One of the most important of these is Vishnu who rose from a second-rank position in the Vedas to that of supreme god and lord of the universe in Hinduism. In the centuries around the beginning of our era his cult became so important that scholars speak of 'Vishnuism', as an aspect or sect of the Hindu religion. It is said that the Gupta emperors were Vishnuites. His cult spread all over India, even into the deep south. Vishnu is mainly venerated as the preserver and restorer, as the giver of all good things. He is young and handsome; his skin has a dark-blue colour. He is portrayed as having four arms and hands. Vishnu is married to Lakshmi, the goddess of fortune. His favourite emblem is the lotus flower; often he is represented seated on the 'padma', the lotus.

This god is 'polytheistic', as well as many-sided, for, as the creator, he is identical with Brahma, while he is also the same as Shiva. The cult of this other supreme god of whom I have already written, represents another aspect or sect of Hinduism, called Shivaism. To return to Vishuism, "Vishnu is the highest Brahman from whom everything proceeds, who is the all, in whom the all is, and to whom everything returns." This proves that, although Vishnuism is far more mythological than philosophical Brahmanism, it nevertheless retains the notion of the Absolute [309]. Furthermore, Shiva has ten 'atavaras', a word meaning 'descent', something like 'incarnation' or 'manifestation'. By means of these atavaras Vishnu is present in the world and keeps it going. The best known of these incarnations is Krishna whose name was made a household word in the streets of the big cities of the west by the Hare Krishnas. Often Krishna is considered identical with Vishnu. Possibly there once was an historical Krishna who grew into a very famous mythological hero celebrated for his great deeds. Later he came to be seen as the eighth atavara of Vishnu himself and sometimes as his most perfect manifestation.

b. Contradictory statements about women

If we transport what was written before on Spirit and Matter to the level of common thought, we are not suprised to hear that Spirit is seen as the male principle and Matter as the female one. Matter is conceived as Nature that must be fructified. "Without the union of the two (i.e. male and female) no creation takes place". Although here again we seem to find the idea of unity in duality, they really are 'dualistic conceptions', as Monier Williams calls them [310]. It always and everywhere has been extremely difficult for mankind to maintain a proper equilibrium between masculinity and femininity. Usually the scales tip in one direction, most of the time giving the males the overweight. We have already seen that it is or was the normal situation in India, with the male seen as the representation of Spirit, and the female as the embodiment of Matter, the one being the giving and the other the receiving party.

But sometimes, when the balance is shifting the advantage is for woman. Dr. Mukherjee, an Indian scholar, was surprised at "the contradictory situation (of women) in our (Indian) contemporary society. At one extreme they are extolled as 'goddesses', and at the other vilified as the roots of all evils" [311]. She gave her little book on Indian women the subtitle of 'normative models' showing thereby that 'ideal women' really exist in Hindu literature, perhaps more for the elites, she adds, than for the masses [312]. She then goes on to describe a great number of such women and to typify them.

c. The Hindu mother cult

There was and is one type of woman that meets with general respect, not to say with veneration, and that is the mother. I was struck by the many times that the volumes of the numerous Hindu scholars I consulted were dedicated to their mothers or to their memory. Generally the position of women, even of married women, was inferior, as we have seen. But when a married woman became older, or downright old, and was the mother of many children, and the grandmother of numerous grandchildren, perhaps even of greatgrandchildren (for she was often married at a very early age), she gradually became a matriarch assuming the traits of a Great Mother. She had triumphed over all her weaknesses and shown that she was in full possession of that magico-mythical power, the procreative force. Her children venerated her and paid her deference to such a degree that we are justified in speaking of a 'cult'. Horner calls this cult 'mother-homage', and says that this is "a fundamental and striking aspect of Indian thought, and one that is not peculiarly Buddhist" [313]. He describes the mother as "the pivot around which devotion and genuine admiration revolved" [314].

d. Mother-Goddesses

There is a religious connotation here; I myself already used the term 'Great Mother', the 'Magna Mater', the Mother-Goddess. Several scholars believe that this somewhat unexpected veneration of the mother is an inheritance of pre-Aryan culture, of the Indus valley civilization. However that may be, Mother-Goddesses, the 'matris' (the word is easily recognizable), were omnipresent in ancient India. Basham states that in the period I am discussing the leading classes took very little interest in female deities in general, leaving their veneration to the agricultural population [315]. There is a kind of social watershed with regard to religious experience on this point. It is an intriguing question whether Hindu religion knew an important cult of the Mother-Goddess. I do not believe that this was the case in by far the greater part of the long period I am treating here. A main characteristic of the Vedic religion is 'the predominance of the male element'. The Vedas do not pay much attention to female deities; they occur, but only in 'a very subordinate position' [316]. There were, indeed, several Mother-Goddesses going by different names, but they were hardly distinguishable from the phenomenon they represented, in particular the earth. "Go to thy mother", says a Rigveda burial hymn, meaning internment in the earth [317]. But no general cult of the one great Mother-Goddess ever developed in India as it did in other religions.

In Hindu religion there exists a heavenly mother - Aditi whom we already met -, and an eartly, a chthonic divinity called Nirrti. Between them, and in a dualistic way, they represent the 'benign and malign aspects of the primitive mother-goddess'. Aditi is associated with the sky and the light; she protects those who pray to her and gives them happiness. But Nirrti is the patroness of death and decay [318]. She looks well enough, what with her golden hair on which a golden crown rests. But beware! The appearance is deceptive. "Underneath her glowing externals there lurks a frightful, terrible, and a wicked soul". She "has a malicious and devious mind" and "represents the anarchic forces of chaos in the universe" [319]. As such she is utterly different from Aditi who is the goddess of cosmic order. The existence of a deity like Nirrti proves that universal order was constantly threatened by disorder, or should we say that order carried the germ of disorder in itself?

e. The come back of the female divinities

According to Wendy O'Flaherty, goddesses very slowly came back into their own during the many, many centuries of our period. After the near-total eclipse in the Vedas there was some slight reshifting of the balance in the epics, till in the Puranas, as this author states, we may even speak of 'female dominance' (in the mythological world, that is) [320]. The 'Puranas' form one of the principal genres of Hindu literature next to the Vedas, the Brahmanas, the Upanishads, the epics, and the law-books. What they contain are legends about the genealogy and history of the royal houses. Or perhaps we should say that they start from these legends but were transformed in the course of time into tracts of religious propaganda exalting the glory and might of the two main Hindu deities, Shiva and Vishnu [321]. This literary gestation and transformation lasted very long, the Puranas getting their final form, in classical Sanskrit, only in the Gupta era, in the fourth and fifth centuries A.D., at the extreme end of our period, that is [322]. It was only then, and later in the Middle Ages, that high society showed an heightened interest in the cult of goddesses [323]. Emerging from their state of vague existence they now were venerated in temples of their own.

In this later development the male deities had spouses, or rather, a female counterpart or feminine aspect. This aspect is called 'sakti', the creative energy or potency of the male god; it is not wholly clear whether with sakti a god's wife, in the most personal sense, is meant, or merely the female side of himself. There was, so to speak, a theological difference between a god and his sakti, since the god himself was thought to be 'inactive and transcendent' whereas the sakti is 'active and immanent' (i.e. in the world) [324]. There is a whole class of Indian writings that give pre-eminence to the saktis, the so-called 'Tantras' ('tantra' means 'system'). The Tantras never gained universal recognition but remained the holy books of a sect called 'Tantrism'. Their central thesis is that "Shiva's wife (is) the source of every kind of supernatural faculty and mystic craft" [325]. The whole world proceeds from the sakti and has, therefore, a feminine origin. Above all they venerate 'Maha-Devi', the 'Great Goddess', the sakti (or wife) of Shiva. Women are seen as the images of Maha-Devi, and, in consequence, must be respected. Tantrism arose only after 500 A.D. and, therefore, falls mainly outside our scope.

The same applies to Saktism. This movement must not be seen as a general Indian movement but as a sect or as a number of more or less similar sects. However pluriform Saktism may appear to us, all its adherents subscribe to the central idea that "potencies conceived as one or more goddesses, directly or indirectly, determine the order of the world". Gonda says that this notion has influenced all Indian thought of the last fifteen hundred years [326].

f. The dual(istic) character of Maha-Devi

In the ultimate phase of our period, Maha-Devi, the sakti of the god Shiva, gained pride of place as the goddess par excellence. She rose to the position of the dominant female divinity in the Hindu pantheon. But, as Wendy O'Flaherty says, "the dominant woman is dangerous in Hindu mythology, and the dominant goddess expresses this danger in several different but closely related ways" [327]. This scholar presents some very cogent reasons why Hindu males even to-day fear that their wives dominate them - apart from the fact that nobody loves to be dominated. First, her sexuality is felt as a threat; the more erotic she is, the more she drains him of his life force (sexual energy seen as as a limited quantity so that a lustful wife may make a man impotent). But erotically powerful or not, she is also the mother of his children; as such she evokes in him the image of his own adored mother which gives him a vague but unpleasant impression of committing incest [328].

This uneasy ambivalence is transported back into the mythical sphere. Maha-Devi is a goddess with a dual, not to say, a dualistic nature since she is mild and fierce at the same time. She goes by many names which shows that her worshippers were none to sure about her identity. She is called 'Parvati' = Daughter of the Mountain (the Himalayas), 'Sati' = the Virtuous, 'Gauri' = the Beautiful, 'Annapurna' = She who gives plent of food, "Mata' = the Mother; all these names refer to her bountiful aspect. Under her malicious aspect she was called 'Durga' = the Inaccessible, 'Kali' = the Black One, 'Candi' = the Fierce One, and 'Bhairavi' = the Terrible. Now she is a beautiful young woman accompanying Shiva, or Shiva is portrayed as half Shiva, half Parvati. Then again she is made into a repulsive hag with long shrunken breasts, her red tongue dangling from her mouth, her head adorned with skulls - a real demoness [329]. I believe that Maha-Devi, ambivalent as she was, mirrored the (dualistic) conception Indian men had of women : givers of life but seducers and vampires as well.

The long process I described did not result in a redress of the balance between male and female divinities. While older Vedic mythology was hardly interested in goddesses and was all about male ones, in the final stages of our period, we observe a certain measure of female preponderance.

g. The Linga and the Yoni : an uneasy balance

Indians expressed their supreme interest in the dual character of the divine world in a drastic way, from a western standpoint that is, viz. by the veneration of the linga and the yoni, Hindi words for respectively the male and female private parts. Since Shiva "personifies the reproductive forces of nature", his linga, or phallus, in an erect position, became an object of general veneration. The cult objects are the omnipresent conical and cylindrical stones [330] or short pillars with a rounded top. The Vedas knew little of this, the Mahabharata somewhat more, but from the beginning of the Christian era the linga cult sprang into full bloom; it became wide-spread, the linga being "the symbol under which Shiva is universally worshipped" [331].

The central idea of the god's inexhaustible sexual potency and his never abating lust has been exemplified in a lot of very explicit erotic iconography, for instance, in sculptured reliefs on temples. There even is a Hindu sect called the 'Lingayat' the adherents of which, men and women alike, carry a linga symbol with them in a silver or bronze case [332]. An acute observer of the Indian scene reports that "childless Indian women will make innumerable offerings and prayers to the basalt Linga of the Shiva temples" [333]. We also know that there existed temple prostitution which granted intimate access to the godhead by means of sexual union with one of his servants [334]. Hindu mythology depicts Shiva as the sexual creator, as committing incest, as the seducer of the sages' wives, as an adulterer [335]. His sexual activities are the prop and mainstay of the universe; his amorous dalliance with his wife Parvati keeps the cosmos going. The moon is full when he has sexual intercourse with her; she is waning when the lovers are separated from one another [336]. In short, he is the patron of 'the phallic world' [337].

But this same Shiva is the shining example of the yogis, himself the greatest of them. On the high slopes of the Himalalaya Mountains he sits on a tiger skin, utterly still, turned inward, wrapped in silence, meditating. On his forehead we see a third eye, the 'emblem of his superior insight and wisdom'. And now we hear it stated that it is his meditation which sustains the world [338]. How must we explain such a flagrant contradiction? Must we believe that the ancient Hindus were cynical enough to depict their great god falsely as an ascetic? We are tempted to believe this when we read that the same text, after having pictured Shiva sunk in deep meditation and utterly deaf to female seduction, goes on to describe him "as possessing a phallus which lusts for a womb and as being maddened with passion" [339]. Are we in the presence of a dualistically split divine personality?

I do not think that O'Flaherty is entirely satisfying when trying to explain this contradiction. In her opinion there is no contradiction or paradox - or dualism - here, but only 'correlative opposites'. 'Tapas' (ascetism) and 'kama' (erotic desire) are 'diametrically opposed' both being forms of 'heat'. Does it really explain anything to say that "Shiva among ascetics is a libertine and among libertines an ascetic"? Although I readily admit that she shows herself fully aware of the ambiguities in Hindu myths, it could be that, on this point, she too becomes the victim of the irresistible western impulse to transform the strongest possible contradictions into harmless oppositions, and then to explain that such oppositions in reality are the opposite sides of the same coin. This scholar weakens her own argument by stating that within the myths "tapas and kama are dynamically opposed, acting against one another in spite of (or rather because of) their similarities" [340].

We find the same ambivalence in several castration myths which have Shiva as their subject. According to these stories, when Shiva observes that Brahma is doing the creational work, he tears off his linga and throws it on the earth or plants it in the ground. And he goes away to meditate, 'ascetic versus sexual creation'. But even cut off his linga bears fruit, for "it results in the fertility cult of linga-worship" [341].

Do I go very far astray if I suppose that the plight of Shiva - his dual character, his unsolvable ambivalence, his dualism - faithfully portrays the eternal battle in mankind's breast, the dualistic opposition between the two opposed aspects of sexuality : sex as the urge to procreate, on the one hand, and on the other as the cause of endless trouble; as the source of vitality and joy, and yet as something tormenting and degrading; as the vehicle of intimate love and yet at the same time leading to hatred and contempt; as at once holy and a sin; in short, as contradictory in its essence as Life and Death? Some myths have it that Shiva's loss of his virility was the result of a curse. Other versions tell us that, when his phallus had fallen on the earth, "it burnt everything like a fire". Like a glowing torch it proceeded even to the underworld troubling everyone and everything on its way. Thus sex is seen as something wild, uncontrollable, and threatening.

The only solution Brahma the Wise has to offer is the union of linga and yoni, the sexual union of man and wife, that is [342]. Here sexual intercourse is not seen as the highest expression of intimate love but only as a palliative and an anodyne. Seen in this way the innumerable phallic pillars and stones are not so much the expression of insatiable lust but rather the petrified cry for help of a tormented masculinity. In consequence, we find also representations of 'linga in yoni' which sounds gross enough but in reality is innocuously symbolized by a pillar in a ring. As such it portrays the man-woman unity. I saw a photograph of an Indian stamp showing the atomic reactor (sic!) at Trombay in India : the dome of the reactor within its protective ring is, iconographically, wholly identical with a phallic stone place in a yoni ring [343].

The yoni symbol itself, without the linga, is also an object of veneration. It is set up in shrines and used as a mascot for bringing luck. Near Bombay there is a cleft which resembles the female organ; it is, indeed, called the 'Yoni'; "to pass through it is seen as a pious act" [344]. But it was in particular by the Saktist sect that the yoni was adored. This sect too based its insights on the Tantras of which I have already spoken; its central thesis is that woman "is the dominating force in the world (and) must be allowed to control it" [345]. What the Saktis venerated was, in fact, femininity, sometimes in an allegorical form but also in a very concrete way, by making statues and paintings of a nude woman, or even a living naked woman, the objects of their devotion. Their meetings are accompanied by the drinking of strong liquors and often end in general promiscuity [346]. There even existed a curious practice of 'inverse sexual union' in which the woman acts as the giver and the man as the receiver [347].

One gets the impression that the Saktists, acting in this way, are not so much trying to restore the balance between the male and female sides of existence but rather that they want to shift the accent from masculinity to femininity. Common Indian thought holds the male for superior, but the Saktists proclaim 'the supreme female principle' [348]. Once again we see what O'Flaherty calls 'a pendulum of extremes' [349]. I close this section with a general remark made by Monier Williams : "We find ... that the Hindus, in dividing divine nature into two halves, formed no idea of any due co-ordination of working power between them as between man and woman" [350].

21. Yoga dualism

a. The way of the atman

Apart from the ritual approach, there is also a subjective approach to the highest god or principle whether he (or it) be called Brahma, Vishnu, or Shiva, the three great divinities of the Hindu pantheon. Here the road upwards starts from the atman, the soul. Perhaps we should not speak of soul but of the 'true self'. We know that for the Hindus the body is only a temporary home to be discarded at death, while the atman will lodge itself in another body. In Hindu thought the relationship between body and soul is distinctly dualistic. The body is temporal and accidental, a product of time and space, subject to every kind of vicissitude, and, finally, destined to destruction. There is no resurrection of the body. The atman, on the contrary, is permanent and eternal, and, basically, destined to unification with the godhead.

To the philosophical Brahmanic mind atman is the subjective aspect of Brahma which means that they are essentially one. "Brahman is Atman"; in this way "the infinite is present in the finite" [351]. In the doctrine of the Upanishads atman is Brahman incarnate in man. The ultimate aim of life is to become united with the Highest Atman, the Brahma, the most supreme lord, the world spirit, or whatever it may be called. The formula of this unity is "tat tvam asi" = you are that"; the individual self is identical with the universal essence 352). The Supreme Atman is Being, and as such the Only Truth; everything changeable and perishable is 'inessential and, therefore, false' 353). This is the same dualistic stance as that of Parmenides (Vol. I, Ch. II, Section 8).

The realization that one's individual atman is Brahman sets man free; this is the only way to get off the wheel of rebirth and to find eternal rest in the total union - or must we say 'reunion' - with the world-spirit. However, what I mean is not an intellectual statement, something like "I now realize that my atman is identical with Brahma"; it cannot be reached by means of logical reasoning. It is rather a kind of 'gnosis', an intuitive knowledge that does not spring from the intellect but has a mysterious origin. And as 'gnosis', it is not given to all and sundry.

b. The 'via negativa'

So the simple conclusion 'tat tvam asi' is not sufficient in itself. Once this is realized, or in order to realize this, it is necessary to strip oneself, totally and consequently, of the world of temporal phenomena since these do not represent Real Being 354). The way upwards is, in fact, a 'via negativa' : the devotee must keep himself as far as possible from the actual world. Contempt for the world is the key-word of Hindu theosophy (as Speyer called it). As Dumont states, "there are two kinds of men in Hindu India, those that live in the world, and those that have renounced it" 355). However, the renouncer, although being thrown back on himself, and utterly alone, does not look down on the religion of his fellow-men; he is no western sceptic 356).

Speyer writes that, more than anywhere else, Indian thought is dominated by the notion of the transitoriness of all and everything. Hindu sages believe that contemplation of the highest things is not compatible with an active life in the world. The most radical of them do not marry, have no children, possess neither rank nor properties, not even a home, but lead a vagrant life 357). Of course, this is not everybody's choice, but being an ascetic of some sorts is absolutely indispensable. O'Flaherty aptly remarks that Hinduism knew "a conflict between the desire, as well as the obligation, to have children ... and the obligation and desire to renounce family life to seek union with god" [358].

Some of the ascetics were, as Basham says, 'solitary psychopaths' lying on a bed of thorns or hanging head downwards for hours [359]. But the normal ascetic too abstained from food and drink, from sex and the comforts of life as much as possible. In this way he became inwardly free to obtain "insight which no words could express ... He solved the mystery beyond all mysteries; he understood, fully and finally, the nature of the universe and of himself, and he reached a realm of truth and bliss, beyond birth and death, beyond joy and sorrow, good and evil. And with this transcendent knowledge came another realization - he was completely, utterly free. He had found ultimate salvation, the final triumph of the soul". In these splendid words Basham describes the path upwards [360]. This path runs through meditation, through long and frequent meditation; it is still a quite normal sight to see a devotee sitting with legs crossed in a position that is not changed for hours. In the present day European and American youth flock to India to learn this art from gurus.

c. What is yoga?

How to be released from incessant transmigration - nothing could be more important to the Indian mind - was the object of much discussion in the beginning of the Christian era. There originated six schools, or doctrines, which may be thought of as six systems of salvation or release. They differ considerably among themselves but dualism of body (or matter) and soul is common to them all. One of these systems, yoga, has become widely known in the west where many of its adherents see it as a kind of higher gymnastics on a vaguely religious basis. The word 'yoga' is etymologically the same as the Latin 'jugum', the English 'yoke', and the Dutch 'juk'. Whosoever practises yoga - he or she is called a 'yogi' - takes a 'yoke' on the shoulders, that is, he or she puts him- or herself under a discipline. In this sense yoga is a generic term, for every Indian religion prescribes yoga. But there is also a yoga doctrine, the fourth of the six systems I already mentioned. The exertions of the yogi are directed towards the ishvara who, here too, is the world spirit or the supreme atman. This spirit is not to be found in matter; there is in yoga an absolute dualism of spirit and matter. This means that the yogi must free himself from matter and become wholly spiritual.

Yoga means a systematic training of the mind; it is, therefore, a practice, but there is, of course, a theory behind it. That a human being is capable of attaining a state of concentrated contemplation during which extra-normal knowledge is revealed to him is, in itself, not a specifically Indian idea. But in India this practice reached its highest perfection. We find the first traces already in the Rigveda 361); we can follow its development through the centuries. Classical yoga got its canonical expression in the so-called 'Yoga-sutras', a collection of 194 short maxims and adages, the authorship of which is attributed to a certain Patanjali; their time of origin very probably is the first century A.D. The first elaborate commentary on this rather short work is the 'Bhashya' whose author is supposed to be a certain Vyasa in the sixth century.

d. Yoga's philosophial background

The philosophical background of the Yoga-sutras is the 'Samkhya', another of the six systems, and perhaps the most dualistic of them all. This too has a canonical book, the 'Samkhya-karika', by Ishvara-krishna, probably dating from the fourth century A.D. For practical purposes we may treat Samkhya and Yoga as one system. According to this school of thought then, 'matter' is uncreated an eternal; it has no divine origin. The western word 'matter' is an approximate rendering of the Hindi term 'praktri'. Matter possesses in itself all the forces that causes its unfolding and development. From itself it brings forth intelligence and self-consciousness; these in their turn produce the ethereal and material elements, the organs of sense and action, and finally, mind. What, at last, emerges may be called 'nature', in the widest sense, or 'universe', conditioned as it is by the categories of time and space [362]. But there is no soul in this universe, that is, no real life, but only mechanical movement and progress. With praktri as its sole cause, nature is fundamentally one [363].

'Soul' exists too, the 'life-monad', or 'true self' (atman), but wholly apart from praktri. It is called 'purusha' of which word 'person' is, again, an approximate rendering. There are countless purushas; they exist independently of the universe, and the universe runs its course regardless of them. This what Zimmer calls "the irresoluble dichotomy of 'soul' and 'matter', of 'purusha' and 'praktri' " [364]. This, doubtless, is one of the rare cases of absolute dualism. But, as I argued in an earlier work, absolute dualism in the purest form is intellectually inconceivable; the human mind is not capable of imagining two worlds that are imperviously separated from each other and will remain so for ever and ever. At some point the two worlds must come into contact. This is the case here too. A number of purushas have the misfortune of getting involved in matter; the combination of purusha and praktri is a human being.

All this means that, according to the Samkhya and Yogi doctrines, man is composed of two utterly different and irreconcilable elements; in other words, he is a dualistic being. The purusha or 'life-monad' does not take part in the development a human being undergoes. Strange as it may sound to western ears, in general what we call 'personality' does not proceed from the purusha but belongs to the material element. The purusha itself is uncreated and brings forth nothing at all; it does not change and transform itself; it does not experience pain or suffering nor even happiness. Although part of man and apparently participating in the vicissitudes of life, it is, basically, 'kevala' = absolutely isolated [365].

There is one important difference between Samkhya and Yoga. The Samkhya doctrine is materialistic and atheistic; its purusha is a pluralistic concept (there are an indefinite number of them), but it acknowledges no unique 'world spirit', not even the one Atman.

Yoga, on the contrary, is 'theistic', for it is aware of the existence of the ishvara. However, we must not think of a creator, still less of a providence, but rather of the supreme spiritual monad, at the greatest possible distance from all the miseries of existence; it is indicated by the word 'om'. The origin of this word are the letters a - u - m which, in later times, represented the 'Hindu triad' of Brahma, Vishnu, and Shiva. I would rather call this notion of ishvara 'deistic', instead of 'theistic'. It seems that yoga adepts found this concept too abstract, and, starting with the commentator Vyasa, began to give ishvara more concrete and personal traits [366].

e. Yoga practice

The first thing the yogi has to learn is that the restlessness he or she experiences does not come from the true self, the purusha, but from the mind, since mind is, at bottom, nothing but matter. The precondition of all further progress is that the yogi must learn to suppress all inner and outer movements, in order to discover the true self that is eternally at rest and totally unmoved. In other words, the yogi must cross the threshold between his existential and his essential being; by doing so he leaves the praktri side in order to reach the dualistically opposed purusha side. Although yoga practice is a 'technique', it is based on a fundamentally gnostic conception. It is not given to everyone to know what the 'true self' is.

The yogi first of all must practise self-control and learn to be non-violent, truthful, honest, chaste, and free of greed. Then he must become 'observant' by being pure, contented, ascetic, a student of the Vedas, and devoted to the godhead. Next he must learn to adopt certain sitting positions because these are necessary for meditation. Since these are difficult to learn, they require a lot of exercise, in particular the 'lotus position' in which one is sitting with legs crossed under him and with the feet laid crosswise on the thighs. In many statues we see gods sitting like this. Then comes control of the breath. Our usual, always slightly irregular breathing is a hindrance to inner concentration; the yogi must learn to breathe in an utterly different way, or rather, hold his breath for long periods of time. The importance of this practice becomes clear when we realize that 'atman' (identical with 'purusha') is etymologically the same word as the Dutch 'adem' and the German 'Atem' both signifying 'breath'. Breath control means coming into contact with the atman which is the godhead.

The next step is restraint which means at once withdrawal into the self and total indifference to one's surroundings. Now the mind must be steadied, by concentrating on one object solely, to the exclusion of all others, as, for instance, the navel - which became the origin of the proverbial 'navel staring'. The yogi is now ready for the first stage of meditation during which he learns to concentrate his mind on one single thing. Having mastered this he may proceed to deep meditation in which its object is gradually relinquished till at last the mind is void of everything. This means that the purusha is now free from all bonds with matter (with existence, that is) and attains a state of absoluteness. The material personality has been dissolved; as long as deep meditation lasts, only the purusha remains [367]. This is the redemption, the return of the true self to moksa, the Nirvana where the om resides.

I wonder whether, up to now, we have ever met another system that is more profoundly dualistic than this one, certainly not in the personal or psychological sphere. Cases of absolute dualism are rare enough anyhow. There is Parmenides' dualism of Being and Seeming, and the heterodox (Zervanite) variant of Zoroastrianism with its opposition of Good and Evil. But we have not yet encountered a technique, a system that allows a human being to step out of his personality. I ask myself whether modern western adepts of yoga fully realize all its consequences.

22. Jainism

a. The founder, Vardhamana

I believe that the most logical continuation of my argument would be to speak of Jainism first (and after that of Buddhism), since this religion, if it is a religion, is almost as dualistic as Yoga. It originated in the same period as Buddhism. Although many legends are told about the life of its founder, Vardhamana, there can be no doubt that he is an historical person who lived in the sixth century B.C. There is no consensus on the exact date of his life. Traditionally Jainist doctrine has it that he died in 527 B.C. but this very probably is much too early. Modern scholarship says that the year of his death was 477 B.C., only a few years after the death of the Buddha (it is, by the way, highly improbable that these two, though contemporaries, ever met). If we accept this date, it is not unreasonable to suppose that he was born about 540 B.C.

His father Siddharta was the chief, or 'raja', of the Jnatrika clan; his mother Trisala was the sister of the chief of the politically important Licchavi clan. Vardhamana, therefore, was a prince. His birthplace is Vaisali (now Besarh), north of Patna (Pataliputra), at some distance from the Ganges. He was married to Yasoda and had a daughter by her who was married in her turn; she became the wife of a Kshatriya and gave birth to a daughter. But regular family life did not suit the instincts of Vardhamana. When he was thirty years of age, he got, with some difficulty, permission from his family to lead the life of the wandering ascetic [368].

b. Jainism's relation to the Parshva creed

This sudden change becomes less astonishing when we realize that Vardhamana had a highly religious background since his parents professed the Parshva creed. According to tradition, Parshva was the son of a king in Benares and lived in the eighth century B.C. At the age of thirty he too underwent a conversion, retired from the world, and spent the rest of his life in propagating the truth. It is said that the became a hundred years old. Having reached that high age, he climbed the top of a mountain, no longer took food and drink, and died after a month. He himself would have said that he did not die but entered Nirvana.

According to Glasenapp, the followers of Parshva hold the following tenets. The universe is uncreated, eternal, and imperishable. It is divided into three parts or layers : the upper world of the gods, the nether world of the demons, and in between the middle world of human beings, animals, and nature. The whole universe is filled with innumerable souls. These souls are morally perfect, possess infinite knowledge, and are all equal. Unfortunately most souls have entered the bodies of gods, human beings, animals, plants, or demons. The fusion with a body makes them imperfect; now they lust after pleasure, power, and riches. Bound up with matter as they are, this element penetrates into them and makes them victims of karma.

It will be clear what the adherent of the Parshva sect will have to do : he must stop the infiltration of matter into his soul and cast out all the matter that has already penetrated into it. But how is this to be done? First of all, the believer must close the gates of his senses, that is, avoid as much as possible all contacts coming from outside; he must also suppress all inner unrest caused by anger, greed, fraud, and pride, and, most poisonous of all, the will to live. He must be strictly honest, speak nothing but the truth, possess only what is given to him (without asking for it), and not kill or maim any living being. Parshvaites live a strictly ascetic life on a vegetarian diet; as far as possible they avoid every contact with the world and very often castigate themselves.

The result is that the believer succeeds in killing all earthly instincts and in purging his soul of every material infection. In Hindu terminology, he makes his soul free from karma. Then the Parshvaite is capable of sinking into deep meditation, or rather, he ascends to the top of the world where he enjoys supreme knowledge of the real nature of the universe. It is said that Parshva won about half a million adherents, considerably more women than men; about fifty thousand of them accepted the last consequences of the doctrine and joined the orders of monks and nuns that were founded [369]. It needs no argument to prove that the Parshva creed was strongly dualistic. Normal life was considered utterly worthless compared with the higher insights that are to be won. Vardhamana's parents were pious Parshvaites and often visited a nearby Parshva sanctuary [370]. This means that he imbibed dualism with his mother's milk.

c. The annihilation of karma

When Vardhamana said goodbye to his family and the world at the age of thirty, he simply followed the example of the great preceptor. For a year and a month he wore a monk's garment but then threw this away and henceforward went about completely bare. Very probably he at first belonged to an ascetic Parshva order but found the monks not strict enough and left. For twelve years he wandered about, fasting, praying, meditating, and castigating himself in the purest Parshva tradition. Often he was mishandled by people who did not want to be accosted by a naked beggar. And then, sitting under a shala tree on the banks of the river Rijupalika (as legend tells us), he suddenly saw the light, received the supreme knowledge, and became 'mahavira' = the great hero, a 'jina', or conqueror who had triumphed over the world. From now on he propagated a renovated Parshva doctrine that is called 'Jinism' or 'Jainism'. For the next thirty years he preached his doctrine everywhere in Bihar and finally passed into Nirvana [371].

In the two hundred years that elapsed since the death of Parshva his order had grown somewhat lax. Mahavira re-established the ancient practice in its full vigour. A special accent was placed on celibacy for the monks and nuns while the deepest respect for every living creature was inculcated on all adherents; Jainists, therefore, are strict vegetarians. There is a tradition that the emperor Chandragupta Maurya became a Jainist after his abdication [372].

Compared with the other religions that have passed the review in this chapter, the Jaina religion is heterodox since it acknowledges neither a supreme being nor a creator. There is no Brahma or any other highest divinity. The universe is uncreated and is running its course according to its own laws. It is unchangeable [373]. The main theory is identical with that of Parshva : the universe is full of 'jivas' = souls, or lives. But there is also karma. In contrast to other systems Jainists take karma as something material, as very fine atomic stuff. It clings to the souls as dust would do and makes them dull and slow. The mixture of jiva and karma produces human beings who, because of this karma, are selfish, cruel, and greedy. This makes them morally imperfect. The karma law of retribution comes into effect; the result is the endless cycle of transmigrations.

One must annihilate karma in one self in order to get off the wheel of rebirth; this, however, is so difficult that most people do not succeed in this, and, are, therefore, condemned to continuous wanderings from body to body. Only the enlightened Jainist will be redeemed and enter Nirvana. First of all, the Jainist must avoid adding any new karma to that which he brought into his life at his birth. The means of achieving this are as follows. He should not lead an active life, he should control his senses strictly, and he should adhere faithfully to the body of doctrine. Yet even so the original karma remains, the sum total of all the experiences of former lives. This karma must be totally destroyed, or else the soul of the Jainist will not enter Nirvana, the 'heaven of Jina', that is reserved for the final victor [374].

The prime condition for entering the ultimate state of bliss is the acquirement of the right knowledge. Of course, this knowledge cannot be won by a simple act of the will or by studying a few handbooks. It is 'gnosis', esoteric knowledge; it can be attained only by going through fourteen long and laborious stages. In the last stages the Jainist becomes a 'kevali', one who is omniscient. Thought, reasoning, impulses from the body, it has all stopped. The devotee sinks away in deep meditation and contemplates the last and eternal things. Finally, all that remains of karma is dissolved. The bondage of the atman in the body comes to an end and is definitely redeemed [375]. The strictest Jainist sects consider it necessary that the kevali should no longer eat so that by starving himself to death he may enter Nirvana immediately [376].

d. The arduous road upwards

The road upwards along the way of renunciation and meditation cannot be trodden without the continuous practice of ascetism, inward as well as outward. There is, first of all, the duty of regular fasting, even up to the point of starvation. Further, one must follow a diminished diet by eating only a part of a full meal. Regarding meals, strict regularity is prescribed; they must be taken only in certain places and at certain hours. What is tasty should be avoided, for instance, milk, honey, and sugar, and, of course, all titbits; spirits are prohibited. The food of course is strictly vegetarian. The ascetic must most carefully shun all that might lead him into temptation by means of the senses, in particular the proximity of women. However, the Jainist is not against marriage. He may be married and have children, with the obvious exception of monks and nuns, but must practice the strictest conjugal fidelity. The body should be tamed, even 'killed', by meditation in suffocating heat or piercing cold. Jainists must not strive after comfort; on the contrary, they must suffer lack of comfort gladly, and not even scratch themselves when it itches somewhere. They are negligent in the care of the body.

Inner ascetism begins with frequent confession of sins before a guru. Deep respect must be shown to the ministers of religion. The devotee must be helpful and subservient to other people, in particular monks and gurus, fellow-Jainists, ill people, etc. He must continuously study the holy books. He must show himself indifferent to everything that comes from the body and from outside, and concentrate on what is in the soul, utterly neglecting and despising everything else. Finally, and this is his most important duty, he must take the road of meditation [377].

Monks and nuns assume the strictest duties. They must live from what is given to them but are not allowed to ask for anything. They must divest themselves of all possessions. They vow to remain unmarried, avoid all thoughts and talks relating to sexual matters, and carefully shun all temptations. Lay people may live somewhat less strictly but their duties too are heavy enough. The layman must always speak the truth, be honest and chaste, and not covet possessions but be content with which he has (the extent of which must be modest). Only the really necessary things must be found in his home. He must avoid hurting other people, even by word or thought, and not carry arms, or any other implement that may inflict harm.

What is common to monks, nuns, ascetics, and lay people, is the strict duty never to injure, still less to kill, any living being, however small and insignificant. Jainists, therefore, are not only vegetarians but have no animal sacrifices. They must also spare the plants. This last injunction makes it impossible for them to be agriculturalists. The most strict sect, the Digambara, does not even wear clothing since this is made of vegetable materials (when they go out in public they do manage, however, to throw a garment over themselves). There are some who drink water only through a gauze to avoid swallowing an insect and have their mouths veiled for the same reason; they carry a broom to sweep the floor so that they may not crush an insect. In their professional life Jainists restrict themselves to handling lifeless objects like gold, jewels, and ... money, with the consequence that many of them, like jewellers and bankers, have become fairly well-to-do people [378]. According to Petech, the Jaina community of the present day is an important financial and economic power [379].

e. Jainism to-day

Jainism pretends to be universalistic and a world religion. It indeed made some converts outside India; there even are some western Jainists in Britain and the US. A Jaina society since 1913 exists in London, the 'Mahavira Brotherhood' [380]. However, the great majority of the two million Jainists live in the Indian Union, mainly concentrated in Rajasthan, Uttar Pradesh, and Gujarat [381]. The Jainist creed has many tenets in common with Hinduism, like the doctrine of karma and rebirth, and the need for redemption by means of deliverance from the body. The personal life of a devout Hindu does not significantly differ from that of a Jainist [382].

There are also many similarities between Buddhism and Jainism. What these two denominations have in common is that neither of them was able to maintain itself against the overpowering onslaught of Hinduism. But whereas many Buddhists consider Jainism a heterodox form of their own profession, many Hindus tend to regard Jainism as little more than a variant of Hinduism, and, indeed, in the last centuries Jainism has moved so close to Hinduism that an expert like Glasenapp believes it possible that the two systems might merge completely [383]. The most important difference still is that Jainism is a carefully formulated dogmatic system, while Hinduism is extremely catholic in this respect; since the most varying and differing opinions find a home in it, there is room for Jainism too [384].

23. Buddhism

a. The life of the Buddha

Many people vaguely believe that Buddha is an Indian godhead. However, though some Buddhist sects to some extent divinize him, he was, nevertheless, an historical human being. It is quite a problem for the historian of religion that in early Buddhist writing no life of him is to be found; furthermore, it is, with regard to the events of his life, often difficult, if not downright impossible, to distinguish fact from legend [385].

The birthplace of the Buddha was situated in the furthest north of India on the slopes of the Himalayas and near to the frontiers of Nepal. The township near which he was born, in the Lumbini Grove, is called Kapilavastu, 300 km north of Patna and the Ganges; it has proved impossible to locate the exact site. He entered life as a member of the tribe of the Sakhyas. All the sources agree among themselves that the Buddha was the son of a king or a chief of this tribe, and that he, therefore, was a prince. The usual date given for his birth is 536 B.C. Some modern scholars believe that his being the son of a king is pure legend, and that he really belonged to a high Kshatriya family [386]. However that may be, he was not of humble descent. His name was not 'Buddha' then but Siddharta. Threading our way through the vast web of legends that surround his birth and infancy, we find as reliable facts that his mother died a few days after having given birth to him, and that he was raised by his aunt Gautami. For this reason he was called Siddharta Gautama.

He was an unusually intelligent young fellow who, at the age of sixteen, married a girl of equal age; it is even possible that he married two or three wives. Later he became the father of a son. His own father seems to have feared that he would choose the ascetic way and offered him all the pleasures of life. But when Siddharta was twenty-nine, he met a wandering ascetic who struck him as a really happy man. He then renounced his family, palace, and position, cut off his hair, clad himself in rags, and began a vagrant life looking everywhere for redemption.

Seven years he wandered about in the country of Patna and sat at the feet of several famous gurus. But none was capable of satisfying his thirst for the redeeming knowledge. Finally, as tradition has it, he saw the light. Sitting under a pipal tree on the banks of the river Nairanjara, looking eastward, and sunk away in deep meditation, he inwardly 'awoke'. He discovered the origin of the law of causation, he discovered how causes and effects were connected, and, most important to all, he discovered the four 'noble truths', that of suffering, that of the origin of suffering, that of making and end to suffering, and that of the road that one must go in order to free oneself from suffering. From then on he was a man 'awake' - in Hindi, a 'Buddha'; in fact, he was the Buddha. There are several dualistic elements in this story, the total renunciation of traditional teaching, the sudden enlightenment, and the new 'knowledge' which, in fact, is a 'gnosis'. Even the former identity, that of Prince Siddharta Gautama, was abandoned in favour of a new one, the Buddha.

The Buddha assembled some disciples around him and started a wandering life that lasted between twenty-five and thirty years. The region where he used to dwell was that between the Himalayas and the Ganges. He everywhere preached his new doctrine, won many adherents, and discussed with the Brahmans. The converts came from all classes, castes, and ranks of society, rich and poor, kings, scholars, merchants, artisans, and peasants, free and slaves, casteless people, and even Brahmans. His most high-ranking convert was King Bimsibara of Magadha. The most consequent of them became monks or nuns (we already heard that the Buddha had to be persuaded to allow women into his monastic orders). The Buddha died during the rainy season of dysentery; he passed away meditating under a sala tree. The town near which he died was Kusinagara the location of which is uncertain; the date of his death is the year 480 B.C. (or another year close to this date) [387].

b. The corpus of Buddhist scripture

There exists an enormous corpus of Buddhist scripture. It is of no use to confuse the reader with an enumeration of all these writings and commentaries, but perhaps it will be helpful to know a few important things. The Buddha himself left no written utterances behind him but a number of his sayings and words were noted down by his disciples. Many legends about this exceptional man began to circulate and were embellished in the process. Extensive commentaries on the doctrine were composed; the rules were explained (and added to). The earliest part of all these writings is to be found in the so-called 'Pali' or 'Theravada' canon. It is called 'Pali' because the only complete collection is written in the Pali language. We have parts of it in other languages, such as Sanskrit, Chinese, and Tibetan. The canon is also called 'Theravada' since it is said to have originated with the 'thera', the venerable ancients who were the immediate followers of the Buddha. The canon must have been composed at some time between the death of the founder and the last quarter of the first century B.C. [388].

c. The spread of Buddhism

The rapid spread of Buddhism is partly due to the fact that many people felt dissatisfied with the cold and rigid ritualism of the Brahmans which had become too complicated for the ordinary devotee. The flood of conversions also means a sort of social reaction, viz. against the aristocratic superiority of the Brahmans. Buddhism was 'democratic', or, perhaps rather, 'populist', for it accepted everyone. Some scholars hold that the Buddha himself did not intend at all to found a new religion but saw his own doctrine, to quote Basham, 'as a sort of super doctrine, which would help his followers further along the road of salvation than Brahmanism or Upanishad gnosis'. If this were true - but Basham considers this point of view erroneous -, then we should not speak of 'conversion' but rather of 'a counsel of perfection'. Anyhow, in the early days there was not much wrangling between Brahmans and Buddhists; there was more discord between Buddhists and adherents of Jainism that originated in the same period. However this may be, Brahmanism and Buddhism steadily grew further apart till finally, about two centuries later, Buddhism had to all intents and purposes become a distinctly different religion [389].

With these two centuries we reach the reign of the great Maurya emperor Asoka (273-232) whom W.F. Thomas calls 'the imperial patron of Buddhism' [390]. It must be stated, however, that although he fostered a predilection for Buddhism, he also protected the other religions. Up to this period the new religion had remained restricted mainly to the Ganges region. But assisted by Asoka, it now began to spread over all India, to Kashmir in the north-west and to the far south, and then further to Sri Lanka where a brother of the emperor went as a missionary. Temples and monasteries arose everywhere, many of them becoming wealthy through large donations made by rich people. Thousands of pilgrims, among them Asoka himself, wandered to the holy places of Buddhism, for instance to the Tree of Enlightenment. It is not impossible that at the time Buddhism was a majority religion. The missionaries concentrated on mass conversions, and less on vocations for the orders; according to ancient sources the numbers of converts ran into the hundreds of thousands [391].

Buddhism penetrated into Burma about 250 B.C.; later it came to Thailand, and then to Tibet, all of them still predominantly Buddhist countries. Enterprising missionaries brought the faith to China first and thence to Japan. But with this statement we are already overstepping the limits of our period.

In India proper the decline of Buddhism had already set in then. It proved no match for popular Hinduism. Furthermore, it became riddled with schims, harassed by heresies, and threatening to fall apart into widely different schools and sects. In the long run it proved impossible to persuade the ordinary layman that Buddhism really was a separate religion and offered a way to salvation that was different from or better than that of Vishnuism, for instance. Many people came to think that the Buddha was an incarnation of Vishnu, and that Buddhism itself was no more than a somewhat heterodox sect of Hinduism [392].

d. Buddhism a 'non-theistic religion'?

It is an almost hopeless undertaking to sort out from the mass of early Buddhist writings what the Buddha himself said and taught, his 'ipsissima verba'. The doctrine that usually is called 'dharma' = law, constitutes, in the words of Bareau, 'an inorganic system of heterogeneous and often contradictory elements'. From the very first it needed to be commented upon and interpreted. Such comments became an integral part of the corpus, with the result that after a hundred years and at the end of the one and only period of doctrinal unity, the dharma did not represent "the Buddha's own teaching but the state of the doctrine ... when several generations of disciples had enriched it with their personal creations" [393].

It is a very vexed question whether or not Buddhism is a religion. The problem is that orthodox Buddhism, just like Samkhya and Jainism, denies the existence of a supreme godhead who is the creator of the world. There is no eternal deity nor an ultimate reality that is the ontological fundament of the universe. According to primal Buddhism, nothing is definite and all is change. "Even the great Brahma is subject to coming-to-be and ceasing-to-be", said the Buddha [394]. Orthodox Buddhists consider the ishvara-idea as nothing but human speculation and as utterly ineffectual; no insight is to be gained from it. As in Jainism, the world is uncreated but not eternal. It will come to an end; after a long interval another world will come into being.

However, the Buddha himself proclaimed that there are gods (in the plural) : "These are (gods). The world is loud in agreement that there are gods" [395]. Somewhat too loud? The Buddha seems to admit their existence rather reluctantly. These gods ('devatas' in Hindi) have no permanence; they are born and they die. There are higher and lower gods; but none of them is very powerful and important. They may help people in distress; they reward good deeds and punish evil ones, and they glorify the Buddha. In this way Shakra = Indra became a much venerated deity for less doctrinal Buddhists. According to Glasenapp, "the Buddhist gods have essentially the same function as the Christian and Islamic angels and saints" [396]. If this holds true, then Buddhism knows no gods at all, since in the monotheistic religions angels and saints are no gods. So Buddhism would be a religion without gods.

But is not the idea of a religion without gods, an 'atheistic' religion, a contradictio in adiecto? Glasenapp says that it must be so "to those who have grown up with the habitual (religious) thought" [397]. He adds that from somebody's idea of there being a personal god "nothing else can be deduced as to (that person's) further religious or irreligious views" - a standpoint that seems to me in accordance with classical Buddhism. However, the fact that someone believes in a personal God - for instance, the God of Abraham, Isaac, and Jacob - must, in my opinion, necessarily lead to questions such as these : does this person believe that his God is a creator, that he is his creator too? And how does he view his relationship to the God who created him? I for one find it very difficult to imagine a religion that is virtually without gods. In my view it is fully justified to question whether a religion without gods is possible. Is it truly a religion? And does the answer to this question only depend on what we understand by religion?

Glasenapp implicitly answers this question by stating that Buddhism is a 'non-theistic' religion. I feel this is begging the question, for it is tantamount to saying that, whatever the tenets of Buddhism may be, it is a religion, gods or no gods. The reason why Glasenapp maintains the opinion that Buddhism is a religion in the full sense of the word is centred on his notion of the 'holy'. "Taking this as the decisive factor, Buddhism shows itself as a genuine religion, and not as a particular metaphysical explanation of the world, or a way of life" [398]. In this the author is following famous authors like Rudolf Otto and Nathan Söderblom. I shall not continue this argument although I am itching to do this. My critics would certainly object that it has nothing to do with my central subject. However, I am not able to study and describe such an important and highly respectable system like Buddhism without feeling personally involved and without giving some expression to this involvement. I felt the same when I was speaking of Pythagoreanism in Volume I, of the religion of Israel and of orthodox Zoroastrianism in Volume IV, and it will be the same when we come to Islam.

e. The road to Nirvana

If then there is no ontological substance of any kind that sustains the world, and if everything is always in flux and nothing, gods not excluded, is permanent, the great question is where the starting-point of the Buddhist creed is to be found. There is no other answer possible than that the hard rock on which the truth is to be built is the human person himself. This truth is not something that can be studied or learned. Of course, the aspirant to it will have teachers and in particular must listen to the Buddha himself. But there is no real body of revelation; the truth must grow inwardly; it will emerge spontaneously and be grasped intuitively. The Buddhist believer in this way becomes a 'Buddha', someone who, like the Buddha, is 'awake'; by the same token he is a 'svayambhu' = one who has attained the truth by himself alone [399]. This makes the discovery of truth a solipsistic affair. However, this does not mean that Buddhism is an esoteric system (although esoteric sects exist within it) since it invites every human being to find the truth in him- or herself. In this respect Buddhism resembles the gnosis.

The truth to be grasped is called 'bodhi' = wisdom. Who already is aware of this truth is a 'bodhisattva' = somebody whose being ('sattva') is 'bodhi'. Such a person is still an aspirant hoping to become, at last, a 'Buddha', by having found the ultimate Enlightenment. All this implies that a human person will not turn into a Buddha overnight; there is a long and arduous road to be followed. The great question now is what the core of this final Truth is. The ultimate aim of the Buddhist is to get rid of this fleeting world in which nothing is permanent, a world that, therefore, is full of suffering and pain, and that, in fact, is incomprehensible because it is subject to the interplay of Good and Evil, and Being and Non-Being, with the result that the non-Buddhist will never know what to think or believe or how to act.

The road upwards ends in Nirvana which is a non-dual condition since none of the non-dual entities is to be found in it. But it is not the One either, since with the dual entity 'the One and the Many' not only the Many but the One too is dissolved. It cannot be stated what exactly Nirvana is; it can only be described in terms of what it is not (not the One, not God, not Being, not another and new world, not heaven, and so on). For the western positivist mind it is impossible to understand this notion. Anyhow, so much will be clear that the Buddhist must cross the dividing-line between the actual world of temporal phenomena (including his own personality) and Nirvana, and these two are dualistically separated. We may, therefore, state that the core tenet of Buddhism is a form of absolute dualism, there being no relation whatsoever between our world and Nirvana. However, as always, there is a connection : the path of the Buddhist who leaves this objectionable world behind him and strives towards Nirvana.

The bodhisattva is convinced of the following elementary truths. First, everything in this world is suffering; orthodox Buddhism takes an extremely pessimistic view of existence (but there is a way out). Not only illness is suffering, and death, but also being born, having to live, not receiving what one wants to have, living with one whom one does not love, or far from the person one loves : our whole existence can be summarized in this one word, suffering. But what is the cause of all this suffering? It is, in fact, a lack of insight, for we do not realize that we are thirsting and thriving after what is not essential, the lust of the senses. We see life as nothing more than becoming and decaying; we believe that samsara, the eternal circular course of events, is self-evident, and that there is no escape from it. What we really should thirst for is 'nothing', Nirvana [400].

f. The Lesser Vehicle

The most orthodox always remained faithful to the doctrine of Nirvana. They strove to become perfect, to become an 'arhat' (in Sanskrit), an 'arahat' (in Pali), that is a 'worthy one'. One who has followed the difficult path to the goal and shed off all fetters with which life binds one is worthy to enter Nirvana. The career of such a disciple is wholly centered on the winning of arahatship. It is often called 'Hinayana' which usually is translated as 'the Lesser Vehicle' (to salvation). Both terms, 'Hinayana' as well as 'the Lesser Vehicle' probably are not entirely correct. F.W. Thomas explains that the ancient texts seldom speak of Hinayana but rather of 'shravakayana' and 'pratyekabuddhayana'. What these three terms have in common is the suffix 'yana' which means 'career' or 'vehicle' as a means of progress. What this vehicle has to achieve is to lift the believer from the wheel of rebirth. 'Hina' signifies 'small'; so 'Hinayana' is 'the Lesser Vehicle', in contrast to 'Mahayana', the 'Great Vehicle'.

A 'shravaka' is a 'hearer', that is one who is beginning to learn; the shravakayana is the pupil who begins to learn what the yana, the career, is. Still more pregnant is 'pratyekabuddhayana'. A 'pratyeka' is one who 'walks alone' on the road the Buddha has indicated, a solitary sage; he is called 'buddha' because he is enlightened. He has grown utterly indifferent to all vicissitudes of life and to all sufferings, not only those of himself but also of his fellow-men [401]. The attitude that the pratyekabuddha takes is, therefore, profoundly and expressly anti-social, anti-existential, and even anti-human since his great Goal is the dissolution of all that is human in him. It is difficult to imagine a more sharply dualistic stance than this one. The school of the Lesser Vehicle became firmly entrenched in Southern India and in Sri Lanka. From there it spread to Burma, Thailand, Cambodia, and Laos [402]. Originally it counted eighteen sects of which to-day only one remains, the Theravada, that was already mentioned.

It is clear enough that the idea orthodox Buddhists have of existence is gloomy to the utmost degree. Life is nothing but misery and woe; in this world there is no escape from the fundamental unpleasantness that is inherent in existence. Ordinary people are full of greed, lust, ambition, desire, and all the possible vices; they are utterly selfish. People are propelled by delusion, or 'moha', which makes them believe that the self is the important thing and that everything is dependent on the senses. This moha causes 'tanha' = thirst, the desire to be different, to have an existence different from that of others, which is egoistical and leads to endless suffering. What is really necessary is that this self should be completely erased. All desire for an individual existence, for individuality, must be abandoned so that the enlightened pratyeka finally will be fused with all and everything in Nirvana.

To western minds it looks profoundly illogical but Nirvana is Being and Non-being at the same time. Perhaps it may be dubbed a state of rest, in contrast to the state of flux that is characteristic of the actual world. "The universe is transient. There is no abiding entity anywhere." There is no telling what somebody or something is, since there is nothing but change. A person who believes that there is any permanence in this world is a dull fellow and very far from being even a bodhisattva. Suffering will be his lot. So the state of Nirvana forms the absolute opposition to actual existence because it is the only stable entity. It has no place, it may be anywhere. The enlightened even enter it before they have died [403].

g. The Great Vehicle

To many Buddhists the Lesser Vehicle appeared much too solipsistic. They looked down on the Lesser vehicle which, in fact, is a term of disapproval, and adhered to Mahayana, the Great Vehicle. This school became firmly established around the beginning of the Christian era and is to be found to-day in Northern India, Tibet, Mongolia, China, Korea, and Japan. It is also called the 'Northern School'. It rejects what, according to its followers, is the egotistical ideal of the strictly orthodox. It teaches that the Buddha, before his Enlightenment, was a bodhisattva, that is one who is on the way of becoming a buddha. The adherent of Mahayana does not really want to become an arahat; it seems rather selfish to him to be mindful of one's own salvation and forget everyone else. About Nirvana he knows one thing for certain : one who has entered it is separated forever from his fellow-men; it is far beyond this world, there is no connection between the two.

The Mahayana Buddhist, however, wants to help his fellow-beings. Although he may already be in the possession of a higher truth and be prepared to become a buddha, he, nevertheless, willingly postpones entering Nirvana in order to be with others who are suffering so much and help them in their plight. These believers preach the ten perfections, among them mercy (or gift), patience, and wisdom. Far more optimistic than its Hinayana counterpart, Mahayana believes that there is much good in the world, not only evil. It is also far less exclusive, for, whereas the pratyekabuddhayana leaves everybody to his own fate, most Mahayana schools believe that basically everybody is a bodhisattva, and that nobody will be shut out from the ultimate bliss that is Nirvana [404].

Finally, many Mahayana followers believe in the return of the Buddha. This, of course, is less than orthodox since the strict ideology teaches that the Buddha at his death was dissolved into Nirvana. Now the Buddha himself seems to have thought that there had been many Buddhas before him, and that he himself was the last incarnation of this line. Some early Buddhist commentators even spoke of twenty-five previous Buddhas. Anyhow, the great Buddha, because of his inner Enlightenment and his adherence to the path, rose to such perfection that at his passing away the succession broke off. He then entered Nirvana where his personality or individuality was dissolved into nothingness, or was fused with it, to put it more positively. Many of his followers found it impossible to believe that he now no longer existed. Since Buddhas had existed before the last one, why then could not a Buddha return on earth? From the beginning of the Christian era belief in a coming Buddha is widespread; he is called 'Maitreya'. Some present-day gurus claim that they are the Maitreya; one or other of them has visited the west [405].

24. Looking back

Very probably the reader will feel somewhat confused now he or she has gone over this whole field of Indian religions. So many names, ideas, concepts, sects, and schools have passed the review that he or she must have got rather flurried. I suppose it will be helpful to this reader if I now try to sketch an overall picture in a few main lines.

First of all, let us omit all those religions that are less than marginal to our subject, that is, early Christianity, Zoroastrianism, and Judaism, the religion of the Sikhs, the animalistic religions of the hill-tribes, and some others. Islam only arrived at the end of our period. Let us also not speak any more of the pre-Aryan religion, that of the Indus valley or Harappa civilization. This leaves us with no more than three religious systems, those of Hinduism, Jainism, and Buddhism, all three of them authentically Indian.

The principal one of these was and still is Hinduism, with at present more than 80 % of the population belonging to it. Hinduism developed in three stages, Vedism, Brahmanism, and Hinduism proper, as the great popular religion. These stages overlap in time and cannot be separated from each other in the cleanest way, elements of all three continuing to exist side by side. Vedism, based on the holy books, the Vedas, is the religion of the early Aryan period, that of the invasions, conquests, and early settlements. It has a predominantly male, even 'macho' character; it recognized supreme gods, above all Indra, the prototype of the Aryan warrior.

The second stage was that of Brahmanism, obviously the religion of a far more settled and civilized period since it had a strongly philosophical and scholarly hue. This tendency led to the development of a highly complicated ritual. It also gave an outstanding position to those who 'knew', the Brahmans, priests, philosophers, scholars, and teachers. Ideologically, it was based on the concept of Brahma, the supreme entity of the universe, probably rather a principle than a god.

The final stage was that of Hinduism proper, a religion that is more mythological and less philosophical and ritualistic than Brahmanism. Next to Brahma, and far more than him, it venerates Shiva and Vishnu as it great gods. Hinduism knew and knows many schools and sects and is extremely liberal with regard to its dogmatics. Of these tendencies a few were mentioned, Shivaism that adores Shiva, and Vishnuism, that includes those who, above all, venerate Vishnu.

The almost exclusive male predominance in these religions in the later stages of our period caused a slowly developing reaction that brought the female element more to the foreground. This was done by Tantrism and Saktism. I hope that I do not add to the confusion of the reader when I mention that Tantrism is also a Buddhist sect.

Jainism and Buddhism originated in the same period, about 500 B.C. Jainism was never more than a minority religion. Buddhism flourished greatly in India but dwindled to a minority status in due time. The difference, however, is that Jainism virtually remained restricted to India herself, while Buddhism almost disappeared from its native soil but spread over all South-East and East Asia. Jainism and Buddhism agree on this point that there are no gods. Jainists distinguish themselves by living a very strict life, and, in particular, by paying an enormous respect to every living being, however small, insignificant, and even obnoxious.

Buddhism, although not so much different from Jainism, is less dogmatic. It knew many schools and sects most of which disappeared in later days. The two main tendencies are the Lesser and the Great Vehicle. The Lesser Vehicle embraces the strictly orthodox, those who, regardless of anything or anybody else, strive only after their own ultimate redemption. The Great Vehicle is less strict and admits the possibility of gods, although these are of minor importance. For the time of this life the followers of the Great Vehicle take much interest in the plight of their fellow-beings rather than in their own liberation.

Diversified as this picture seems to be, it must not make us lose sight of the fact that all religions and sects of ancient India acknowledged the same basic tenets. To all of them there is an almost unbridgeable distance between actual life and the state of rest that ultimately may be attained. They all agree that this state of rest, Nirvana, is not like the Christian afterlife in the presence of God with all other blessed souls but a complete loss of individuality and the fusion of the self with 'nothingness'. All of them are of the opinion that attaining Nirvana is an extremely difficult thing, and that one life, human or other, is by no means sufficient to reach it - if ever it is reached at all.

The world, as we know it, is 'samsara', flux, unrest, change, suffering, moving about in cycles, endless repetition. Man is doomed to this because of his 'karma', the sum total of the qualities of his former lives and his present one - which always spells imperfection. The effect of karma is to be born and reborn ever again. One may lessen the impact of karma by faithfully living up to 'dharma', that is, by obeying the law, the rule, or whatever it may be called, of the universe - which is given a concrete form in the dharma of the (sub)caste. Practising dharma, however, does not suffice to get off the wheel of rebirth. To obtain this more radical measures are required.

'Measure' is not really the correct word suggesting as it does a purely human activity. What is needed is an inner revelation of the Truth. It is a long and arduous road that leads to this. The necessary preconditions are a life of the utmost probity, on the one hand, and the severest ascetic practice on the other. These are conducive to that state of deep meditation in which the Ultimate Truth may be grasped. This means that, how much the Indian religions may differ from each other, they are basically built on a dualism between personal existence, fundamentally selfish and thoughtless as it is, and the state of unworldly contemplation that leads one to the final loss of all that is self.

NOTES TO CHAPTER II

1) Petech 353.
2) Rapson, Peoples 34.
3) Renou-Filliozat I 45-50. There is also an older classification by Risley; it is mainly based on lingistic characteristics; it ranges from Indo-European, or Indo-Aryan, to Mongoloid, see Rapson, Peoples 36-43. This classification was combated by several scholars, see Chatterji 141 sqq.
4) Described by Rapson, Peoples 36-43.
5) Piggott 27.
6) Wadia 82.
7) Wheeler, Early India 22/23.
8) This difference in attitudes is very tellingly borne out by William Golding in his fine novel 'The Lord of the Flies' (1954). A group of boys on an uninhabited island splits into two parts; the larger one becoming hunters (for wild swine), the smaller one sticking to the original diet of fruit from the trees. The 'hunters' change into 'savages', painting themselves, and becoming dangerously aggressive against the more orderly and civilized group of food gatherers. For this passage with citation from Gordon Childe, see Basham 11.
9) Wheeler, Indus Civ. 2.
10) Wheeler, Indus Civ. 89.
11) Petech 360.
12) Petech 359/360.
13) Basham 29.
14) Kosambi 72.
15) Piggott 245.
16) Piggott 246.
17) Kosambi 73.
18) Piggott 247/248. The problem is amply discussed in Childe's work on 'The Aryans', especially in Chapters VI and VII.
19) Piggott 250.
20) Kosambi 73.
21) Piggott 250.
22) Ghosh, Vedic Lit. 218/219.
23) Ghosh, Indo-Iranian Rel. 219/220.

24) Suggested by Arthur Christensen in his 'Kulturgeschichte des Alten Orients', 211/212, cit. by Ghosh, Indo-Iranian Rel. 220.
25) Keith 69/70.
26) Gordon 94.
27) Gordon 97.
28) Petech 370.
29) Majumdar, Outline 79.
30) Majumdar, Outline 80.
31) Basham 409.
32) Petech 416.
33) Hopkins, Princes and People 219.
34) Renou-Filliozat I, Filliozat 196-198, and Renou 532/533.
35) Spear 83.
36) Majumdar, Outline 123/124.
37) Rhys-Davids, Early Hist.Buddh. 162.
38) Raychaudhuri 97.
39) Rhys-Davids, Early Hist.Buddh. 163.
40) Kosambi 128.
41) Petech 380.
42) Petech 383.
43) Basham 48.
44) Basham 47.
45) Raychaudhuri 109.
46) Petech 383.
47) Petech 383/384.
48) Basham 49.
49) Majumdar, Outline 127-129.
50) Majumdar, Outline 130.
51) Adv.Hist. 68/69.
52) Spear 95.
53) There is also a possibility that she was his grandmother.
54) Adv.Hist. 98.
55) Plut., Alex. LXII.
56) Just. 15.4.13-23.
57) Basham 51.
58) F.W.Thomas, Chandragupta 425.
59) F.W.Thomas, Chandragupta 426.
60) Majumdar, Outline 132.
61) Adv.Hist. 101/102.
62) Basham 53.
63) Adv.Hist. 102.
64) Basham 53.
65) Majumdar, Outline 139.
66) Majumdar, Outline 140; Basham 53.
67) Adv.Hist. 103.
68) Majumdar, Outline 140/141.
69) Rock Edict no. 13, cit. Basham 54/55.
70) Basham 55.
71) Rock Editc no. 13, cit. Basham 54/55.
72) Adv.Hist. 105.

73) F.W. Thomas, Acoka 454.
74) F.W. Thomas, Acoka 454.
75) Basham 56.
76) Rock Edict no. 13, cit. Basham 54/55.
77) Rock Edict no. 13, cit. Basham 54/55.
78) In his novel 'Look Homeward, Angel' (1929).
79) Rapson, Successors 487.
80) Strabo XI 56.
81) See for this passage Basham 58-61; Adv.Hist. 116-118; Rapson, Successors 487-507 (Ch. XXII).
82) Rapson, Scyth. and Parth. Inv. 510.
83) Rapson, Scyth. and Parth. Inv. 508-536 (Ch. XXIII); Adv.Hist. 118/119.
84) Rapson, Scyth. and Parth. Inv. 526.
85) Adv.Hist. 119-123; Majumdar, Outline 150-159.
86) Adv.Hist. 144/145.
87) Adv.Hist. 145.
88) Adv.Hist. 144.
89) Majumdar, Outline 317.
90) Basham 66.
91) Basham 66.
92) Piggott 133-136.
93) Malik 104/105.
94) Kosambi 97.
95) Kosambi 98.
96) Other historians think that there was no distinction between assembly and council; in that case 'sabha' would only mean the place where the assembly met. See Keith 80 and Adv.Hist. 30.
97) Petech 369.
98) Adv.Hist. 26; Allchin 154/155; Kosambi 80. Not every scholar adheres to this explanation of certain passages in the Rigveda the meaning of which, in their opinion, is uncertain.
99) Härtel 99.
100) Kosambi 87 who erroneously believes that there was real mating.
101) Petech 384.
102) Petech 384. The discussion on the character of early Indian kingship has been summarized by Dumont, Conception of Kingship.
103) In the Taittiriya Upanishad 1.5, cit. Basham 82.
103) Basham 82.
104) Cit. Basham 82/83.
105) For the two theories see Dumont, Conception of Kingship 70-72.
106) Basham 83.
107) Drekmeier 250.
108) Basham 84.
109) Drekmeier 251.
110) Drekmeier 256.
111) Härtel 213.
112) Prasad 290/291.
113) Prasad 286.

114) Härtel 207.
115) Mahony s.v. 'Dharma' (Hindu), Enc.Rel. 4, 329-332.
116) Skorupski s.v. 'Dharma and Dharmas' (Buddhist). Enc.Rel. 4, 332-338.
117) Härtel 208.
118) Skorupski s.v. 'Dharma and Dharmas' (Buddhist), Enc.Rel. 4, 332.
119) Glasenapp, Phil.d.Ind. 237; the words between brackets presumably are Glasenapp's.
120) Mahony s.v. 'Dharma' (Hindu), Enc.Rel. 4, 329.
121) Gonda, Veda und ält.Hind., Rel.Ind. I 208.
122) Mahony s.v. 'Dharma' (Hindu), Enc.Rel. 4, 329.
123) Smith s.v. 'Samsara', Enc.Rel. 13, 56/57.
124) Smith s.v. 'Samsara', Enc.Rel. 13, 56.
125) Mahony s.v. 'Karman', Enc.Rel. 8, 261-266.
126) Härtel 208; Gonda, Veda und ält.Hind., Rel.Ind. I 208.
127) Smith s.v. 'Samsara', Enc.Rel. 13, 56.
128) Chattopadhay 3 (preface) says that "some scholars had occasionally mentioned some aspects of slavery in our country in the course of their discussion of the social and economic history of India". He himself was the first to compose 'a complete picture of slavery in our country'.
129) Rhys-Davids, Buddh.India 219; Basham 151; Gokhale 112.
130) Bevan 373.
131) Rhys-Davids, Buddh. India 120.
132) Raj 40.
133) Apte 354/355.
134) Basham 152.
135) Mahabharata III 256.11, cit. Basham 152.
136) Rhys-Davids, Econ.cond. 183.
137) Apastamba II 4.9.11, cit. Basham 152.
138) Basham 152.
139) Mookerji II 361; Hopkins, Princes and people 239.
140) Adv.Hist. 819 and 826.
141) P.Thomas 6/7.
142) Shastri 10/11.
143) P.Thomas 44-46.
144) Sengupta gives a long description of the life of women in the early Vedic age in his Chapter X, The Position of Women.
145) P.Thomas 48.
146) P.Thomas 53.
147) P.Thomas 55/56; see also 13.
148) Rigveda VIII.3.17, cit. Indra 9.
149) Rigveda X.95.15, cit. Indra 9.
150) Indra 9.
151) Atharva Veda VI.11.13, cit. Shastri 43 (the Atharva Veda is the youngest of the four Vedas).
152) Rigveda VIII.6.24, cit. Shastri 43.
153) P.Thomas 57.
154) Shastri 76/77.
155) Mahabharata I.159.11, cit. Meyer I 7.

156) Mahabharata XII.243.20, cit. Meyer I 7.
157) Ramayana VII.9.10-11, cit. Meyer I 8.
158) Meyer I 156.
159) Indra 59.
160) And perhaps later too. There is a passage in the Mahabharata in which five brothers share one wife, Basham 175.
161) Mahabharata XIV.80.15; see Meyer II 471.
162) This custom is sometimes compared with the so-called 'Levirate marriage' in biblical Israel; however, when a man had died without offspring, his brother had to marry the widow and have children with her on the name of his brother. So a Jewish woman did not have two husbands at the same time.
163) Basham 174/175.
164) Cit. Indra 59.
165) Basham 175.
166) Mahabharata II.68.81 sqq., cit. Basham 175.
167) Basham 175.
168) Basham 187.
169) Vana Parva c. 16, cit. Indra 99 note.
170) Manu V.168, cit. Indra 99.
171) Basham 188.
172) Basham 188.
173) Inscription on pillar of 510 A.D., cit. Basham 189.
174) Basham 189.
175) Indra 118/119.
176) Indra 117.
177) P.Thomas 50.
178) Altekar 49.
179) Altekar 52.
180) Altekar 53-55.
181) Altekar 56-62.
182) Altekar 95.
183) Altekar 97.
184) Altekar 100.
185) Altekar 69.
186) Altekar 9/10.
187) Altekar 94.
188) Altekar 109.
189) P.Thomas 228.
190) Sengupta 159/160.
191) Cit. Indra 12/13.
192) Sengupta 158.
193) Cit. Indra 12.
194) Cit. Sengupta 1
194) Cit. Sengupta 158.
195) Cit. Indra 14.
196) Cit. Indra 15.
197) Cit. Indra 14.
198) Sengupta 157/158.
199) Altekar 208.
200) Altekar 208.

201) Paul 8.
202) P.Thomas 80/81.
203) P.Thomas 82/83.
204) P.Thomas 83.
205) P.Thomas 84.
206) Paul 6.
207) Paul 5.
208) Hutton 7. In his preface to this book Prof. Louis Renou asserts that Hutton's work will be the only one to be read in the coming years. Alas, the pages of the copy I took in hand in the library of the South-East Asia Insititute at Amsterdam had not even been cut open in the forty years since its publication. At present the most authoritative work is that of Dumont, Homo hierarchicus.
209) Hutton, Ch. IX, 138 sqq.
210) Ketkar 12/13; Dumont, Homo 36/37.
211) Hutton 168-173.
212) Anant 20.
213) Dumont, Homo 147/148.
214) Rapson, Peoples 47/48.
215) Rapson, Peoples 49.
216) Basham 150.
217) Basham 149; Dumont, Homo 101-103.
218) Basham 152.
219) Ambedkar's book is called 'Who were the Shudras?', see bibliography.
220) Sharma 33-35.
221) Sharma 36-38. This thesis was defended by Ambedkar in his Ch. 7, entitled 'The Shudras were Kshatriyas'.
222) Sharma 38.
223) Ambedkar's Ch. 5, 'Aryans against Aryans'.
224) Sharma 40.
225) Petech 375.
226) Ambedkar 192.
227) Sharma 44.
228) Sharma 48.
229) Sharma in his Ch. IV.
230) Radhakrishnan I, 26/27.
231) Glasenapp, Phil.d.Ind. 4.
232) Glasenapp, Phil.d.Ind. 12.
233) Glasenapp, Phil.d.Ind. 17/18.
234) Mandala X 129.
235) Petech 376.
236) Petech 376.
237) Glasenapp, Phil.d.Ind. 13.
238) Gonda, Inl. 32-35.
239) Rigveda 1.164.16.
240) Agrawala 49.
241) See for an extensive treatment of this subject Kamrisch, Ch. VIII, 'The Androgyne God', especially 220/221.

242) Monier Williams 85.
243) Monier Williams 225.
244) Glasenapp, Phil.d.Ind. 385/386.
245) Gonda, Veda u. ält.Hind., Rel.Ind. I, 42.
246) Heesterman s.v. 'Vedism and Brahmanism', Enc.Rel. 12, 221.
247) Gonda, Ind.godsd. 17.
248) Macdonell s.v. 'Vedic Religion', Enc.Rel.Eth. XII, 603.
249) Gonda, Ind.godsd. 11/12.
250) Gonda, Ind.godsd. 15-17.
251) The Rigveda once calls Indra a son of Aditi which obviously is an attempt to harmonize him with the others, Heesterman s.v. 'Vedism and Brahmanism', Enc.Rel. 12, 221.
252) Petech 372 and 376; Heesterman s.v. 'Vedism and Brahmanism', Enc.Rel. 12. 221.
253) Gonda, Veda u. ält.Hind., Rel.Ind. I, 77.
254) This opposition is, of course, not peculiar to Indian existence alone.
255) Gonda, Veda u. ält.Hind, Rel.Ind. I, 76/77.
256) Quotation from a Brahmanic source, Gonda, Veda u. ält.Hind., Rel.Ind. I, 75.
257) Heesterman s.v. 'Vedism and Brahmanism', Enc.Rel. 12, 221.
258) Macdonell s.v. 'Vedic Religion', Enc.Rel.Eth. XII, 610.
259) Gonda, Veda u. ält.Hind., Rel.Ind. I, 37/38; Macdonell s.v. 'Vedic Religion', Enc.Rel.Eth. XII, 610.
260) Heesterman s.v. 'Vedism and Brahmanism', Enc.Rel. 15, 217.
261) Gonda, Veda u. ält.Hind., Rel.Ind. I, 17.
262) Heesterman s.v. 'Vedism and Brahmanism', Enc.Rel. 12, 220.
263) Heesterman s.v. 'Vedism and Brahmanism', Enc.Rel. 12, 220.
264) O'Flaherty s.v. 'Brahma', Enc.Rel. 2, 293.
265) Heesterman s.v. 'Brahman', Enc.Rel. 2, 294.
266) Heesterman s.v. 'Brahmans and Aranyakas', Enc.Rel. 2, 296.
267) Jacobi s.v. 'Brahmanism', Enc.Rel.Eth. III, 799.
268) Glasenapp, Phil.d.Ind. 382/383. Although "his name is invoked in in religious services ..., Pokhar is the only place where he receives worship", Class.Dict. s.v. 'Brahma', 57
269) Gonda, Inl. 40/41.
270) Dr. Lacombe remarks that the authors of the Upanishads reason by means of analogy, in an indirect way, that is, from the microcosmos to the macrocosmos which are connected with each other 'by long chains of ontological correspondences'. "All this consonant diversity", he says, "is only the variegated expression of a unique principle the names of which have been changed to the advantage of the most prestigious of them all, the Brahman", Lacombe, L'Absolu 83. If I stick to the way Thomas of Aquinas used the analogy concept, there is no analogy at all here but rather 'panessentialism', or whatever term with which one would care to dub it, since the terrestrial subjects lose their identity in favour of the godhead.
271) Radhakrishnan 186-190.
272) Radhakrishnan 190.

273) Kuiper 10.
274) Kuiper 19.
275) Kuiper 21.
276) Kuiper 10.
277) Kuiper 9.
278) The Upanishads became known to Europe through a French sailor with a scholarly mind, Anquetil-Duperron (1731-1805); he discovered them in Iran in a Persian translation, Challaye 19.
279) Radhakrishnan 150.
280) Radhakrishnan 203.
281) Glasenapp, Phil.d.Ind. 381/382.
282) Gonda, Veda u. ält.Hind. I, 105.
283) Heesterman s.v. 'Vedism and Brahmanism', Enc.Rel. 12, 227.
284) Heesterman s.v. 'Vedism and Brahmanism', Enc.Rel. 12, 227.
285) Gonda, Veda u. ält.Hind., Rel.Ind. I, 110/111.
286) Heesterman s.v. 'Vedism and Brahmanism', Enc.Rel. 12, 223.
287) Monier Williams 2.
288) Gupta 48.
289) Monier Williams 22.
290) Described in detail by Gupta, Ch. 3, 'Sacrificial Activities and the Brahmanas'.
291) Heesterman s.v. 'Vedism and Brahmanism', Enc.Rel. 12, 227.
292) Basham 140.
293) Keith 113/114; Apte 432/433 and 483/484.
294) Gupta 75.
295) Gupta 76.
296) Gupta 74.
297) Gupta 85 sqq.
298) Gupta 82/83.
299) Gupta 89.
300) Gupta 90-94.
301) Basham 140.
302) Basham 202 and 357/358.
303) Gupta, Ch. 7, 'Temples and Temple Priests'.
304) Gupta 148.
305) Gupta, Ch. 8, 'Some degraded Brahmans'; Rhys-Davids, Econ.cond. 181; Basham 141.
306) Basham 139/140 and 163.
307) Basham 121.
308) Basham 139-142.
309) Gonda, Ind.denkers 259.
310) Monier Williams 224.
311) Mukherjee VII.
312) Mukherjee VII.
313) Horner 4/5.
314) Horner 11; see for this subject also Paul, Ch. II, 'The Mother'.
315) Basham 313.
316) Adv.Hist. 39.
317) Bhattacharji 83.
318) Bhattacharji 160/161.

319) Lal 109.
320) O'Flaherty, Women, Ch. III.4, 'The Shifting of Power in Indian Hierogamies'.
321) See Rapson, Puranas.
322) Hopkins, Period of Sutras 201.
323) Basham 313.
324) Basham 313.
325) Monier Williams 184.
326) Gonda, Tantrismus and Saktismus, Rel.Ind. II, Ch. I.2., cit. p. 40.
327) O'Flaherty, Women 77.
328) O'Flaherty, Women 77.
329) Basham 314.
330) Pusalkar 187.
331) Bhattacharji 198; Basham 311/312; Class.Dict. s.v. 'Linga, Lingam'.
332) Macmunn 157.
333) Macmunn 164 sqq.
334) Temple prostitutes are called 'devadasis'; they enter the temple precincts often as very young girls, many of them unwanted daughters who are sold to the temple by their parents; they are at the service of priests as well as of worshippers, Macmunn 164.
335) The reader will find all the issues fully described and richly documented in O'Flaherty, Ascetism.
336) O'Flaherty, Ascetism 296.
337) Thus called by Bhattacharya, Saivism and the Phallic World, see bibliography.
338) Basham 310.
339) O'Flaherty, Ascetism 173.
340) O'Flaherty, Ascetism 35/36.
341) O'Flaherty, Ascetism 131.
342) O'Flaherty, Ascetism 257.
343) O'Flaherty, Ascetism opp. 81.
344) Macmunn 164.
345) Macmunn 161/162.
346) Monier Williams 192 and 190; see his informative Ch. VII, 'Saktism'. The book of Dr. Pushpendra Kumar, Sakti Cult in Ancient India. Varanasi, 1974, remains piously silent on this kind of thing.
347) O'Flaherty, Women 38.
348) Bhattacharji 173.
349) O'Flaherty, Ascetism, Ch. X.
350) Monier Williams 181.
351) Radhakrishnan 169.
352) Basham 253.
353) Speyer 64. Prof. Speyer was the teacher of the famous Dutch historian Johan Huizinga who began his intellectual career as a Sanskritist.
354) Speyer 64.
355) Speyer 49/50.

356) Dumont, Renunciation 37.
357) Dumont, Renunciation 45/46.
358) O'Flaherty, Women 115.
359) Basham 246.
360) Basham 247.
361) Glasenapp, Phil.d.Ind. 218.
362) Gonda, Ind.denkers 136/137; Frauwallner I 386 sqq. and II 89.
363) Gonda, Ind.denkers 137.
364) Zimmer 281.
365) Zimmer 286; Frauwallner II 65.
366) Glasenapp, Phil.d.Ind. 223/224; Class.Dict. 224.
367) Glasenapp, Phil.d.Ind. 228/229; Basham 328.
368) Glasenapp, Jainismus 23/24; Guérinot 39-41.
369) Glasenapp, Jainismus 19-23.
370) Guérinot 40.
371) Glasenapp, Jainismus 24/25.
372) Basham 291.
373) Glasenapp, Jainismus 214-222, 'Die Beweise gegen das Dasein Gottes'.
374) Buhler 8/9.
375) Glasenapp, Jainismus 192-199.
376) Buhler 11.
377) Glasenapp, Jainismus 208-210.
378) Glasenapp, Jainismus 202-205; Buhler 11/12.
379) Petech 393.
380) Glasenapp, Jainismus 79/80 and 314-316.
381) Petech 393.
382) Glasenapp, Jainismus 442/443.
383) Glasenapp, Jainismus 449.
384) Glasenapp, Jainismus 443/444.
385) E.J.Thomas, Life 20-28.
386) E.J.Thomas, Life 28.
387) E.J.Thomas passim; Bareau, Ind.Buddh. II.1. 'Der Buddha und die frühe Gemeinschaft'. Rel.Ind. III.
388) E.J.Thomas, Life, Appendix, 'The Buddhist Scriptures', 249-277; Bareau, Ind.Buddh. II.2, 'Die Literatur'. Rel.Ind. III; Pusalkar, Pali Canon, 396-410.
389) Basham 264. See for 'An outline of the most ancient form of Buddhism', Vetter XXI-XXXVII.
390) F.W.Thomas, Acoka, The Imperial Patron of Buddhism, see bibliography.
391) Lamotte III.1. 'La Chronique sinhalaise', 319-339, see the table on 324.
392) Basham 268.
393) Bareau, Ind.Buddh. Rel.Ind. III 32.
394) Cit. Glasenapp, Buddh. 36.
395) Cit. Glasenapp, Buddh. 19.
396) Glasenapp, Buddh. 23.
397) Glasenapp, Buddh. 16.
398) Glasenapp, Buddh. 125.

399) Glasenapp, Buddh. 72.
400) Glasenapp, Phil.d.Ind. 302 sqq., Bareau, Ind.Buddh., Rel.Ind. III, 32 sqq.
401) E.W.Thomas, Hist.Buddh.Thought 176/177 remarks that 'yana' is not correctly translated with 'vehicle'. Humphreys' Pop.Dict.Buddh. proved more than once very useful to me, also on this point.
402) Basham 274.
403) Basham 272-274; Glasenapp, Phil.d.Ind. 326 sqq.; Bareau, Ind. Buddh., Rel.Ind. III, 69 sqq.
404) E.W.Thomas, Hist.Buddh.Thought 177 sqq.; Bareau, Ind.Buddh., Rel. Ind. III, 120 sqq.
405) Basham 275/276.

CHAPTER III

SINENSIA

1. The cradle of Chinese civilization

Where in this immensely vast domain shall we begin, in this China that, at present, stretches over 3.600.000 square miles, from the arid Gobi desert in the north to the jungles of Burma in the south, and from the cool waters of the Yellow Sea in the east to the snow-clad peaks of the Pamir in the west? Where shall we start in this country where to-day more than a billion people live, by no means all of them vintage, or 'Han', Chinese, but belonging to a great many other nations and tribes with a rich diversity of languages, religions, and cultures? Westerners often believe that China is the oldest political entity of world history and that its annals go back thousands and thousands of years, to a period in which neither the civilizations of Egypt and Sumer nor that of India had dawned. This is a profound misunderstanding which needs to refuted. But that refutation will mean that we cannot start from a Celestial Empire that already existed when no other people in the world had any form of political organization. This seems to make our problem still more acute but in fact the answer to our initial question is rather easy to give. Before 1000 B.C. the area of Chinese civilization proper remained restricted to the regions north of the Yangzi (Yangtze) river at some distance from the Pacific coast while at the same time reaching westward till it comprised the fertile territories around Lanzhou (Lan-Chou) in the province of Gansu (Kansu) [1]. This is only a relatively small part of modern China [2].

2. Times of legend

True enough, China has an incredibly long prehistory. Father Teilhard de Chardin, who was a palaeontologist before he acquired fame as an author, discovered the remains of the so-called 'sinanthropus pekinensis', the 'Peking man' who is said to have lived in caves near Beijing (Peking) five hundred thousand years ago. China underwent the usual stages of development, from the Old Stone Age through the Neolithicum to the Bronze Age that, in that country, began about 1500 B.C. Apart from archaeological finds, there is no historical evidence whatsoever for this extremely long period; all we have is pure legend. No historical chronicles concerning highest Antiquity have been preserved [3].

Like many other culturally important peoples who possess only vague time indications with regard to their earliest history, or like biblical scholars of earlier days who even pretended to know on which day of which year the world had been created, the Chinese too wished to have an exact date for the beginning of their history, and their scholars presented them with it : 2582 B.C. From this year onward China is said to have been ruled by the Three Sovereigns followed by the Five Rulers, all of them mythical kings. Legend makes them into great benefactors of mankind and 'cultural heroes' who delighted their peoples with the invention of fire, house-building, farming, the silk culture, medicine, the calendar, and Chinese script; in short, all the main elements of Chinese culture were attributed to them [4]. Later Chinese historians describe this period as a paradise, a Golden Age; in their trail some modern Marxist authors see in it the period of Marx' 'primal communism' [5].

After these wholly legendary rulers came the Xia (Hsia) dynasty traditionally dated from ca. 2200 to 1700 B.C. (or 2033 - 1562). They are supposed to have been the rulers of a Xia realm for which, however, not the slightest archaeological evidence has been found - this in spite of the fact that about 500 B.C. Confucius described these kings as model rulers [6].

3. The Shang dynasty

The ground under our feet becomes somewhat firmer with the advent of the Shang dynasty. The dates of the Shang period are only approximate, from between 1766 and 1523 to years varying from 1122 to 1028 B.C. [7]. Artefacts found over a wide area from Beijing southward into the province of Henan (Honan) and along the Wei river prove that the existence of a Shang civilization is an historical fact. The most important of these finds were made between 1928 and 1937 in a region that is known as 'the cradle of Chinese civilization', at Anyang in the great bend of the Yellow River. Innumerable bones inscribed with characters - the oldest form of Chinese script - have been found there [8]. Very probably the region over which the Shang kings ruled, on both sides of the lower course of the Yellow River, was much smaller than the area of its cultural influence.

Respect for human life was not the most conspicuous feature of Shang civilization. In the tombs of the kings and other important people a great number of human skeletons were found. In groups of ten, the victims were beheaded with an axe and buried along with the king becoming in this way his retinue in death. This custom seduced Marxist historians to speak of the 'slave society'. Very probably, however, the beheaded were prisoners of war and members of wandering shepherd tribes [9]. These tribes, surrounding the Shang region on its northern, western, and southern boundaries, were seen as 'barbarians'. It has been a constant feature of Chinese national ideology to make a very sharp difference between the sons of the Celestial Empire and all others who were dubbed barbarians. Perhaps great civilizations, in particular when they have a high opinion of themselves, show a deep-lying craving for being surrounded by 'barbarians' - in order to shine the brighter in the encircling darkness. We have already seen that this was the case with the Greeks (Vol. II, Ch. II) and with the Egyptians (Vol. IV, Ch. I); to some extent the people of Israel manifested the same tendency with regard to its religion (Vol. IV, Ch. II). The civilized Chinese certainly never thought poorly of their culture.

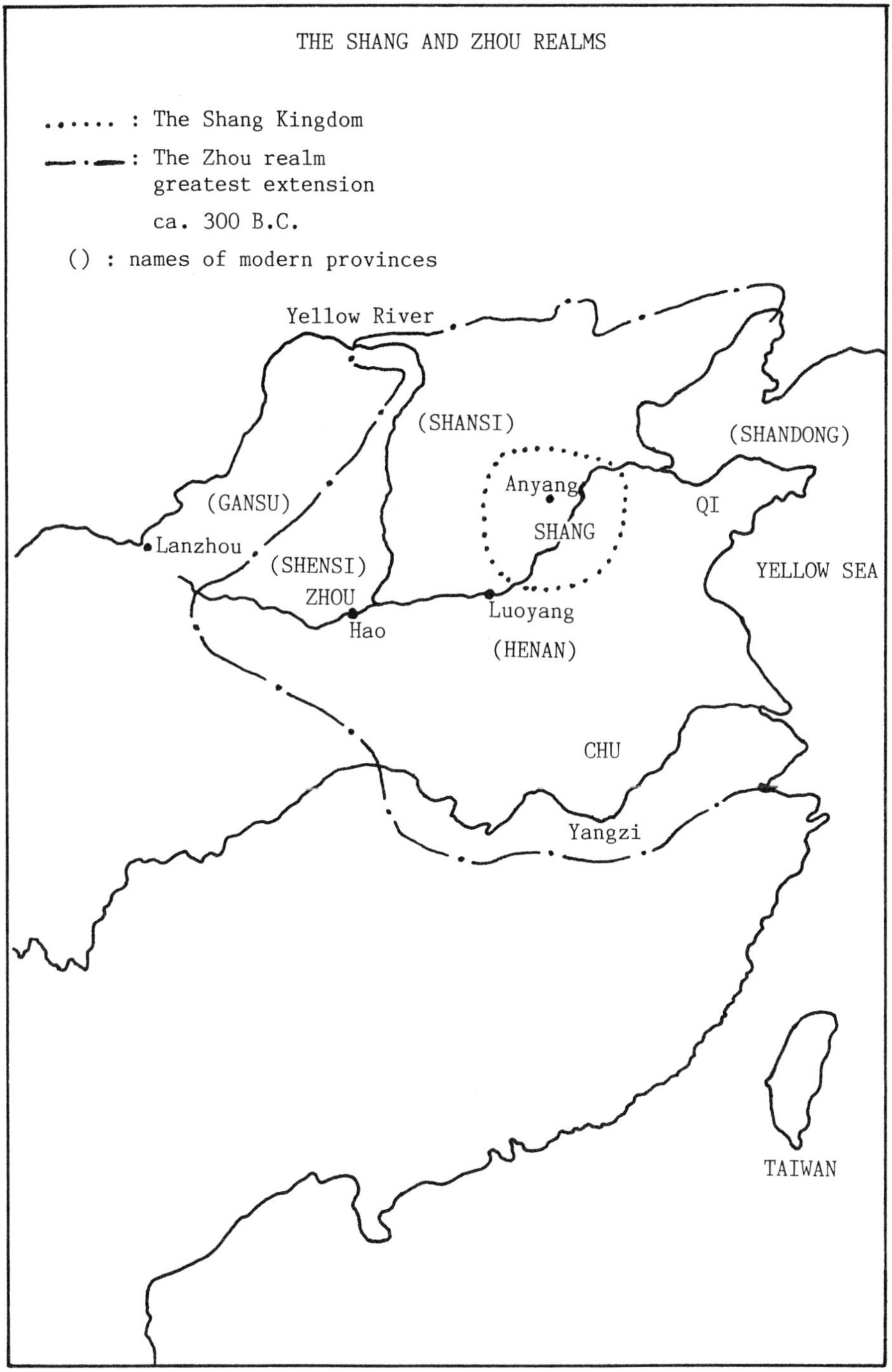
THE SHANG AND ZHOU REALMS
: The Shang Kingdom
: The Zhou realm greatest extension ca. 300 B.C.
() : names of modern provinces
Yellow River
(SHANSI)
(SHANDONG)
Anyang
SHANG
QI
(GANSU)
Lanzhou
(SHENSI)
ZHOU
Hao
Luoyang
(HENAN)
YELLOW SEA
CHU
Yangzi
TAIWAN

Even historians who do not subscribe to the Marxist theory of an early slave society in this period freely admit that "there were sharp social and economic cleavages within Shang society" [10]. The monarchy had an authoritarian character; kingship was hereditary, but younger brothers were preferred to sons. Excavations show that the rulers lived in large palaces while the common people had to be content with 'crude pit dwellings'. They formed a dense mass of peasants governed arbitrarily by the king and the nobles.

There has been much speculation on the question how the manifest 'tendency of the Chinese throughout their history to establish and accept a unified absolutist state' originated. It has been supposed, for instance, that the ruling classes had a monopoly of the bronze production which provided them with weapons and chariots the others could not come by. Another factor may have been that the Chinese family fosters a deep respect for the authoritarian father - feelings that were easily transferred to the father-figure of the monarch. Yet another theory says that the Chinese always felt threatened by their nomadic and barbarian neighbours and, therefore, showed a marked tendency to make their state as strong as possible and to fence themselves in. In this context, of course, the Great Wall must be mentioned.

Then there is the possibility that the need to control the unruly waters of the mighty Yellow River forced them to cooperate under strong leadership - a theory that we also find stated with regard to natural conditions in Egypt. However, Reischauer remarks that this theory does not apply to the Shang period, since then there were not yet 'great efforts at water control' [11]. Without denying the general validity of the water-control theory in connection with the rise of the unified state, I might point out that in my country, the Netherlands, common defence against the waters of the sea, the rivers, and the great lakes has always been and still is a dominant feature of national life. Nevertheless, it has never led to authoritarian political tendencies; the unification of the Netherlands - historically a late event - was brought about by totally different factors. One could equally well maintain that the need to cooperate and to join hands in the common task fostered the development of democracy, since everyone had a personal stake in the joint effort.

4. Zhou rule

The end of Shang rule must be dated somewhen about 1050 B.C. and was caused by the people of the Zhou (Chou). These Zhou lived to the west of the Shang area in Shaanxi (Shensi), in the horseshoe formed by the bend of the Yellow River. Although ancient sources often decry the Zhou as barbarians, they were, to all intents and purposes, just as Chinese as the Shang, less civilized perhaps but undergoing Shang cultural influence. But it is true that when they attacked the Shang, they did so in alliance with many barbarian tribes. The Zhou had moved eastward under the pressure of Turco-Mongolian or of Indo-European nomadic peoples; perhaps the Yuehzhi (Yüeh-chi) we met already, were instrumental in this. Anyhow, at some point in the eleventh century B.C. the Zhou, under the leadership of Wu-wang (= 'the warrior king'), threw themselves on the Shang kingdom and conquered this in successive stages.

In the truest Confucian manner this conquest, however brutal it had been, was placed in a moral context. The last Shang king was said to have been a cruel person luxuriating in his own power and committing the most horrible crimes. As a consequence he gambled away his 'Mandate of Heaven', his 'Tianming', which naturally devolved on the pious King Wu, the 'Son of Heaven'. The bad Shang got what he deserved : bedecked with his jewels he threw himself into the flames of his palace. For the godfearing King Wu this was not yet punishment enough; the corpse was beheaded and the severed head hung on the white ensign of the conqueror [12]. This event is often seen as the beginning of Chinese history.

The Zhou rule spanned a period longer than that of any other Chinese dynast, from the invasion in the eleventh century to 249 B.C. From now on every Chinese supreme ruler, till the last one in 1912, was a 'Tian-zu', a 'Son of Heaven', and the bearer of a celestial mandate. Of course, this put the ruler far above all others, even of the highest dignitaries. This does not mean that Wu and his successors ruled over a centralized empire. By no means! Wu's realm consisted of perhaps hundreds of principalities which paid allegiance to the sovereign. Its political situation reminds one of the Holy Roman Empire; there too the power of the emperor was only nominal at most times. What gave coherence to the Zhou state was the permanent struggle against the surrounding barbarians. There were the Xianyuan in the upper reaches of the Yellow River, the Quanrong and the Di to the west of the great bend, and the Huai-Yi on the Yangzi river to the south [13].

In the Zhou period the distance between the upper and nether layers of society did not grow smaller. Just as the Normans after 1066 were endowed with land in England, the Zhou chiefs after the conquest were presented with landed property. These new lords divided all the territories among themselves. The great lords - who can be compared with dukes and earls in medieval Europe - had many vassals, some of whom possessed rather large fiefs while others had to remain content with a domain 'smaller than a large ranch in Texas' [14].

The nobles ruled, and the peasants were ruled. Agriculture being the main, almost the only, means of subsistence, the lower classes nearly exclusively consisted of peasants. These were not the owners of the plots of land they tilled. Part of the harvest had to be handed over to the noble proprietor. There were corvées too, like the building of bridges and the repair of the roads. Thus the whole life of the peasant and his family was dependent on the lord and his goodwill. At the lowest rung of the social ladder we find the slaves. Prisoners of war, condemned criminals, peasants unable to pay their debts were sold into slavery; even a nobleman captured in war (and not ransomed) was turned into a slave. Just as in other slave-holding societies enslaved persons were the property of their masters and could be sold and bought; they were treated wilfully, sometimes leniently, often badly. Their fate was far from enviable [15].

In the first period of the Zhou era, the time of King Wu and his immediate successors, the power of the king, who lived in the capital Hao on the Wei, seems to have been fairly great. But as time wore on, their grip on their vassals became weaker and weaker. King Yu (781-771 B.C.) is sometimes compared with the last Shang ruler, being more concerned with the whims of his favourite concubine than with the interests of the state. He too got the fate he deserved, for he was murdered by one of his courtiers; the capital Hao was taken by rebellious vassals with the help of barbarians. The crown prince who had been deposed in favour of the concubine's son was abducted to Luoyang (Loyang), where he was set up as king. This new capital lies in Henan, hundreds of miles east of Hao; it was chosen because it was more out of the reach of the barbarians. From then (771 B.C.) the Zhou realm is called the 'Eastern Zhou', whereas the older state is named the 'Western Zhou'. The reader should be aware of the fact that these names do not refer to two states of the same period that were geographically apart, but to two different states that existed the one before 771 B.C. and the other after that date [16].

5. The Eastern Zhou

a. The position of the ruler

Before the year of the unification of China it is preferable to refer to the supreme ruler as 'wang', or 'king'; after that date, 221 B.C., he is called 'huangdi' = emperor. The king then of the Eastern Zhou did not possess much real power. He had to be content with direct rule over his capital Luoyang and its immediate environs, but for the rest he was dependent on his feudal lords. Politically minded Europeans and Americans are perhaps apt to write him off for this reason, but that would be a grave mistake. For although the king was politically powerless, he was all the same a sacred person. Wasn't he the Son of Heaven? Since there is only one heaven, there is also only one Son of Heaven on earth. This means that the Chinese supreme ruler had an importance, a significance, a function that was not, and could not be, shared by any one else in the world, not even by fellow-rulers elsewhere, like the emperors of Persia and of Rome. The ruler could not be done away with since his main task was to bring all the necessary sacrifices. This sacrificial function was an indisputable one since the well-being of the world, with all mankind, was dependent on it. There being, according to Chinese thought, a strong congruity between heaven and earth, the royal offerings served to maintain the equilibrium between the upper and nether parts of the universe. Should the sovereign fail in the fulfilment of his task, there would be no end of catastrophes [17].

The fact that the sovereign was considered the Son of Heaven had yet another consequence. As I stated above, there could be no other emperors. Perhaps in the Zhou era this political concept was not yet so sharply delineated as it became in the Qin period but the main outlines were already visible. We must draw the line still further : there simply could be no other political entities. Just as Heaven stretches itself over the whole earth, the Son of Heaven was entitled to reign over the whole world. In so far as there were political entities of some kind, they could never exist in their own right but had to be subject to the emperor of China. The universal ruler expected that all other princes would pay him homage [18]. We have met this basic political ideology before, for instance in the history of the Mesopotamian empires (Vol. IV, Ch. III); there I have dubbed this as absolute dualism since between the supreme ruler with his otherworldly mandate and the rest of the world there is simply nothing at all : all other political entities are all and sundry considered non-existent. Here, with the Chinese sovereign, this dualism is, if possible, still more radical and undiluted.

b. Chinese imperialism

This explains why China is such an enormously big country. Her rulers have always felt free to annex, to absorb, to incorporate other nations, tribes and states. We are, therefore, entirely justified to speak of Chinese imperialism. Dualism, however, is always connected with fear, and political dualism with political fear. The supercilious attitude of the Chinese of the Zhou era hid their fear of the surrounding barbarians. The tribes on the north and west were very probably pastoral ones, with those in the north considered the most dangerous. Those on the east coast were mainly fishermen. The tribes in the Yangzi area, although perhaps semi-civilized, in Chinese eyes were ostensibly different and did not speak Chinese but an unintelligible gibberish - which always is a clear proof of barbarism [19].

The mighty vassals of the sovereign extended Zhou power in many directions. The feudal state of Qi (Ch'i) reached the coast and occupied the Shandong (Shantung) peninsula. This move gave its rulers the virtual monopoly of the salt production which, together with the river traffic in iron and bronze, made them very rich [20]. Other feudal lords made themselves famous as protectors of the Chinese against the barbarians by pushing southward and extending their sway beyond the Yangzi and into the regions south of this river along the Yellow Sea [21].

This expansion was outward bound. But there was also an inward movement. For in between the Zhou cities and purely Chinese territories many tribes still lived, sedentary and agriculturally occupied, that were not Chinese. They underwent the irresistible pressure of Zhou civilization; in the course of time they became thoroughly sinicized. This process of Sinization also stretched beyond the pale of the political power of Zhou. The pastoral tribes of the north and west became settled, and, in this way, 'part of Chinese agricultural civilization' [22]. Thus during the Zhou period a more or less homogeneous Chinese culture gradually arose in an area stretching from the Yellow Sea westward on both sides of the Yellow River to the provinces of Shanxi (Shansi) and Shaanxi (Shensi), and reaching southward to some distance beyond the Yangzi. This area constituted only a small part of what now is the People's Republic comprising as it does only seven of the present twenty-two provinces (and the smallest at that); it covered most of the North China plain. I mention in passing - for I shall have to come back to it - that this was the time of classic China and of famous philosophers like Confucius.

c. The ruler and his vassals

Although inside the Zhou realm the age-old opposition between the civilized Chinese and the uncouth barbarians was steadily disappearing, other oppositions were strengthened in this period. I have already drawn the reader's attention to the unique position of the sovereign. As a sacred being he stood apart from everybody else. The nobility too, though not sacred in itself, was considered essentially different from the commoners. What the nobles possessed, in contrast to the others, was 'te'. An exact translation of this word is not possible; it is something like the Latin 'virtus' or the Greek 'aretê'. It is a mythical or magical force or potency, perfection perhaps or excellence. At any rate, only the nobles have it; it is 'te' that makes them noble and entitles them to superiority. A young nobleman was put into full possession of te during a long and laborious initiation service after which he had the right to wear the man's cap, which meant that he now possessed the right and duties of an adult noble.

Only the nobles held land in fee and were the holders of offices; almost all economic and administrative power was in their hands.
Later there were too many nobles for the existing feudal positions; many of them served in the army. They rode on chariots while the peasant soldiers fought on foot. Another difference was that the agricultural population lived on the land while the nobles had their fortified settlements or lived in the cities. There was not the slightest trace of popular influence or any form of democracy; the power of the lords over their domains was unlimited. Sharp as the opposition was in the first centuries of Zhou dominance, the gap between nobility and peasantry gradually grew somewhat smaller. Impoverished noblemen had no better life than a peasant; many a farmer got somehow in the possession of his parcel of land and was, therefore, no longer wholly dependent on a feudal proprietor [23].

As I have already written, the political power of the Zhou ruler over his vassals was only nominal. All the feudal lords tried to make themselves virtually independent. Around 700 B.C. there must have been some two hundred of such feudal states. But their lords fought endlessly against one another; the stronger states absorbed the weaker ones, with the powerless sovereign only looking on [24]. In the seventh century B.C. a fierce opposition developed between the northern and southern principalities of the Zhou domain. The northern states, like the already mentioned Qi, were thought to be more authentically Chinese than the southern ones, like the aggressive and not wholly sinicized state of Chu (Ch'u). Bloody battles were fought to keep Chu in check [25]. The pretensions of the Chu rulers were openly demonstrated by their styling themselves 'wang' = king, in defiance of the Zhou ruler in Luoyang.

Actually, Chu's struggle for power may be seen as a reaction of the south, that is of the area beyond the Yangzi, against the north, the true Chinese. It is not so that the southern states rejected the notion of 'Chinese'. On the contrary! The southerners, more or less sinicized already and proud of their culture, did not see themselves as inferior to the Zhou Chinese; moreover, they had their full share of the growing wealth which gave them economic power. For these reasons they refused to play second fiddle to the north. Bloody as the clashes were, they must be seen as steps on the road to China's unification [26]. There was, for this period, an exceptionally long spell of quiet - forty years - after the peace treaty that was concluded in 546 B.C. between north and south.

The next period, 481 - 526 B.C., is called that of 'the Warring States'. It was a time in which the still existing feudal states fought each other relentlessly till finally only one remained. Luckily it is not incumbent on me to describe this period in detail; the situation was a confused one which would only bewilder the innocent reader. The general pattern resembled that of Greece, with her internecine warfare, in the fifth and fourth centuries B.C. (Vol. II, Ch. II). The main lines were as follows. Armies became larger and fighting became more fierce once iron weapons came into use. Cavalry with large masses of mounted archers became a normal feature of warfare [27].

The warring chiefs, without any regard for their Zhou suzerain, acted as virtualy independent rulers. Most of them came to calling themselves 'wang' but none of them dared to usurp the title 'Son of Heaven' or act as the sacrificial high priest of the kingdom [28]. The ritual position of the Zhou 'Son of Heaven' was the only symbol or token of unity that remained intact. There were always coalitions of warring states; one alliance fought against the other, and the enemy of to-day could easily be the ally of to-morrow. As in ancient Greece, sometimes a 'hegemon', a 'ba', was appointed to give military leadership to an alliance. From time to time a state perished in the turmoil and was annexed by others so that the number of warring states grew steadily smaller [29].

The confused political situation of the Zhou kingdom invited foreign enemies to take their share of the booty. The problem of the barbarians in the interior was successfully solved in the course of time but now another kind of barbarian appeared. These were nomads living in the steppes to the west, mounted herdsmen who drove their herds from pasturage to pasturage. They were not economically self-sufficing since what they raised from their herds did not provide them with certain kinds of food which they needed or with silk for their clothing. To acquire these commodities they tried to force their way into the western parts of the Zhou area where they were available in abundant quantities. This led to constant frontier warfare since the western war-lords tried to keep the predatory nomads out; lines of defence were built that were the forerunners of the Chinese wall [30].

6. Qin, the first unified Chinese empire

a. Qin and China

The period of fratricidal Chinese wars was brought to an end by the final victory of the state of Qin. 'Qin' is the official, or 'pinyin', rendering of 'Ch'in' which is the root of our word 'China'. It is, indeed, 'our' word because the Chinese do not call their country thus; their favourite (and older) name is 'Tianxia' (T'ien-hsia) which is translated by the well-known term 'the Celestial Empire' but more literally meaning 'All under the Heaven'. Another indication of the Chinese territory is 'Zhongguo' (Ghung-kao), the 'Realm of the Middle' which remained in use after the disappearance of the empire in 1912. In imperial times this name, or rather title, signified that China is situated in the centre of the world under the dome of heaven; from this central position Chinese civilization, Chinese virtue, was thought to radiate in all directions and convert the 'barbarians' [31].

To return to the state of Qin, we find it when we go westward from the Zhou capital of Luoyang and ascend the course of the river Wei that forms the bottom line of the horseshoe bend of the Yellow River. Tracking up the Wei we arrive at the town of Xianyang (Hsienyang), the capital city of the Qin state. It is located west of the heartland of Zhou and, in the past, was a peripheral state of the Zhou realm. Li compares the relationship between Qin and the states to the east of her to that between Macedonia and the Greek city-states. The eastern states viewed Qin as a semi-barbarian country just as the Hellenes saw their neighbour to the north [32]. Qin was a prosperous agricultural country and strongly inclined to expand. Tradition has it that she annexed two semi-barbarian states, Shu and Ba (Pa), in Sichuan (Szech'uan, Szechwan) with which move Chinese political influence reached the upper course of the Yangzi [33].

b. The foundation of the Chinese empire

In the middle of the third century B.C. Qin felt strong enough to turn eastward. This became a momentous move, for Zhou was annihilated and the last wang was dethroned. The year 249 B.C. saw the end of the time-honoured Zhou dynasty [34]. A few years later, in 246 B.C., a man ascended the throne of Qin who was destined to become the first real emperor of a unified empire. Helped by able administrators and generals he made his state very powerful; in the years between 230 and 221 the still surviving feudal states were conquered one after the other. From then on the new universal ruler styled himself, not wang ('a much deflated title), but 'Qin Shi Huang-Di' which means so much as 'the First Emperor of China' (literally Huang-Di means 'august ruler') [35].

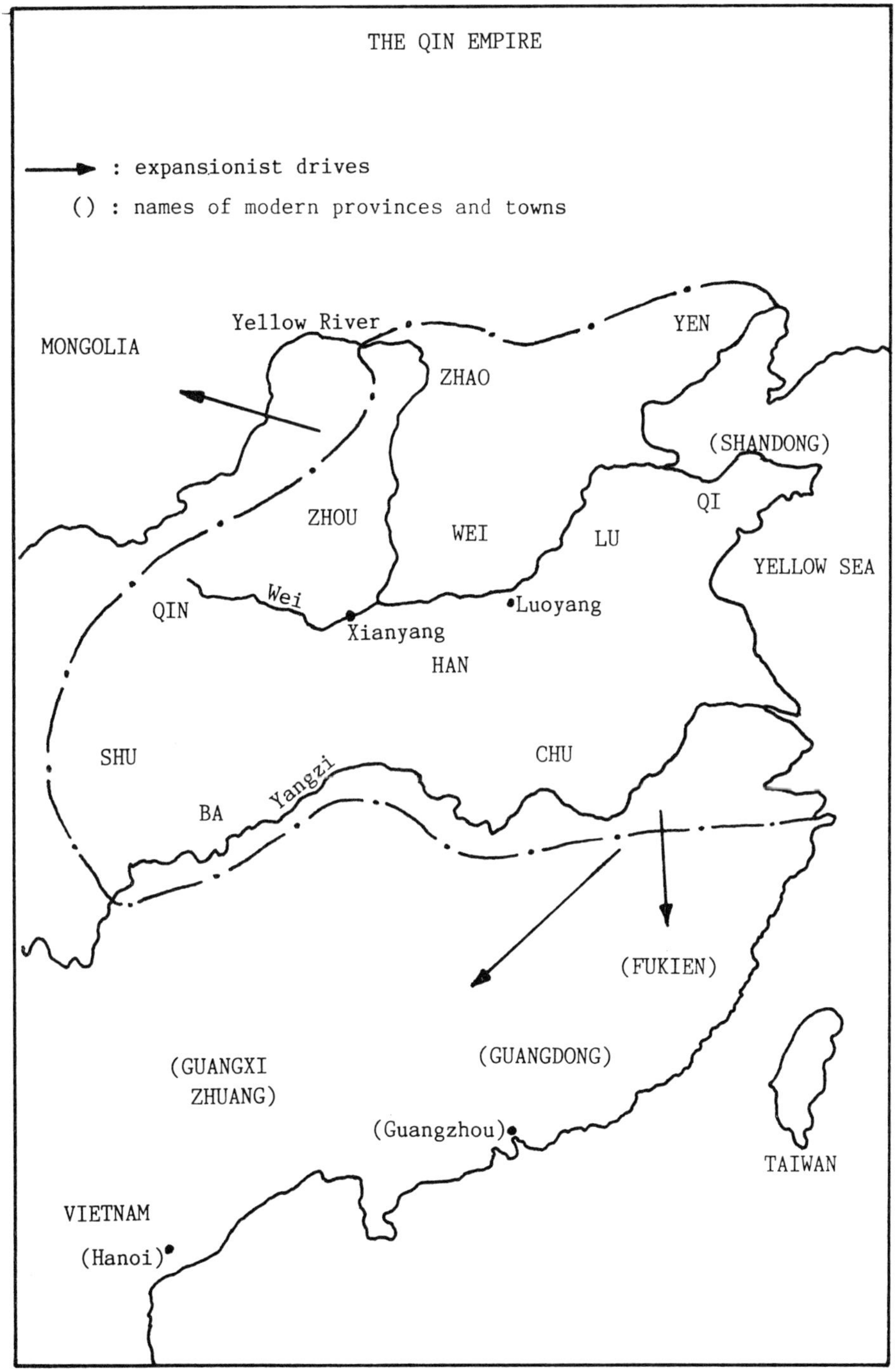

THE QIN EMPIRE

True enough, in the pre-Xia period one of the legendary Five Rulers, the so-called 'Yellow Emperor', was also referred to as 'huangdi'. But here 'huang', written with another character, means 'yellow'. Apart from its political meaning the word 'di' had strong religious connotations. During the Shang dynasty, 'di' had been the name of a godhead who, probably, was seen as the divine ancestor of these kings [36]. So with the First Emperor no common mortal came to the throne. 'Huang-di' was to remain the official title of the Chinese emperors for more than twenty-one centuries. The year 221 B.C. saw China's unification. The year 220 A.D. was the year in which she disintegrated again for a few centuries. The unifying process was completed in 219 B.C., when the First Emperor travelled to 'Taishan' (T'ai Shan), a holy mountain in Shandong on which he, in a religious ceremony, received the Celestial Mandate and thus became the Son of Heaven - which implied that he must 'rule all that is on earth' [37].

c. The promotion of national unity

The first Qin emperor made it perfectly clear that he would have none of the old feudal system that had so successfully put out of joint the fabric of the Zhou kingdom. The feudal entities were all of them abolished with one stroke. The whole country now became divided into thirty-six units of command each of them subdivided into counties. The administrative staff that governed these new divisions was without exception civilian; the offices were not hereditary. It constituted a tricky problem what to do with the deposed aristocrats. Their number traditionally is given as a 'hundred and twenty thousand families' which certainly is much too high; nevertheless, there must have been a great many of them. They were deported far from their former seats of power to the capital Luoyang where they were provided with palaces and stipends that would enable to vegetate till the end of their lives. Furthermore, all (non-military) weapons had to be handed over to the central government; the fortifications of the walled cities were demolished [38]. The new emperor assuredly made a clean slate!

Cultural and national unity was much promoted by the official measures with regard to Chinese script. The regional variations in the characters were abolished; the system was at once simplified and rationalized, and made obligatory for the whole empire [39]. A common law code was introduced [40]. Next a large network of imperial highways was organized; the total length of the new roads is estimated at about 6.800 kilometers. They radiated from the capital in all directions. The pride of the road-builders was the 'zhidao' (chi-tao), the Straight Road, which ran north-south over a distance over eight hundred kilometers. Parts of it still survive [41]. This makes us think of the highways of Persia and imperial Rome; reliable roads obviously belong to the infrastructure of universal empires.

d. Qin authoritarianism

The mentality of the new government was thoroughly authoritarian, even totalitarian. The rulers did not feel inclined to suffer deviating opinions. The Qin empire believed in a juridical and political ideology which is called 'Legalism' and which the rulers served very well in their purposes. Its authentic name is 'fajia' (fa-chia), the 'School of the Law'. It was based on a number of legal treatises. In legalist thought only one political entity is important, the all-powerful and omnipresent state. Here we hit on a dualistic element of great importance : the state did not recognize citizens but had only subjects. This implied that nobody had rights but only duties; traditions and rites were not allowed to hamper the role of the state. The value of the subjects was measured by the rod of production : peasants and soldiers were the productive class but scholars and merchants were of no use to the general human well-being. The state had a very low opinion of human frailty [42].

Confucian scholars of the later Han period give us a highly unfavourable picture of the Qin state. To-day several historians basing themselves on an accurate study of the often contradictory and enigmatic Qin sources and on archaeological finds believe that Qin rule in reality was not so harsh as others suppose it to be. This still is a controversial subject. What Confucian texts tell us is the following; I relate this with all due reserve. The state (personified by the emperor) was everything, the subject was nothing - a truly dualistic relationship, that is. The government disposed of its subjects at will. And not only of their persons, of their ideas too! In 213 B.C. there was a banquet in the imperial palace during which the emperor was lavishly praised by tail-wagging scholars. But one man had the courage to protest openly against the ruthless centralization. The omnipotent prime minister, Li Si (Li Ssu), flew into a rage and forthwith ordered the burning of all documents expressing deviating opinions. Many doubtless invaluable books were consigned to the flames [43].

The end of the feudal period had not spelled the abolishment of corvee duties. On the contrary! People were still called up to build roads and to repair bridges. A brandnew feature was that conscripted workers often were sent far away from home, sometimes thousands of miles; many of them died on the roads or during their work. It is said that half a million men were transported south to cultivate the newly won territories; others were employed in the north and northeast to construct large fortifications against the nomads. This was the period in which the Great Wall, with its imposing lenght of 2.100 kilometers, was built [44]. When the emperor visited the Shandong peninsula and saw how sparsely populated it was, he decreed that thirty thousand families should leave their homesteads and be settled there [45].

It is to be expected that such a vigorous ruler as the First Emperor wished to extend the frontiers of his realm. This indeed he did but in his view the Celestial Empire had no frontiers. The Mandate of Heaven entitled him to rule the whole world. His attitude with respect to foreign peoples was just as dualistic as that respecting his own subjects. There were ten years of relentless campaigning. In the north the Qin armies penetrated into Inner Mongolia. To the south the successes were even more spectacular. A considerable part of Fujian (Fukien) was conquered, and, still further south, most of the provinces of Guangdong (Kwangtung, with the region of Guangzhou = Canton) and Guangxi Zhuang (Kwangsi). The imperial armies even entered Vietnam and reached the environs of Hanoi [46].

At the end of his reign the emperor seems to have become paranoiac. He connected his palaces with each other by means of subterranean corridors so that he could fly from the one to the other. He kept all his movements carefully secret. When he visited one of his palaces nobody might reveal his presence there; the punishment was death [47]. Dualistic attitudes exact their price. There is always a grain of insanity in them.

7. The foundation of Han rule

It was, indeed, the pitiless imposition of corvees, with the accompanying punishments, that triggered off the great rebellion. In the year 209 B.C. we see two poor peasants struggling along in disastrous weather over flooded roads; they are on their way to the spot where corvee duties await them. They arrive too late and know that, because of this contravention, they will be executed. Their only line of escape is rebellion. They organize a revolt, and soon the whole labour force is up in arms. Large masses of disgruntled labourers arrive to swell their ranks [48]. The rebellion spread far and wide; the two initial leaders soon disappeared into the background. In 206 B.C. rebel armies stormed the capital and captured it. No member of the imperial family survived this event; the last Qin emperor was executed. All the palaces, built at such great cost of human labour and tax money, were burned to the ground. This was the inglorious end of the Qin empire [49]. Now the two main rebel leaders fought each other for four more years, till one of them, Xiang Yu, was killed; the other, Liu Bang (Liu Pang), ascended the throne on February 28, 202 B.C. [50].

The new emperor - he was the fourth one - dated back the beginning of his reign to 206 B.C., the date of the death of the last Qin ruler, and by this device was supposed to have been sovereign for eleven years. His real span of government was only seven years (202-195 B.C.). Nevertheless, this short reign was momentous enough, for it ushered in a new period of Chinese history. Liu Bang is posthumously called 'Gaozu' (Kaotsu), the 'High Progenitor', since he inaugurated a new imperial dynasty, the Han, that ruled China for four centuries, from 206 B.C. to 220 A.D. The name 'Han' is that of the river in the vicinity of which the emperor was born. The Chinese are often called 'Han Chinese', vintage Chinese as it were, to distinguish them from other 'Chinese' nations, like the Mongols, the Tibetans, or the Miao-Yao (minority tribes in South-China). The Han empire is roughly contemporaneous with the Roman Empire in the west and the Parthian Empire in Iran (Ch. I); it parallelled the Roman Empire in power and prestige and surpassed it in the size of its population. Its structure became the authoritative model for all later regimes of China.

8. Some thoughts on the unification of China and on history writing

Before we proceed we must meditate somewhat on the historical problem that is presented by unification, or, to put it in Toynbean terms, by the creation of the 'universal state'. On a more theoretical level such a meditation would parallel the factual description of the unifying processes we met in Volume IV and the present one.

When the First Emperor, only forty-nine years old, died in 210 B.C., he was buried in a big mausoleum on the Shandong peninsula. Over his dead head, on the inner side of the cupola, the starry sky was pictured [51]. Even when dead, the Supreme Ruler, consorting now with the celestial beings, was no less grandiose than when alive. But grandiose or not, Shi Huang-Di had a bad press from later Confucian authors who had the habit of looking at history with a moral eye. They found him cruel and tyrannical. In an essay significantly called 'The faults of Qin', the author, Jia Yi (Chia Yi, 201-169), gives as his opinion that the Qin dynasty was so shortlived "because it failed to display humanity and righteousness or to realize that there is a difference between the power to attack and the power to consolidate" [52].

It is perhaps to be expected that modern Chinese authors should look at the other side of the coin; after all, they are more or less the defenders of a once again unified and strong state whose policy does not err on the side of mildness. But I feel disconcerted with the glibness with which European and American authors condone the evil side of Qin politics. Although Bodde readily admits that the Qin regime operated 'cruelly and exploitatively' [53], he also says in the First Emperor's defence that he "was obviously intensely conscious of his extraordinary role as the creator of an unprecedented universal empire" [54]. Morton too states that Shi Huang-Di was 'a ruthless tyrant', but "he laid down the main lines upon which the empire subsequently developed. In particular he produced a unified and centralized realm which remained the Chinese ideal for empire" [55]. Eberhard dismisses Confucian criticism which he explains by the fact that the First Emperor was an opponent of Confucius' doctrine [56]. This means that, in his view, these critics were motivated by their own interest and were, therefore, not capable of an independent moral judgment.

We may well ask whether this 'ideal', that of the unified and centralized Chinese state, really was worth all these immense sacrifices. After all, for hundreds of thousands of people the whole fabric of their lives was destroyed. Countless numbers of them were deported, robbed of their own private existence, and put to uncongenial tasks, never to see their homesteads again. Scholars like those I mentioned (in spite of themselves, I am sure) give the impression that this selling-out of human life is justified if only the aim (the centralized state) is reached. They do this because they believe, probably unconsciously, that History (with a capital) has an inherent tendency to create such states, that this even is the essence of history.

Maybe there also is a more practical reason for this. History is a manifold thing, utterly unsurveyable at first sight and wholly incomprehensible to the untrained eye. Historians try to create order in the immense mass of persons and events by following the political line, in particular that of the development of states. The bigger the empire the easier history becomes to handle. What a godsend the Roman

Empire was! For centuries it dominated the historical scene, and had longlived successors in the Holy Roman and Byzantine Empires. They supply grateful historians with a frame by means of which they are able to lend coherence to long stretches of history.

The readiness with which not only politicians but also historians, history teachers, and the general public accept the existence of states - particularly of large, unified, and centralized states - as self-evident comes very near to the notion of historical necessity. States are, unconsciously, believed to be the most natural entities of history. But actually they are not. For enormously long periods of human history people did not live in states simply because these did not exist. Even up to the threshold of contemporary history there were tribes that did not have the slightest idea that they were the subjects of a colonial or post-colonial state. When around 1930 or later white officials and missionaries reached Papua tribes deep in the jungle of Irian (New Guinea), these people were totally unaware of the fact that they were the subjects of Queen Wilhelmina of the Netherlands. By the same token, one may imagine a situation in world affairs in which the political entities called states no longer exist. A politico-economic construction, such as the European Community, will after 1992 be very powerful in many respects but it will not be a state.

Thus the state is not self-evident, and neither was the Chinese state. We must not lose sight of the fact that Chinese emperors often were usurpers annexing and subduing many regions, nations, and tribes that, originally, were not Chinese at all, and subjecting them to a thorough and often successful process of Sinification. This means that the Chinese Empire, like so many realms of this kind, was an artificial structure not growing out of the wishes of those who were to be made Chinese or even of those who already were Chinese. If such had been the case, the rulers would not have been forced to be so cruel and pitiless.

To return to professional historians, they are much too ready to overlook all the human tragedies that are the unavoidable consequence of these unifying policies. Canetti, himself not an historian, has some scathing things to say about this. In his opinion historians are, openly or secretly, fond of power. "Historians who are not adorers of power are not capable of writing a coherent history of the state", he says. According to him, Ranke, however famous as a scholar, gave a bad example : "(he) acknowledges power, and realization by means of power is, to him, history". "History", Canetti says, meaning history writing, "presents everything in such a manner as though it could not have happened in a different way. But it could, in a hundred different ways. History puts itself on the side of what really happened ... Among all the possibilities it bases itself on the only one, the surviving one. History thus operates as though it were on the side of the stronger, that is of that what really happened. It is impossible that this would not happen; it simply had to" [57].

What does this signify for the philosophy or ideology that underlies history writing? That "historians who are professionally obsessed by power (Canetti seems to see this as a kind of occupational disease - F.) use to explain everything by Time, behind which they, as experts, can hide comfortably, or by Necessity that, under their hands, may assume every shape" [58]. It is for this reason that the American scholar Dwight D. Hoover, describes historians as 'secular theologians, explaining the ways of society to man. In this role, historians are conservative and success oriented, showing how changes had to occur and why these changes were all for the best" [59]. Harsh words, indeed! But are they wholly unjustified? The examples I mentioned do not belie them. In former volumes I have given other instances; it would not be difficult to multiply these.

What I myself have been saying, coupled with the quotations by Canetti and Hoover, has some pertinent consequences that are valid within the frame of this work. First, there may be, there often actually is, a dualistic opposition between the state and the interests of the citizen. I have already expained this at some length when writing of the Greek polis (Vol. II, Ch. II); in the Qin state, and to some extent also in the Han Empire, we have other telling examples. We shall have to pursue this line further; even modern democratic states show a tendency to play havoc with the rights of the individual citizens.

Second, there exists an opposition, not free from dualism, between History and history, between that what is written and is transmitted to pupils and the general public, and that what really happened. I do not mean at all - I want to stress this most emphatically! - that modern historians wilfully and intentionally distort history in favour of the powers that be (although in Nazi Germany, in Marxist states, and under many authoritarian regimes this happened on a large scale). But their 'obsession with power' causes a bias of which they themselves probably are not aware. It produces not only a far reaching justification of the state and its works, but also, still more important, a (hidden) hypostatizing of history, i.e. the creation of History, standing apart from and even above actual happenings, that alienates history writing from the public and gives it the idea that it, in fact, is powerless, even in democratic states.

9. Early problems of the Han regime

a. The initial situation

Shrewd as he was, Liu Bang decided not to repeat the mistakes of Huang-Di. He somewhat loosened the shackles of unification by introducing feudalism again. About two-thirds of the extent of the empire were parcelled out to deserving fellow-combatants of the victor and to his brothers and sons. All of them received smaller or greater fiefs and were allowed to call themselves 'wang' = king. Later, at one feudal step lower, a hundred margraves were installed. However, this did not mean a total return to the more or less anarchical situation of Zhou times. No feudal lord was entitled to nominate vassals of his own; so there was not an endless fragmentation of power. Furthermore, no office was hereditary [60]. Finally, a not insignificant part of the empire was ruled, directly and uncompromisingly, by the emperor himself.

The initial situation of the Han Empire was, therefore, that two political systems subsisted side by side, the imperial and the feudal ones. Li calls this a 'dyarchy' [61]. The relationship between the two never was easy. The reason for the antagonism was not only that the two systems were so diverse but also that Liu Bang and his successors never whole-heartedly accepted this state of affairs; in their view feudalism was no more than a transitory expedient. They saw the existence of powerful feudal lords as a very real threat to their ambition to centralize China once again. So the relationship between the emperor and his great vassals was, on principle, inimical. We may describe this conflict between centripetal and centrifugal forces as dualistic, and, what is more, as dualism of a fierce kind, since one of the two systems had to disappear.

The emperors relentlessly pursued an anti-feudal policy by deposing wangs whenever they could, and by steadily enlarging the extent of their centralized domain. There was one moment when the monarchy seemed on the verge of collapsing. In 154 B.C. a number of wangs rose in revolt, in the so-called 'Seven States", or 'Seven Kings' Rebellion', but the state-appointed generals, loyal to the throne, succeeded in crushing this insurrection. After this rebellion little was left of feudal power; under the Emperor Wudi (Wu-ti, 140 - 87 B.C.) the last vestiges of feudalism were abolished [62].

Thus, in the first centuries B.C., the centripetal forces had triumphed, at least for the time being. The new subdivision into smaller units had a purely administrative character; a hundred provinces were established, each divided into twenty districts. The provincial governors and the district magistrates were all state-appointed. At the top, just below the emperor, we find the central government consisting of the Three Chancellors (superministers) and nine secretaries of state (ministers), all nominated by the emperor, at least formally [63].

b. Modernists and reformists

The establishment of the new regime provided yet another opportunity for conflict. Michael Loewe says that, among the leading circles of the empire, two attitudes occurred that may be denoted as 'modernist' and 'reformist'. He warns us that this opposition is not identical with that between 'Legalists' and 'Confucians' that had played a role in the late Zhou period and would continue to do so. This scholar defines the modernist line as 'positive and expansionist', more directed to the future than oriented to the past. Its leading idea was the unification of China; this meant that the central government, under the aegis of the emperor, had to be powerful. Politics had to be based on a strong economy controlled by the authorities. The population should be kept in check by a system of rewards and punishments. Finally, the empire must be enlarged by the acquisition of new territories both for economic reasons and to keep foreign peoples at bay [64].

Reformists agreed with the modernists that China should be a unified and centrally administered state. But less 'political' and materialistic than the opposite party, they considered Heaven 'the supreme arbiter of the Universe'; their ethical background was the doctrine of Confucius. In economics they felt inclined to private enterprise rather than to state control. They rejected the idea of expansion for the sake of revenue. With regard to foreign policy, they were more inward looking and somewhat isolationist [65].

Loewe states that both sets of ideas had their influence on imperial policy. "The conduct of Han government was frequently marked by compromise" [66]. Perhaps oscillating between the two parties suited the emperors very well since the existence of two political ideologies enabled them to rule in conformity with the adage 'divide et impera'. Although in the last centuries B.C. modernist policy most of the time carried the day, the reformists were not without some influence. Juridical practice became more lenient than the modernists would have it, while in 44 B.C. the existing state monopolies were abolished [67].

c. The beginnings of Chinese bureaucracy

It is more or less reliably stated that in the year 2 A.D. the Han Empire counted 55.594.978 inhabitants [68]. This is more than the Roman Empire had in the same period and about the size of the present population of the Federal Republic of Germany. If this huge mass of people had to be governed from a central point according to strict rules, an extensive bureaucracy was needed. The number of state officials in the first century B.C. is said to have been 130.528. This would mean one civil servant per four or five hundred citizens; compared with the state of officialdom in modern states this is not excessive. This rate remained unchanged in the centuries to come [69].

We find the first beginnings of a bureaucratic system already in the Zhou and Qin periods but only during the reign of Wudi was it thoroughly organized. During the later dynasties this system basically remained the same. In respect to our theme its main element is that it constituted, so to speak, a higher echelon in the human hierarchy, situated between the emperor with his ministers and the commoners, but much closer to the Son of Heaven than to the illiterate mass of peasants. Since the emperor was a sacred being, even the lowest district official shared to some extent in the religious respect everyone had for the mythical personality of the highest ruler. Furthermore, officials were literate; they could read and write and consult registers and codes of law. This is no mean achievement in a country where the number of characters in the writing system grew to be some fifty thousand, where the reading of even the simplest texts necessitated the mastery of some two or three thousand characters, and where many of these characters are extremely difficult to draw, some of them consisting of more than twenty-five strokes [70].

It is easy to imagine how the simple peasant looked up in awe at an official who unfolded a scroll and read from it. It must have seemed sheer magic to him, and, indeed, originally, and even nowadays, Chinese characters are supposed to possess a magical force. Reischauer adds that "prayers to the gods were not spoken but written". And he goes on to say that "in the East Asian civilization the written word has always taken precedence over the spoken ... The magic quality of writing is perhaps one of the reasons why the peoples of East Asia have tended to place a higher premium on book learning and formal education than any other civilization" [71].

To supply this formal education Emperor Wudi around 100 B.C. founded a central university in his capital Chang'an (Ch'ang-an) where all future civil servants received their professional training. They were recruited from the ranks of the rich, land-possessing families or were the sons and siblings of acting bureaucrats; however, sons of commoners were not excluded. The necessary qualifications for entering the civil service were talent and education. Since education could only be acquired by those who were wealthy enough, the mass of poor peasants was virtually shut out. Some of those who possessed wealth, namely the merchant class as such, were nevertheless specifically barred from the civil service; elitist societies always are distrustful of merchants [72]. Needless to say that all functions were salaried and not hereditary.

Thus the Chinese bureaucratic system became highly refined, 'unequalled anywhere in the contemporary world' [73]. But it is also true that a system like this one [74] promoted the growth of authoritarian and elitist government, with the almost inevitable result that the system became an end in itself. Although bureaucratic methods doubtless were much less harsh now than under the Qin dynasty, and although more clemency and leniency were shown, we cannot say that the principal and all-directing aim was solely the welfare of the people. Surely the people was 'a major concern' of the government but only 'as tax payers or corvée labor' and ... 'as potential rebels'. The interests the bureaucrats whole-heartedly served were those of the emperor and his family and the army [75]. So the old dualistic bipartitioning of society into those privileged and the lower orders remained in full force.

10. The showdown with the Xiongnu

The Han emperors used the first half century of their rule for a policy of consolidation. This period ended in 154 B.C. with the crushing of the Seven States' Rebellion. With this threat to imperial unity safely out of the way, the Emperor Wudi felt secure enough to inaugurate a policy of expansion. His rule was more modernist than that of his predecessors. The laws grew more severe, and his hard hand rested heavily on the peasants who, in corvée labour, were called up to dig canals [76]. This was done partly with a view to the conquests he planned. Wudi set his face in many directions against enemies real and imaginary. The danger that the Xiongnu (Xiung-nu) spelled was, however, far from imaginary; perhaps they were identical with the Huns.

The Xiongnu formed a confederation of Turco-Mongolian tribes living in the steppes to the north-west of Han China. From 209 to 174 B.C. they were governed by a dynamic emperor called Maodun (Mao-tun). This man expanded his sway eastward through eastern Mongolia and into Manchuria along the northern flank of the Han empire. Northward he pushed on through Gansu and always further and further; Xiongnu influence perhaps even reached to Lake Aral. The real danger spot for Han lay in the Ordos region beyond the bend of the Yellow River and just outside the Great Wall. Starting from this region the incredibly swift mounted archers of the Xiongnu, glued to their saddles, raided the most western districts of the Chinese Empire to the utmost terror of the inhabitants. What complicated the problem for the Han ruler was that discontented Chinese chiefs defected to the invading forces [77].

About 200 B.C. the stage seemed set for a showdown, given the fact that Xiongnu sovereign considered himself no less a ruler than his Han colleague [78]. The first great Han offensive, led by the Emperor Gaozu (Kao Ti) in the winter of 200 B.C., ended, however, in a disaster; the imperial commander himself fell into an ambush and barely managed an escape [79]. After this the Chinese ruler tried to pacify his opponent by means of dynastic marriages. This did not make Maodun less arrogant; on the contrary, he not only went on to extend his realm, but in 192 B.C. he dared to ask for the hand of the widowed Empress Lü - a proposal that the ageing lady furiously rejected. Her answer was not in the style of a young bride : "Both my hair and teeth are falling out, and I cannot even walk steadily" [80]. It will, however, be perfectly clear that the

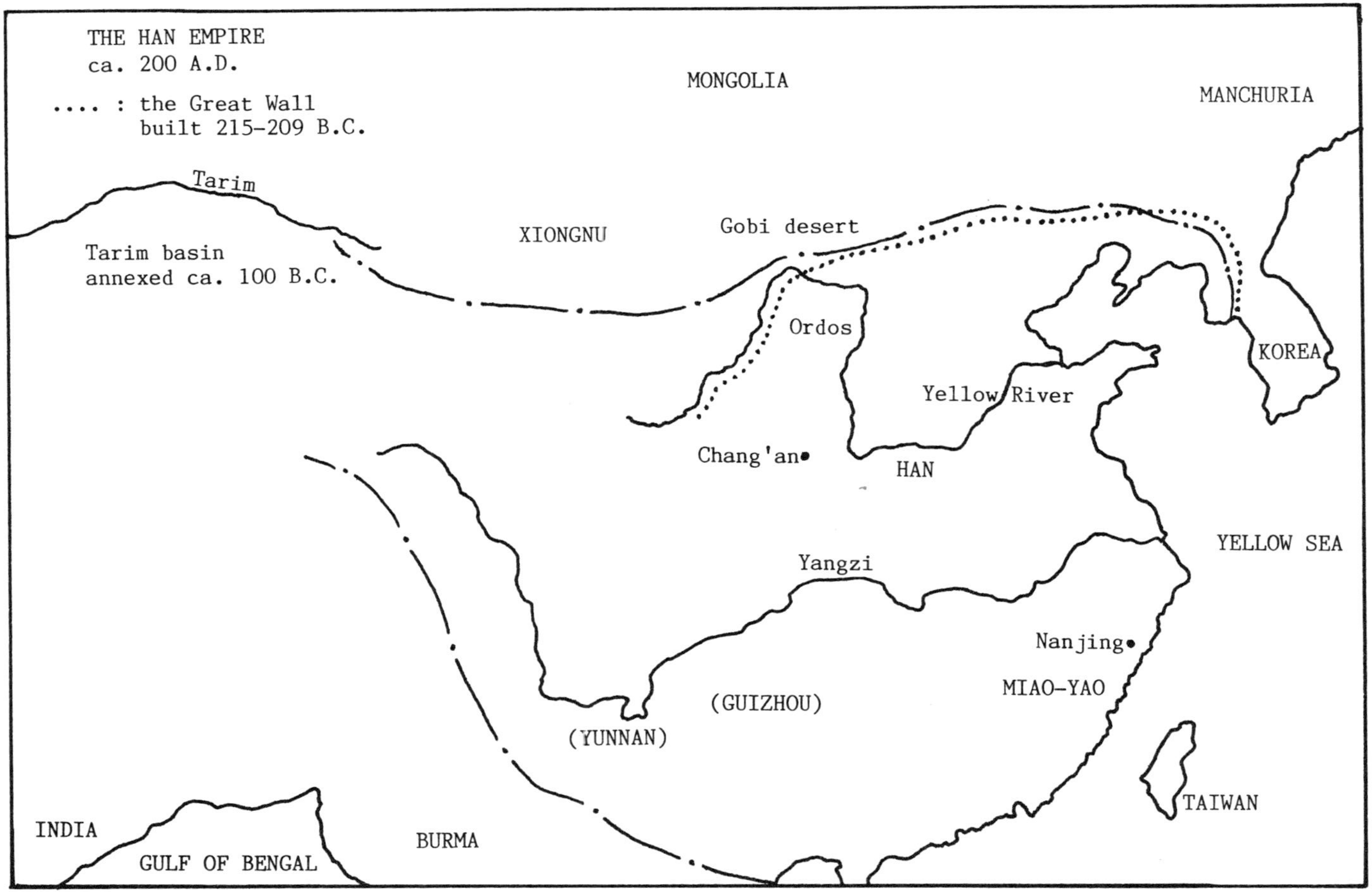
THE HAN EMPIRE
ca. 200 A.D.
.... : the Great Wall
built 215-209 B.C.
MONGOLIA
MANCHURIA
Tarim
Tarim basin
annexed ca. 100 B.C.
XIONGNU
Gobi desert
Ordos
KOREA
Yellow River
Chang'an
HAN
YELLOW SEA
Yangzi
Nanjing
MIAO-YAO
(GUIZHOU)
(YUNNAN)
TAIWAN
INDIA
GULF OF BENGAL
BURMA

marriage-candidate was not seeking the pleasures of love; what he really aspired to was to combine his empire and that of the Han in a personal union so that he might become emperor of China. Later, not long before he died, Maodun told the Han emperor Wendi (Wen Ti, 179-157 B.C.), that he (the Xiongnu ruler) was 'the great Shanyü of the Xiongnu, established by Heaven' [81], with which he claimed the Celestial Mandate for himself. All this signified that the conflict had assumed a dualistic character : it now was the one or the other, with the Xiongnu sovereign clearly intending to be the victor.

After the passing away of Maodun his successors continued their raids into China, often penetrating very deeply, once even to the summer residence of the Han emperors [82]. But with Wudi a man of very hard mettle came to the throne of China. In quick succession heavy blows were dealt to the Xiongnu. The well-organized armies of the Han counted up to a hundred thousand cavalry, to say nothing of the infantry. This, however, did not spell any easy victory. By no means! Sometimes whole armies were fruitlessly frittered away [83]. But in 127 B.C. the Chinese succeeded in securing the most dangerous area, the Ordos region; from there the Chinese forces steadily pressed on northward forcing huge enemy armies to capitulate. In 119 B.C. the Han generals had driven the Xiongnu into the Gobi desert in Mongolia.

This meant an extension of Han rule beyond the Great Wall [84]. From now on the area that to-day is formed by the Ningxia and Inner Mongolia Autonomous regions definitely belonged to China [85]. To the north-east the Chinese obtained a firm footing in eastern Mongolia and Manchuria; the tribes living there had formerly acknowledged Xiongnu supremacy but now recognized the overlordship of the Han ruler [86].

This did not mean the end of the Han campaigns. The ferocious struggle for the leadership in East and Central Asia went on for decades, long after the death of Wudi. In 108 B.C., with Wudi still living, Chinese armies began a first offensive in a westerly direction. This move inaugurated a period of Han expansion in Central Asia [87].

The object of the Chinese generals was not only to outflank and finally destroy the Xiongnu but also to secure the routes of the profitable silk trade. Between 104 and 101 B.C. one of the ablest Han commanders, Li Guangli (Li Kuang-Li), succeeded in crossing the Pamir mountains and occupying Ferghana (in Chinese Danyan, now Soviet-Turkestan), a region, however, that never became an integral part of the Chinese Empire. What, however, was incorporated into China was the Tarim Basin in the utmost west of the country (now in the Xinjiang - Sinkiang - Autonomous Region).

After these incredible successes of the Han, the Xiongnu no longer were much of a menace, although their final defeat had to wait till 88 A.D. An important effect of the western campaigns was that they brought the so-called Silk Road into Chinese hands. This was the road along which the lucrative silk trade took place; it began in Luoyang and ran for more than six thousand kilometers through all Central Asia to the shores of the Mediterranean. However, there never was any direct contact between the Han Empire and its Roman counterpart, the 'Da Qin', as the Chinese called it [88].

11. The Son of Heaven and his Celestial Mandate

The story of the western conquests by no means exhausts the catalogue of Han acquistions. In 112 B.C. the most southern provinces of modern China, Guangdong and the Guangxi Zhuang Autonomous Region, were firmly brought under Chinese control followed by parts of northern Vietnam. Shortly afterwards, in 111 B.C. regions somewhat more to the west and north were added, namely Guizhou (Kweichow) and Yunnan (Yünnan) now bordering on Burma and Laos [89]. All this means that already in the first century B.C. China acquired her present geopolitical shape. Two expeditions in the north of Korea obtained the Chinese a strong foothold in this peninsula.

All these conquests were made in the name of the Han emperor. The first ruler of this race was, after all, no more than a brutal usurper but he had received the Mandate of Heaven and bequeathed this to his successors. Their great successes showed that they indeed were worthy to be the Sons of Heaven. By this claim, as Michael Loewe states, "emperors ... showed themselves as recipients of power imparted by a superhuman authority; it could be asserted that they were acting in response to a mission" [90]. This assured the emperor of a degree of loyalty and allegiance such as would not be given to another type of ruler since it had a religious character. Nobody could have any direct contact with Heaven except the emperor who was the highest religious functionary of the state. He had to carry out many important rites some of them kept secret.

As he was the guarantee of the spiritual well-being of his subjects, he also had to be 'a moral example' in possession of de. Failing to live up to the required standard could even endanger his throne. This standard implied that he was 'a patron of learning, literature, and the arts' too, occupations that could be instrumental in heightening the moral and spiritual level of the nation. All laws emanated from him. This does not mean that the emperor was deeply engaged in practical politics or led armies in the field. The ideal was that of 'wu wei', non-action (not : inaction) : the emperor 'reigned with arms folded, in a posture of ease'. That he should exert himself was seen as unbecoming [91].

12. The unhappy end of the First Han Period

At the end of the first century B.C., a series of natural catastrophes - earthquakes, inundations, solar eclipses - seemed to prove that the Han emperors had sunk below standard and, in consequence, had lost the Heavenly Mandate. An energetic and ambitious high official, Wang Mang, saw his chance and proclaimed himself emperor in 9 A.D. He reigned for fourteen years (9 - 23 A.D.), roughly contemporaneous with the Roman emperors Augustus and Tiberius. In his Confucian zeal to establish a just society he with one stroke abolished large landownership and 'nationalized' the land, after which he began distributing it to the peasants. Of course he thereby ran into trouble with the dispossessed landowners. What was worse, the breaking of the dikes of the Yellow River after exceptional rainfall, and the subsequent large floods, made it clear that Wang Mang was no more than a usurper and not in the possession of the Mandate. The terrified and desperate peasants rose in a revolt that is known as that of 'the Red Eyebrows' since, in order to look like demons, the rebels painted their faces. Wang Mang lost his life in the turmoil [92].

13. The Latter Han Period

The downfall of Wang Mang marked the beginning of the Latter Han Period (23 - 220), for it was again a member of the Han dynasty who now ascended the throne. The commotion of the end of the First Han Period had loosened the grip of China on the western regions in Central Asia. In 73 A.D. a very able general, Ban Chao (Pan Ch'ao) was nominated Protector General of the Western Regions; he succeeded with his headquarters in the Tarim Basin; he succeeded in restoring Chinese supremacy in the west. From his far western outpost he tried to establish diplomatic relations with the Parthian and Roman Empires. His envoy failed to reach Rome; perhaps he was deterred by the Parthians, who did not relish the idea of being caught between two mighty empires. However, Ban Chao came back to Luoyang in 102 with much information about Rome. "It is evident", writes Morton, "that the Chinese knew more about Rome than the Romans knew about China" [93].

In general the Latter Han Period was a time of consolidation. This process, however, was increasingly threatened by the continuous growth of large landownership. The court was weakened by intrigues in which the imperial wives and concubines, influenced by overbearing eunuchs, played an important role. The central government experienced steadily growing difficulties in controlling the more outlying provinces of the empire. With this enfeebling of central authority the dualistic opposition between centripetal and centrifugal forces reared its ugly head again. Successful generals - comparable to the 'war-lords' of twentieth-century Chinese history - founded power centres of their own in the provinces. It was highly important for these generals to have the emperor in their control. More than once the last emperor of the Han line became a prisoner in the hands of one of his army commanders. The decisive element was that each general wanted to dispose of the imperial seal [94].

On top of this there was serious agrarian unrest. The peasants were poor but had to pay heavy taxes. This led in 184 to a queer and dangerous rising known as that of 'the Yellow Turbans' that shocked the empire to its foundations. It lasted for years and was from 190 onwards accompanied by yet another rebellion in the western provinces. The Yellow Turbans rising started in the coastal regions and from there spread westward. Soon there was a peasant army on foot of about three hundred and sixty thousand men. However, we do not not know for certain whether the leaders of the eastern and western rebellions were in contact which each other and played the same game.

The leader of the western rebellion, one Zhang Ling or Zhang Daoling, was a Daoist (Taoist), a charismatic patriarch who founded a theocratic state in Sichuan, a sort of Utopia. This man was firmly opposed to the official imperial state cult that had superseded the old popular rites everywhere. There was a very evident dualistic rift here between the peasantry who followed Zhang Ling and the gentry that was seen by the former as the representative of imperial power. Zhang Ling gave the peasants rites of their own, like confession and communal meals. Eberhard says that after Zhang's downfall these rites subsisted for hundreds of years in Central and South China; he suggests that Daoist elements in the religion of present-day Mongolian and Tibetan tribes may derive from Zhang's or Yellow Turban times. However, the whole movement, without a clear ideology and without consistency, finally ended in failure [95].

The end of the Han period was marked by an atmosphere of scepticism and despondency. It had become less than evident that there was a healthy correlation between moral ideas and politics. As the Sino-American author Ch'en Ch'yün formulates it : "the tensions within the Han Confucian synthesis led to a gradual breakdown of the grandiose holism" [96]. Scholars became increasingly disillusioned with the official optimistic doctrine. While the older view of human nature maintained that it is basically good, pessimistic authors now said that it is wholly bad, while a third party took a middle course [97]. More and more the emphasis was laid on the incomptability of the state and the individual - a schism, says Ch'en, a dualism I prefer calling it -, in striking contrast to the vision cherished by former Han thinkers of an all-embracing unity within the world [98].

It is obvious that Han rule had outlived itself. In 220 a highly successful general formally deposed the last Han emperor and assumed the title himself. Centrifugal tendencies now gained the upperhand for some time, for soon there were three different empires on Chinese soil, one in the old heartland on the Yellow River, one in Sichuan, and a third on the lower course of the Yangzi. The subsequent period, 220 - 280, is called the era of the Three Kingdoms.

14. A time of disunion

a. A failure of nerve

If one is allowed to describe the history of nations in human terms, we might say that the following period of more than three centuries till 589 was one of a failure of nerve. The urge to unify, to centralize, even to expand seemed to have disppeared, apart from some short bouts of aggressiveness. Barbarian and only half-sinicized tribes tried to profit from China's weakness; the old particularisms everywhere were rampant again. But, in spite of all this confusion, some of the work begun by the Qin and Han rulers silently went on, almost automatically. The impulses given by them to Chinese history could not wholly be discounted. Under the surface of turmoil and strife the process of sinicization was continued, with the result that the less 'Chinese' south slowly but certainly became the equal of the north. Buddhism, having arrived from India, gained many adherents and became a new spiritual force, somewhat to the detriment of the older Confucianism. Next, as the third great ideology, there was Daoism (Taoism) that also displayed a great vitality in this era [99]. Both Confucianism and Daoism will be the subject of a fuller treatment further on.

The vicissitudes of the Three Kingdoms need not occupy us. All three of them succeeded in making a few new conquests; however, they spent most of their energy in fighting each other. After about six decades one of the two kingdoms that were located in the south re-unified China under its aegis in 280. This new unity under the Jin dynasty lasted only twent-six years, till 306. There was much in-fighting in the imperial family. After 290 the successive emperors were completely dominated by rival court cliques whose history became increasingly bloody. At least seven emperors, empressess, and claimants were murdered, to say nothing of their families that, more often than not, shared their fate [100].

From 306 onward there is a great difference between the north and the south. While the north lay prostrate and powerless, a prey to succeeding waves of barbarians, the south gradually seemed to come into its own and find its proper place in the Chinese context. This means that although for a few centuries there was an apparently dualistic rift between the northern and the southern half of the country, this rift did not reach deep enough to prevent the later realization of a new imperial unity.

Between 317 and 589 five ruling houses followed each other in the southern realm. All of them had their capital in the city that is now called Nanjing (Nanking). Several abortive attempts were made to conquer the north, the last one, in 417, being almost successful (the northern capital Luoyang was for a short time in southern hands). When, from 311 onwards, the barbarians made themselves the masters of the north, an unending stream of northern refugees began to emigrate to the south; there were, indeed, millions of them, 'probably the largest migration ever recorded in history' [101]. The southern regime settled them to the south of the Yangzi, and area that still was less predominantly 'Chinese' then. There the newcomers established themselves with their wealth and their technical know-how and in this way upgraded the cultural and economic life of the south [102]. In consequence the southern half of China became more thoroughly sinicized than ever before. This is an instance of how an originally dualistic division gradually disappeared, not by means of a deliberate policy but under the weight of external events.

b. 'Darkness at noon' in the north

The emigrants acted prudently, for over the north 'darkness at noon' descended. The internal strife around 300 enticed the barbarians to risk their chance. To the Han Chinese "all nomadic tribesmen living in a grand semi-circle extending from Tibet in the southwest to Manchuria in the northeast, for a distance of more than 2.500 miles" were 'barbarians', for they were not settled, not agricultural and not cultured (in the Chinese sense) [103]. In 311 a tribe of China's old enemy, the Xiongnu, appeared. They did their work thoroughly; Luoyang was looted, and it is said that more than thirty thousand state officials lost their lives. In the wake of the Xiongnu other Mongolian tribes arrived; soon the whole north was flooded by them. Curiously enough, many a tribal chief tried to make himself emperor, only to be toppled by a rival. Havoc was the catchword. According to a contemporary witness, Luoyang looked 'like a gigantic garbage dump' [104]. The old dualistic opposition between Chinese and barbarians was lived out to the full in this period.

But, in spite of appearances, the barbarians finally became the 'losers'. In such frantic dualistic encounters one of the two parties has to go; in this case the barbarians had to cede their place. Not that they evacuated North China. On the contrary! Till far into the fourth century there were new arrivals. But these alien tribes lost their barbarian identity. They became settled and agricultural, they built houses, they began adopting Chinese names massively. The tribesmen were not able to run the country without the help of Chinese officials; they were forced to adopt Chinese political institutions. These rulers, and the members of the upper class in general, were great admirers of Chinese female beauty; the princes collected large harems, while interracial marriages became quite normal. The obvious result was that offspring from such marriages were more thoroughly sinicized than their fathers. Li states that about 500 "the so-called barbarians were in every respect Chinese, and barbarians only when they took pains to trace their genealogy" [105].

In 439 the entire north became a unified state under a Mongolian ruler. Later, from 471 on, sinicization was the official policy carried out by means of legal measures. The regime made Luoyang, the ancient centre of classical Chinese culture, its capital. Many conservative subjects feared that this would mean the definitive loss of their Mongolian heritage; rebellions had to be crushed, the crown prince was executed. Chinese became the official language the learning of which was made imperative for young people. Everyone had to adopt a Chinese name, while the wearing of non-Chinese costumes was forbidden. This process of sinicization was so powerful that later waves of barbarians were sinicized soon enough. Thus the roles were completely reversed : the ci-devant barbarians were just as Chinese as the Han and in their turn sinicized others [106].

We may conclude that in the last resort the north and the south steered the same course, that of sinicization. This, combined with the historical, deep-seated urge towards unity, suggests the future reunification of China. This eventually happened but not before 589. Towards the end of the sixth century an authentically Chinese dynasty, the Sui, came to the throne of the north. The Sui emperor had very little difficulty in evicting the ruler of the south. So, in 589, after three hundred and sixty years of separation, China was a unified state once more. Centralization had triumphed over particularism in the end. What followed falls outside the scope of this work.

15. Chinese philosophical concepts

a. A universe in three parts

We are fully justified in calling Confucius the first Chinese philosopher. This, however, must not be taken to mean that, before him, nobody 'thought', but that such thoughts were not committed to bamboo, or, if this did occur, the 'books' have disappeared without leaving any trace. Excavations and inscriptions teach us that the earliest inhabitants had a religion. One of the most important elements of Chinese religiosity was - and always remained - the ancestor cult. However, in the earliest period the commoners had no part in this cult; under the Shang dynasty it was only the royal family that venerated its ancestors, joined in this by the vassals during the Zhou period. Ancestors were believed to be still present among the living; they wanted to be venerated. They had their own temples which were centres of ritual life [107].

In the view of these ancient Chinese the universe was partitioned into three : a superior world where the divine beings dwelt, the middle world, that of mankind, and a nether world, the abode of the demons. According to Eichhorn this threepartitioning always remained a main element of Chinese ideology. Divine beings were, for instance, 'Dongmu' (Tung-mu), the East Mother, or the sun, 'Xiamu' (Hsia-mu), the West Mother, or the moon, and, in addition, the stars, the winds, the clouds. They were 'gods of nature', though it remains unclear whether they were simply personified natural forces [108]. The dominating godhead was the divinized ancestor of the dynasty, the 'Shangdi' (Shang Ti), or Supreme Emperor.

b. Heaven as the supreme godhead

Under the Zhou dynasty, when the compass of Chinese civilization was widened far beyond its original borders, it proved impossible to maintain a tribal ancestor as the supreme ruler of the universe. Another sovereign lord came to the fore with a far more universal range,

'Tian' (T'ian), or Heaven. In the course of time the two supreme divinities were combined into one godhead, Haotian Shangdi (Hao-t'ian Shang-ti) = Great Heaven and Supreme Godhead [109]. This well-known Chinese concept of Tian is, in fact, a fairly intricate one. The word may denote the sky in a psysical sense, as opposed to the earth, Heaven and Earth constituting the universe between them. Then there is a more personal meaning of Tian as the Supreme Godhead. But Tian may also mean Fate, the inexorably destined course of events to which everyone and everything on earth is subjected. In the fourth place Tian has a significance that is more or less equivalent to Nature. And finally it is the moral order, 'the highest primordial principle of the universe' [110].

This enumeration can initially give us the idea that, with regard to Heaven, that is with regard to supernatural order, the position of mankind is one of subordination, dominated as it is by an impersonal moral order, by Fate, by Destiny. This made things like divination and magic necessary. The Chinese scholar Fung Yu-lan says that the latter were based on the belief that "a close mutual influence existed between things in the physical universe and human affairs" [111]. True enough, of course, but one or two things must not be forgotten. Resorting to magic and the like also means that the 'physical universe' - which never is seen as purely physical in the western sense but as animated - is experienced as potentially not trustworthy, as adversely disposed, on occasion even as inimical. There is no harmonious relationship between man and nature; the secret intentions have to be discovered in order to be forestalled. This sounding of Nature's hidden plans is by no means everybody's work; it is the special task of experts - sorcerers, magicians, witch doctors - who know the right words and gestures but prefer to keep their knowledge secret.

c. The square earth

Next to the heavenly beings there are also terrestrial godheads. Just as the clouds and the winds belong to Tian, the spirits of land and grain, the 'Sheji' (She-chi), were ruled by the paramount terrestrial deity, She. This brings us to a very important and general Chinese notion, viz. that Earth is square, whereas Heaven is round and stands like as a cupola over the earth. Time too is circular and revolving. That Earth, a flat surface, is square implies that every decent object has to be square. If there also exist objects that are round or oblong, this is the effect of Time. The square earth in its turn is also divided into squares. In the middle square the emperor of China lives. In the exact centre of this central square stands the main altar the dimensions of which are also square. Its centre is covered with yellow earth, and, therefore, represents the earth as a totality. This altar is, of course, dedicated to She; the emperor comes there to sacrifice, implying that the whole earth is his property. On another altar and in a different rite the emperor addresses the Sun God; this he does in his capacity as Son of Heaven.

In four adjoining squares the vassals live, in theory albeit by no means always in practice totally dependent on the Supreme Ruler. The four edges of the central Chinese squares are surrounded by four concentric regions inhabited by different kinds of barbarians, the non-Chinese peoples, varying from nearly civilized to utterly wild (in Chinese eyes). The Chinese used to call these outlying territories the 'Four Seas'. They probably did not believe that these nations actually lived in a sea but rather that their land was inhabitable and could not be cultivated. The consequence of this is that inhabitants of these regions did not share in the fulness of human capacities and qualities that were common to the Chinese. They were considered less than human. Even those Chinese who were banished from the soil of their fatherland and were forced to live among the barbarians lost part of their identity. This is dualism with a vengeance [112].

d. Pairs of oppositions

It is a remarkable fact that the Chinese have no creation story nor do they dabble in cosmogonical speculations (although they were highly interested in cosmology) [113]. In their opinion the history of the universe coincided with that of civilization - a civilization that, self-evidently is Chinese. The starting-point of all history is the biography of the (mythical) first Supreme Ruler. The macrocosm is in a state of perfect harmony which imparts itself to the microcosm of man. This means that, in the Chinese conception of the universe, there is no fundamental dualism.

Nevertheless, there exist several pairs of oppositions. Chinese philosophers speak of Being and Non-Being. Non-Being is usually seen, not as 'nothing', but as a state of formlessness and indeterminancy prior to Being. Being then means concreteness, possessing form, in short : creation. There was a time in which not even Heaven and Earth were differentiated; this was the Great Beginning. The treatise that is ascribed to Laozi (Lao Tzu) states that "Heaven and Earth and the ten thousand things (= all that heaven and earth contain) are produced from Being; Being is the product of Non-Being" [114]. Laozi held that the duality of Being and Non-Being was not the original state of things but that both resulted from Oneness [115]. We see philosophy at grips here with the old problem of the One and the Many; we shall have to return to this.

Another treatise neglects this philosophical notion of Oneness. It says that once there was 'not yet a beginning of Non-Being' nor even 'a beginning of the not yet beginning of Non-Being' [116]. It is extremely difficult to guess what is meant by these rather clumsy or deliberately obscure expressions. This not-yet-beginning before the beginning of the Great Beginning at any rate is not the state of amorphous formlessness from which Heaven and Earth proceed. Was it what in western cosmology is meant by 'chaos'? Or perhaps what European thinkers term 'nothingness'?

Anyhow, in this early period this meaning of initial chaos does not seem to have made the impact on Chinese thought as it did later in Daoism. To the Chinese mind the essential thing was civilization which signified that (ideally) everything was well-ordered and had its own appropriate function; continuity was the key-word. There is a charming story by Zhuangzi (Chuang Tzu) who lived in the fourth century B.C. Two friends succeeded in laying hands on Chaos; since it desired to become civilized it deserved to be received among men. The friends undertook to humanize it which they did by boring holes in its head, every day one hole, for the eyes, ears, etc. But on the seventh day Chaos died of the operation. Whatever this story may mean exactly, it does not betray a great fear of Chaos [117].

According to Chinese feeling, Time, as I said, is circular and revolving; it makes seasons, years, reigns, dynasties return regularly; when one disappears another comes to the fore. Succeeding generations are continuous; always a younger one emerges which implies that Time is constantly rejuvenating itself. There really is no end of it. This sentiment is expressed in several ways, for instance, by wishing one another on New Year's Day 'ten thousand years' [118].

Summing up, we must conclude that the basic Chinese world-view does not imply a fundamental dualism. But we must not overlook an important element. The Chinese system is not so much cosmological or even philosophical but rather political. Society, as the Chinese view it, is essentially a polity, under the aegis of the Son of Heaven. Well-ordered as this polity (ideally) is it mirrors the harmony of the macro-cosm and microcosm. But this ideology contains a strongly dualistic element of which I have already spoken. To be civilized, to live in an well-organized state, to be human, to be in harmony with Heaven, means to be Chinese. China is congruent with the Universe. This implies that peoples and nations outside China do not possess a fully human existence. There exists a deep cleavage between Chinese and non-Chinese.

Some dualistic oppositions that are rampant in western ideologies do not occur in Chinese thought, for instance that between Pure and Impure, or between Good and Bad. This, of course, does not signify that the Chinese were indifferent with regard to Good and Evil, or that it was all the same to them. But the Gnostic, Manichaean, or Cathar distinction of 'either - or' was alien to them. The same applies to the distinction of Right and Left which, however, is of real importance in Chinese thinking. In general, the things of the Earth belong to the Right, while those of Heaven are the province of the Left. But whereas in the Pythagorean list of oppositions (Vol. I, Ch. I, 11 and 12) 'right' is good, and 'left' is nefarious, this is not the case with the Chinese pair. 'Left', indicating what is of Heaven, even has some precedence over 'Right', this, however, being no more than a slight qualitative difference [119].

But as we know, every opposition may grow into a stronger one, and, slowly but imperceptibly, develop into a downright dualism. I do not believe that this happened in China but there are traces of it. Although Left takes some priority over Right, Chinese are normally right-handed, they are taught to be so; they also eat with their right hand. Most of the time Left is favourable and bringing good luck, but sometimes it is equivalent with something sinister, with 'the forbidden roads'. Is it therefore that, when swearing or making friends, a Chinese uses the right hand? Or, that in order to seal an oath, blood is drawn from the right arm [120]?

e. Yin and Yang

The distinction between Right and Left brings us to the pair that is the best-known and the most popular in the west, Yin and Yang. Several persons who knew that I was preparing this section asked me not to omit Yin and Yang. Linking up with the foregoing paragraph we must say that Yang is Left and Yin is Right. Like Left and Right, Yang and Yin are complementary principles together making a whole. Everyone knows the famous vignette in which they lay closely nestled to one another. But although they seem to be resting, they are in fact very active, for they have command over the world [121].

It would be entirely misleading to see philosophical or intellectual concepts in Yin and Yang, or to look for similar or identical concepts in western thinking. For Yin and Yang are not ideas but matter, albeit matter of the most ethereal sort. Yang is the extremely subtle stuff of which brightness, the light, and the sun are made, while Yin, equally fine, is to be found in the moon and in darkness [122]. Eichhorn develops a speculative theory, not generally accepted, that initially

Yin had priority over Yang, since everything and everyone, although wanting to strive upwards to the light, nevertheless ends in the nether region where all is wet and 'maternal'. Perhaps we must think here of the maternal womb from which we all have originated. But at the end of the Zhou period the roles were reversed for then Yang, the luminous, got the upperhand. Eichhorn thinks that this may have happened under the influence of a religion of the light, like that of Iran [123]. I present this with all due reserve.

The ancient Chinese treatise that was already mentioned, the Zhuangzi, says this : "The perfect Yin is majestically passive. The perfect Yang is powerfully active. Passivity emanates from Earth. Activity proceeds from Heaven. The interaction of the two forms a harmony from which things are produced" [124]. Another treatise, the 'Guanzi' (Kuang-tzu), adds that Yin and Yang are the great principles of Heaven and Earth, and that they manifest themselves in the seasons. As we may expect, in spring and summer Yang is supreme, in autumn and winter, on the contrary, Yin [125]. There is, of course, far more to say about the Yin - Yang couple, but almost all of it would fall outside our scope. Yin and Yang are complementary forces, but at the same time they are antithetic with a slight tendency towards dualism (the life-giving urge of spring and summer, the destructive forces of autumn and winter).

Looking outward Chinese society took a strongly dualistic stance but looking inward and closing in upon itself (which it preferred doing), it was for agreement and harmony. Ideally, at least, since in reality, as the first part of this chapter showed us, there was much strife, war, oppression, and cruelty. As so often in world history, there was in China an enormous distance between ideal and practice. For everyday life, and also the exercise of government rule, was, more often than not, just as disharmonious as the ideal situation was supposed to be harmonious. The most recent proof of this discrepancy, at this moment of writing, is that the bloody suppression of the student protest movement in Beijing in the autumn of 1989 took place exactly on Tianan-men, the Square of Celestial Peace. What Confucius set out to do was to bridge this gap.

16. The life of Master Kong

"Among a large fraction of mankind, Confucius has for many centuries been considered the most important man that ever lived". With these words Herrlee G. Creel opens his biography of this Chinese thinker [126]. He adds that "in eastern Asia his name is still invoked in ideological struggles by the most conservative and by some of the most radical, who seek by means of varying interpretations to show that Confucius favoured their views". While already this spells little good for somebody who wants to give an exposition of Confucius' way of thought but who is not an expert, to make it all the more daunting there is the subtitle of Creel's book : 'The Man and the Myth'. It obviously is difficult to distinguish between fact and fiction in this field.

However, as far as I know, nobody doubts that Confucius is an historical person. The dates of his life usually are given as from 551 to 479 B.C. Raymond Dawson, commenting on these dates, thinks that they give rise to suspicion just because they are so definite "in an era when the dates of private individuals were not preserved" [127]. Then there is his name. 'Confucius', of course, is Latin, and not Chinese, this being the transcription of his authentic name by the learned Jesuits who reached China in the late sixteenth century and who were the first to transmit his philosophy to Europe. His family name was 'Kong' (also rendered as 'K'ung'); as an individual he was named 'Kong Qiu' (or Zhongni (Chung-ni)). Kongzi (K'ung tzu), or Kong Fuzi (K'ung fu-tzu), means 'Master Kong'; it was this appellation that the Jesuits latinized [128].

Of the facts of his life very little is known with certainty. The region where he saw the light is the southwestern part of the modern province of Shandong. There a city is situated to-day that is called Qufu (Ch'ü-fu), in the vicinity of which the ancient town of Zou is to be found, the birthplace of the philosopher. A unified China did not yet exist in the sixth century B.C. Confucius happens to be born in one of the smaller states, in Lu [129]. The philosopher himself always said that he was 'of humble status' [130], but there is also a tradition that he was of royal descent - perhaps a later legend to enhance his social status [131]. Anyhow, his family was poor; his father died when he was still a small child. At the age of nineteen Confucius married and begot a son and a daughter. In order to sustain his family he was obliged to serve in subordinate positions, as supervisor of granaries for instance [132].

The young man was ambitious enough. But the higher offices were closed to him because of his humble background; forcing his way upwards by means of an army career or in politics did not seem congenial to him. He was not eloquent, he was incapable of flattery, and was not of a practical turn of mind [133]. In some way or other he amassed an enormous amount of learning, or perhaps rather of wisdom, for he was averse to book learning [134]. This does not mean that he did not study books; he had a predilection for poems and for documents (consisting of bamboo strips) on history and ritual [135].

Later legend pictured him as a prolific author, but modern scholarship does not believe that he really wrote all the books that are imputed to him. One of the few things we may be reasonably sure of is that he composed the 'Chungqiu' (Ch'un-ch'iu), the Spring and Autumn Annals. Nevertheless, he was a great pioneer in the cultural development of his people [136]. The Sino-American scholar Wing-tsit Chan puts it like this : "he started a tradition of liberal and American (sic) education in China that was to eclipse the utilitarian and professionally orientated one that had hitherto dominated Chinese culture" [137]. The Chinese scholar Liu Wu-chi calls what the Master created 'the brave new world of education' [138].

Failing to make any headway in the official line he turned to study and teaching. Creel says that "the first students were simply a group of friends ..., an informal debating society"; there was as yet no 'Confucian school' [139]. The Master, not so much older than his disciples then, put a heavy accent on moral training. We should, however, not think of a kind of elitist Pythagorean society (Vol. I, Ch. I, 5); in Confucius' view education must be open to all without any class distinction. "I have never refused instruction to anyone", he is reported to have said [140].

Wishing to widen his horizon, the Master visited the neighbouring states of Zhou and Qi where he consulted experts on ritual and music. Later his old wish to play a political role in his own state of Lu became fulfilled. The man who exercised power there from 492 B.C. onwards was Ji Kangzi (Chi K'ang Tzu) who sympathized with the Confucian group [141]. In some period after 500 B.C., Confucius very probably held office, although it cannot be stated with any degree of certainty what kind of office this was. Perhaps it was no more than a sinecure. We may hardly expect that a despotic ruler like Ji and a radical reformer like Confucius did see eye to eye. Possibly Ji tried to associate the Master with his rule to make him less dangerous [142].

Anyhow, if Confucius has cherished the idea of being able to reform Lu, he had to give up this ideal. He was nearly sixty when he left his native state and began to travel. His journeys lasted fourteen years and brought him to all the neighbouring states. Towards the end of his life he returned to Lu where he died in 479 at 73 years of age.

17. Not a religious reformer

According to Hulsewé, all early Chinese thinkers saw human action as highly questionable; they were searching for an ideal solution. In their opinion human beings would behave correctly and according to ethical norms only in a well-disciplined society. But the actual society in which they lived did not please them at all because, since the seventh century B.C., the power of the state had become considerably weakened; war followed war, tradition seemed to have lost its meaning [143]. The 'feudal code of rites and etiquettes' is called 'li'. What Confucius did was to transform this into 'a universal system of ethics', which is something different from a code of social behaviour [144]. To him it was the spirit that counted in the observance of li, rather than the scrupulous observance of ritual or social rules. As he once said to a disciple : "In funerals and ceremonies of mourning, it is better that the mourners feel true grief than that they be meticulously correct in every ceremonial detail" [145].

We should not think of Confucius as a religious innovator. In fact I do not believe that he was a deeply religious person. If he had been, he would have raised this issue far oftener than he really did; he seemed reluctant to speak of it. In general, he loathed to discuss the supernatural [146]. It was, however, not his intention to abolish the traditional system of religion. He himself took part in the usual ceremonies. But in response to a question about wisdom the Master said : "It (wisdom) is to attend diligently to those concerns that are proper to the people; and to respect the spirits and maintain the proper distance from them" [147]. Still more telling is this : "He sacrificed to the spirits as if they were present" [148]. First, this seems to shift the emphasis from the field of religion to that of society; second, it betrays a certain coldness with regard to celestial beings. Nevertheless, he judged it necessary to venerate Heaven in which he probably saw an abstract entity instead of a personified divinity. As Creel writes : "Confucius though of Heaven as an impersonal ethical force, a cosmic counterpart of the ethical sense in man, a guarantee that somehow there is sympathy with man's sense of right in the very nature of the universe" [149]. He conceived of himself as mandated by Heaven, that is, acting as if prompted by a superior moral power [150].

18. Confucius the humanist

Confucius' way of thinking was humanist or socio-political rather than religious or philosophical. He observed that in his day society, or rather the state, had taken precedence over the individual. The commoner seemed to be at the bidding of the state; he only existed to obey, to pay, to serve, or even to be sacrificed for what was supposed to be the common good. The Master was no upholder of sheer individualism to the detriment of society; in his view man is a social being moulded to no small extent by society. But likewise he did not consider society a hypostatic entity higher and more exalted than the sum of the individuals who constitute it. Man doubtless has social duties and he must co-operate with his fellow-beings, but he should not sacrifice his own moral conscience to society [151].

The fact that the idea of society, of the state, had no metaphysical connotations for Confucius goes a long way to explain why he never called the ruler 'the Son of Heaven'. Did he deny the famous 'Heavenly Mandate'? At any rate, he did not speak about it. In his opinion there existed no hereditary right to rule : the ruler's claim to sovereign power must be based on character and fitness to govern. This enabled him to hope that in the future one of his disciples would ascend the throne [152]. There should be no class distinctions of any kind; all government action should be taken on behalf of the people and for the good of the people as a whole [153]. This does not make the Master into a democrat western style. By no means! Innately conservative as he was, he found that the best must rule, and he understood by 'the best' those who were well-educated and well-trained and had a talent for government.

Here a rather sharp opposition, even a somewhat dualistic element in Confucius' ideology emerges. With all his high ideas of 'the people' he did not think the commoners fit to govern. This task had to be entrusted to the gentlemen. Of course, these must take care to win and to preserve the confidence of the people by not acting against its interests. But nothwithstanding all this, he viewed the people 'as a large passive force'. Commoners would only behave in the desired moral way if they were presented with models of ethical behaviour. And these, of course, were to be provided by the gentlemen. They, and they alone, had been educated in the proper, i.e. in the Confucian way and possessed 'the requisite vision' [154]. No wonder then that, as Dawson states, "this Confucian message was used by imperial governments for political control". However, in order to exonerate the Master somewhat from the accusation later brought forward against him that he strove to keep the people down, it must be remembered that he was thinking of the small states that existed in his day and not of the enormous Celestial Empire of several centuries later [155].

It seems to me that Confucius's great attempt to find an equilibrium in the relationship between rulers and ruled is not without a trace of dualism. It is somewhat biassed in favour of those who govern and makes a distinction between the active governors and the passive commoners, between those who give the example and those who follow the example of their betters. Respecting this point Creel too admits that "there was a very obvious weak point in this political program that Confucius proposed ... The common people of his day were, in any case, both uneducated and without political experience. Almost the only thing he (Confucius) could do, therefore, was to try, through education, to influence young men who were to be ministers" [156]. Some of his disciples indeed acquired positions of rank.

19. Confucians and Legalists

During the confused period that followed the Master's death, the time of the Warring States, Confucian scholars of different brands were much in vogue with the rulers. Many of these seem to have believed that Confucian philosophy was political magic. And, as Creel adds, "the philosophers did not discourage this opinion". Several of them propagated the view that "if only a ruler could get hold of the right philosophy (Creel's underlining), it would enable him to control the entire Chinese world" [157].

In this same period there was strong competition from the side of those Legalists who have already been referred to in these pages. In many respects they formed an absolute contrast to Confucianism. It is somewhat dangerous to speak of 'the Legalists' as though they formed one single school. This was not the case. Legalists were hard-headed practical men who did not bother to reach their goal by means of education. Whereas Confucius was at bottom a conservative trying to preserve the best of the Shang and Zhou periods, the

Legalists were bold and radical. They desired to abolish feudalism, and, in its place, establish a centralized state. To many rulers this seemed, of course, a highly attractive idea, probably more so than the somewhat vague ethical precepts of Confucianism.

The evident consequence of the political theory of the Legalists was that the freedom of the individual that Confucius had proclaimed was nothing to them. The people had to be kept ignorant; educated commoners were considered dangerous. "The reason why the people are hard to govern is because they know too much", the Laozi complains [158]. The Legalist Han Fei (he died in 223 B.C.) expresses his contempt of Confucian scholars in the following terms : "Cultivating benevolence and righteousness they are trusted and given governemental posts; cultivating literary learning they become famous teachers, renowned and exalted; these are the accomplishments of a common fellow. Thus it comes about that without any real merit they receive posts, and though without noble rank they are exalted; when the goverment follows such practices the state must fall into disorder, and the ruler be endangered" [159]. What is so remarkable in these words is not the obvious jealousy they reveal but rather Han Fei's opinion that there is no real merit in righteousness and learning. Legalism and Confucianism are dualistically opposed ideologies. They, however, agree in one point : the good of the people should be entrusted to the supreme ruler. But then they part ways on the question how the good of the people should be interpreted.

20. The Qin and Han emperors and Confucianism

The First Emperor was delighted with Han Fei's ideas. Han Feizi (a legalist treatise) told him that a ruler should not be benevolent and that the commoners had to be at his beck and call. Idealism was nothing but weakness; force was the prop of supremacy. It was utter nonsense to look for virtuous ministers; these would never be available in sufficient numbers. And they must not be too clever, for then they would hoodwink the sovereign. The supreme norm of everybody's conduct must be the interest of the state. Strictly in accordance with Legalist ideology it was stated that "all speech and action which is not in accordance with the laws and decrees is to be prohibited" [160].

The First Emperor was exactly the man to relish such lofty notions. The reader already knows how ruthlessly he rose to power and with what a hard hand he governed his empire. We also have seen how this ruler raged against dissidents. For the time being Confucianism had to keep a very low profile whereas Legalism was the dominating ideology of the state. But the Qin dynasty was extremely short-lived; already the first Han emperor was more favourably disposed towards Confucianism. The Emperor Wendi is even said to have been a full-blown Confucianist which did not prevent him from appointing a Legalist tutor for his son.

Actually, the Han rulers never became wholly Confucian; Confucian scholars were not political enough for their taste; therefore they continued to lean to some extent on Legalists, at least as advisers. Then, under the Emperor Wudi (140-87 B.C.) the 'triumph of Confucianism' came. The Confucian examination system became the basis for official promotions; a Confucian university was founded while adherents of the Legalist doctrine no longer could hold government posts [161]. But this emperor was at the same time a very stern ruler, heavily punishing evildoers, imposing very severe penal laws on the people, and cherishing warfare and annexations. His model seems to have been the First Emperor. So, if Confucianism triumphed, its victory was only partial. Creel states that in this process (of official recognition) "Confucianism was perverted and distorted in a manner that would have horrified Confucius ... as in fact it horrified genuine Confucians of Emperor Wu's own day" [162].

What I am asking myself is whether this distortion - the way the autocrats made use of a noble doctrine - was not the inevitable consequence of the original sin of Confucianism. From the very first this ideology wanted to influence state policy directly and always showed a predilection for officials far more than for the people. It did not act according to the prescript Jesus Christ gave his disciples

: "Give to God what is of God, and to the emperor what is of the emperor" [163]. This doubtless means that the spheres should be kept apart; Jesus of Nazareth did not want to gain influence by means of political power.

21. Confucian education

Confucianism booked its most conspicuous successess not in the field of politics but in that of education. The Master himself was a very informal teacher; his method consisted in what English scholars would call 'tutoring', i.e. suggesting, discussing, indicating books, also listening attentively to what the pupils bring forward. There were as yet no examinations. Later, however, schooling became much more formalized; examinations acquired pride of place in the educational system. This system produced what we call 'mandarins', cultivated administrators. What would have pleased the Master is that the educational system enabled members of the non-priveliged classes to obtain office (although in practice sons of bureaucrats always had the best chances). What would have angered him is that the subject matter mainly consisted of book-learning, the Confucian classics. Though it is certainly true that the examination system narrowed down the original Confucian ideals, on the other hand it ensured that government functions were not hereditary, and that officials were men of some culture. But it can also be argued that it created some sort of dichotomy in the Chinese population, between those who qualified for the examination and those for whom this was out of reach, i.e. between the cultured and the uneducated, between those who governed and those who obeyed.

22. Mohist pessimism

a. Mo's puritanism

Probably the first to break away from Confucianism was Mo Di, or Mozi = Master Mo. Of his life we know next to nothing. He was born either in the state of Lu or in that of Sung and lived in the late fifth and early fourth century B.V., between 481/480 and 390 or 381 B.C. He is reported to have been of humble origin and to have held a minor office. Mo was educated in the Confucian doctrine but was not wholly pleased with the Master's way of thought. He agreed with Confucius on several points : that governors should rule in accordance with the wishes of the people, that instruction was the basis of a good education, that there existed no hereditary right to rule, and that only capable and well-instructed persons should be administrators [164].

Basically, Mo took a pessimistic view of human nature. Man was innately egoistic, he found. According to him, the worst egotists were the aristocrats, what with their expensive meals and all those weddings and funerals that could last for days and weeks. He also frowned on the religious festivals that were much too costly for his taste. At heart he remained a plebeian who abhorred the aristocratic pleasures of life such as music, dancing, and elegant clothes. He himself and his disciples, lived ascetically, 'all clad in coarse garments and straw sandals' [165]. This opposition to the privileged classes also made him averse to the political institutions that were the prop and mainstay of the Zhou regime. Being in this respect still more conservative than Confucius, he harked back to the legendary times of the Emperor Yu who is said to have been a model of self-discipline and mortification [166].

b. Mo's concept of universal love

The doctrine that Mo Di preached placed him four-square opposite the ideology of the rulers of the day, and even to that of Confucius. True enough, the Master had also preached love, but Mo Di thought that there were questionable degrees of love in his predecessor's system. One should love one's parents and ancestors first and foremost, Confucius taught, so that there only remained a lesser love for one's fellow-creatures. Further, one should love one's country which, argued Mo, implied that one had to condone the warlike and aggressive acts of the state [167].

No, if love had to be truly universal, it should be egalitarian, with the same amount of it shown to everyone. Of course, Mo Di would not satisfy himself with a vague sentiment of all-embracing sympathy. One of his greatest tenets is his total condemnation of wars of aggression. Without denying the right of the state to defend itself against an attack by another state, he considered aggressive warfare, for whatever reason, as utterly detrimental to the well-being of the people; even victories in the long run had a bad effect [168]. A notion like this one would be highly explosive at any time but especially in this period that was called that of 'the Warring States'. Mo Di believed that the original state of civilization had been peaceful and warless; he wanted to reintroduce this ideal situation. Politics should serve the interests of the people and enrich it. The population should grow in numbers steadily; he pleaded for a law that would oblige every young man of twenty to found a family, and every young girl of fifteen to marry [169].

Does not an ugly element of compulsion creep into the sublime concept of universal love here? Mo Di is not the sole social reformer in history for whom general happiness is not incompatible with some amount of pressure; think only of Plato's Republic (Vol. III, Ch. III, 14). Quite in accordance with this but contrary to what the reader might expect, Mo Di "advocated a rigidly disciplined organization of the state". The ruler was the representative of Heaven and, therefore, the final arbiter of good and evil [170].

Failing to inculcate the politicians of his day with his ideas, Mo Di bound his adherents together in a well-organized body. It is for this reason that we are speaking of the 'Mohist School', or 'Mohism', and of 'Mohists'. After the death of Mo Di himself, the Mohist movement was led by a Grand Master. Although on principle peaceful, it was cast in a military mould, and as such was feared by the authorities of that time. The Mohists, indeed, were quite ready to take action if the need arose; for instance, they defended by force of arms the city walls of Song with three hundred men against aggressors from Chu [171].

Mohism flourished during the time of the Warring States but seems to have lost much of its significance once China became unified.

c. Mohism and Confucianism at loggerheads

It goes without saying that Mohism stood at right angles to the dominany political ideology and practice of that confused period and was, therefore, not popular with the authorities. But how must its relationship with Confucianism be envisaged? Strange as it may sound, there was very little love lost between the two schools in spite of the important tenets held in common. For Mohists the precept of universal love did not apply to Confucians. We surely are justified in speaking of a dualistic opposition here. As Liu states, "the battle between the two camps was particularly violent" [172]. The deviating doctrine of the Mohists infuriated the Confucians. Social discrimination also played its role since the Confucians were aristocratic and the Mohist plebeian. As far as I know the parties did not actually come to blows but resorted to abuse [173].

Let us now take a dispassionate look at the real differences between Confucianism and Mohism. First of all, Mo Di was more traditionally religious than Master Kong. To him Heaven was the supreme power but he also believed in spirits and demons. In this he was probably more in accordance with popular sentiment [174]. Second, education is the corner-stone of the Confucian system, whereas Mo Di thought more of practical accomplishments; music, for instance, that for the Master was a great civilizing, even humanizing force, meant nothing to Mo Di [175]. Then, whereas Confucianism may be dubbed 'humanist', with an aristocratic flavour, Mohism is more 'populist', more socially minded, and placing the emphasis on the plight of the underprivileged. But the greatest difference doubtless is that Confucius' leading idea is 'righteousness', and that of Mo Di 'profitableness'. It is for this reason that scholars speak of Mo Di's 'utilitarianism'. Music, for example, may give pleasure but is not profitable. Real profit is brought about by augmenting the population, by establishing peace, and by ameliorating the economic condition of the people [176]. Thus, although both schools wanted to promote general well-being, they were radically at variance with regard to the means for achieving this as well as to the underlying philosophy.

23. Mengzi's optimism

Tradition has it that, at his death, Confucius had seventy disciples who scattered in all directions. Some succeeded in becoming ministers in feudal states, others were active as teachers. But, on the whole, Confucianism did not prosper in this period of continuous warfare. After some time proper Confucian education only existed in the states of Chu and Lu. It was in one of these states that Mengke (Meng-Ko) was born, later called 'Mengzi' (Meng-Tzu) = Master Meng, which name was latinized by the Jesuits into 'Mencius'. His dates are traditionally given as from 371 to 289 B.C. Of his life too very little is known. He worked as a teacher until he was forty, then spent twenty years of his life in persuading feudal lords in adhering to his ideas, and finally returned to Lu to take up teaching again [177].

What Mencius set out to do was to preserve and to transmit the Confucian heritage, he was a fervent admirer of the Master : "Now what I desire to do is to study to be like Confucius" [178]. Actually he considered himself the only person to whom Confucius' work could be safely entrusted. "If there is a desire that the world should enjoy tranquillity and good order, who is there to-day, besides myself, to bring it about?" [179]. To bring tranquillity and order to the world is a lofty claim, even if we assume that Mencius's horizon very probably was limited to his direct environment. This claim, however, becomes more understandable when we know that the philosopher took a highly optimistic view of human nature. "Human nature is disposed towards goodness just as water tends to flow downwards" [180]. This does not mean that the people are always doing the right thing : "In its (human nature's) reality (what is meant is its essence - F.), it is possible to be good. This is what I mean by saying that it is good. If men do what is not good, it is not the fault of their natural powers" [181].

But if doing wrong is not the fault of the people's innate nature, it must be the political institutions and the economic conditions that lead them astray.

In the disorderly situation of the period of the Warring States Mencius was looking for an 'ideal king' who would show the people the 'wangdao' = the royal way. His subjects would readily obey him since they were sure that all laws and decrees promulgated by such a king would only serve to further their real interests [182]. This ideal sovereign would, of course, receive the Mandate of Heaven. He would have no revelations from Heaven but "it (Heaven) indicates its will through his personal conduct and by his conduct of affairs" [183]. The proof that the Imperial Mandate really comes from above is whether or not the people obeys the royal rule. The commoners are the most important element in Mencius' political theory. If they reject a bad ruler, he must be deposed [184].

Does this make Mencius into a 'democratic thinker', as Liu suggests [185]? I don't think so! What the people must do is obey, and no more. Even the right to depose a wicked ruler is left to his ministers. In his purely theoretical optimism about human nature Mencius is forgetting that potentates use to interpret a celestial or popular mandate in their own favour. That people obey them proves that they have a sublime mandate; so they make people obey them. In this way the proof is always demonstrated. May the ministers depose them? Very well! They surround themselves with their favourites who never will act against them. History abounds with potentates who, whether or not they were aware of it, made a very subtle use of Mencius' theory. Well-meant as this is, in the end it only strengthened and widened the gulf between the authorities and the population.

24. One of the Hundred Schools

Mencius showed himself sometimes irritated by what he called would-be philosophers. "Unemployed scholars indulge in unreasonable discussions" [186]. In his day philosophical schools were indeed proliferating so much so that an ancient Chinese treatise spoke of 'the Hundred Schools' [187]. Since it is not my intention to present a review of ancient Chinese philosophy but only to discuss some special aspects of it, I shall restrict myself to a few points.

The Confucian pope who followed Mencius was Xun Qing (Hsün Ch'ing), or Xun Kuang (Hsün K'uang); he too is known as 'Xunzi' = Master Xun. He was born between 340 and 298 B.C., in the feudal state of Zhao (Chao), not far from Lu, the cradle of Confucianism. The first fifty years of his life are covered in obscurity. Later he acquired fame as a scholar, led for some time the life of the wandering sage, and finally got a magistrate's office in the state of Chu. He is reported to have died around 235 B.C.

In contrast to Mencius, he had a very low opinion of human nature. Man simply is bad. What he wants to do is to follow his wicked lusts inhibitedly. Every tendency to be good is only articificial; it must be implanted by means of education and kept in its place by severe laws. Master Xun obviously belongs to the genre of the disillusioned idealist. A very important role falls to the 'wise ruler' who alone is capable of steering society into the right direction. How such a ruler manages to be wise while all others are unwise is not explained. It will be self-evident that in Xun's system, the people remain even more unemancipated, and that the distance between ruler and subjects is still greater that it is in the systems of Confucius and Mencius.

The corner-stone of this master's practical philosophy is education. No good can be realized without it. Ritual observance and music were very important to him. We must, however, not think of him as a very religious man. As Liu remarks, he divorced religion from philosophy [188]. Or perhaps we should say that he emancipated philosophy from religion? For, to quote Liu again, "he set out to prove that the salvation of man lay in himself alone, and not, as religious people would say, in Heaven ... It was his disbelief in Heaven's dispositions that had convinced him of the necessity of man's own exertions" [189].

This process of growing agnosticism had already started with Confucius and was completed by Xun for whom philosophy and religion seemed to be in dualistic opposition. He was, of course, not the only one to think in this way. Liu calls Xun's efforts 'a laudable undertaking'. He (Liu) declares that religion "never again would become the chief concern of Chinese intellectuals except for a few erratic souls" [190]. The dualism I spoke of shines very clearly through this highly denigrating term 'erratic'!

25. Dao, the Way

a. What is Daoism?

During his peregrinations Confucius met persons, sometimes grouped around a master, who were wholly impervious to his teaching and even loathed it. They were peasants, or rather, they chose to live like peasants shunning public life and in particular the courts. This was because they despaired of society. There can be no doubt that, with these peculiar people, we are in the presence of Daoism (Taoism) or of the way of life that would develop into Daoism [191].

'Dao' (Tao) is a very common Chinese word signifying 'road' or 'pathway' [192]. However, it soon acquired the status of a basic philosophical concept [193] coming to mean 'the right way', the manner in which things should be done. This widening of the meaning of Dao occurred during the Zhou period, roughly between 770 and 250 B.C. [194]. In its sense of right conduct it is common to all Chinese doctrines including Confucianism; in fact, this meaning of the term first appears in Confucian texts [195].

Herrlee Creel, an expert on ancient Chinese philosophy, who wrote an article with the intriguing title 'What is Taoism?', on his very first page adjures the reader that he is not going to answer this question. For there is not one school of Daoism but a whole congeries of doctrines. However, seeing from behind his writing-desk the bewildered faces of his readers, Creel admits that "if one is to discuss Taoism, he must at least have a reasonably clear conception of what it is" [196]. Our starting-point is that the term 'Dao' means far more to Daoists than to Confucians [197], to Confucius it is a principle, to Daoists it is a substance.

Before I proceed the explain the Daoist philosophy, we must ascertain from where exactly we derive our knowledge of early Daoism. The Daoist Bible is the 'Dao De jing' (Dao Te Ching) or 'Laozi' (Lao Tzu). 'Dao De jing' means 'A Classic Work on the Way and its Power' (de = virtue or power); Laozi is the man reported to have written it. Its origin is shrouded in mystery. Tradition has it that Laozi was a somewhat older contemporary of Confucius. No modern scholar, however, believes that the book that bears his name originated around 500 B.C. A great Sinologist like Waley suggests ca. 240 B.C.; an equally great one, Maspero, would rather think of 400 B.C., while Fung more vaguely assigns it to the third century B.C. [198]. To the layman as well as to the expert it is highly confusing book, since it contains a great number of contradictory statements [199]. There exists yet another early Daoist classic, the 'Chuangzi' (Chuang Tzu); this is usually dated around 300 B.C. [200].

b. About Laozi

Now, what about a prophet called 'Laozi'? First of all, this is no name but an appellation meaning 'old master', and later latinized into 'Laotius'. Many reputable scholars do not believe that a man called Laozi ever existed. To them it is all legend. He is said to have been born on September 14, 604 B.C. in the present province of Henan, in a village where a temple with a big statue of the man still honours his birthplace. It is not certain whether his real name was Li Er (Li Eul) or Li Dan (Li Tan). We also find Lao Dan (Lao Tan) which evidently is a surname meaning 'the old one with the long earlobes', and, as already stated, Laozi, the Old Master. This last name is said to have been given to him not only because he is believed to have grown extremely old, but also because it is said that he was born with grey hair, then already an old man. Sages reach a very old age and have long ears. Tradition goes on to inform us that Laozi married, had a son, was a functionary of the Royal Palace at Loyang, met Confucius, and gathered disciples around him without ever founding a school. He died when he was a hundred and sixty or even two hundred years old [201]. But whether or not he is an historical person, or whenever he may have lived (those scholars who assume that he really existed assign him to a much later period), the final remark of Kaltenmark that Laozi the man "for us remains wrapped in impenetrable obscurity", is valid in all cases [202].

c. Dao, what it means

Kaleidoscopic as Daoism is, there is, as Creel states, 'one relatively fixed star : the term tao' [203], the Way. It is an substance as well as a method. It precedes all visible things; it is an eternal and primordial substance, a principle of supreme and absolute unity [204]. As such it may also be described as the way the universe operates, or as the ultimate reality [205]. Notions such as these often seduced western scholars to translate Daoist concepts into western ones, making in this way an incomprehensible Asian ideology palatable for European and American minds. Thus Dao will be rendered as 'God'. Dao was also compared to the intelligent and intelligible cause of all that is, often called the 'Logos'. Others preferred 'reason' [206].

Now Logos, reason, cause are intellectual concepts, and God, although not an intellectual concept, is the subject of a science called 'theology'. But hard as this may be to understand, Dao is not an idea nor a concept, and not even an entity and still less a thing but an all-pervading substance immanent in all things. As such it is 'formless but complete', undifferentiated but 'all pervading and unfailing'. It is the beginning of Heaven and Earth. "One may think of it as the mother of all that is beneath Heaven. We do not know its name but we term it 'Dao' " [207]. So, if Dao had to a god, it would be a 'deus ignotus'. He would be more at home in esoteric sects like the Gnosis than in Christianity. But although Dao is a substance, it is not an object (in the sense of western philosophy). Therefore, since objects have

Being, Dao may be described as Non-Being. But as it cannot do without Being, it is also Being [208]. This is one the many paradoxes that bedevil Daoist notions for western observers.

That Dao is also Non-Being does not mean that it is nothingness. On the other hand, it cannot be circumscribed in logical terms. "It is incommensurable, impalpable, yet latent in all entities ..." [209]. Being essentially primordial unity, even the unity of Being and Non-Being, Dao "brings the principle of all things into single agreement. Therefore it can be be both one thing and another, and is not in one thing only" [210]. In consequence, it is nameless.

d. Once again, the One and the Many

Here a very intriguing problem poses itself, that of the One and the Many, of unity and multiplicity. According to the Laozi [211], Dao (the absolute unity) produces oneness. This oneness is the Great Beginning, still a state of amorphous formlessness. Then 'an empty extensiveness' (= space) is produced; once there is space the cosmos can originate. From space a kind of cosmic energy flows forth, a 'primal fluid' or 'primordial breath' called 'yuanqi' (yüan-ch'i) in Chinese [212]. Now duality is produced; it is named 'Heaven and Earth', or also 'yin and yang'. From these 'the ten thousand things' (= all the phenomena of the cosmos) spring [213]. As we already know, yin and yang are complementary forces creating harmony, but they also differ from each other, sometimes sharply so.

On the face of it, it seems that the key-word of the universe is harmony. Multiplicity springs from duality, duality from oneness, oneness from the indescribable unity, all in a direct line of descent. This picture apparently grows still clearer when we look at the human body 'incorporating the totality of the universe'. Its parts correspond to the subdivisions of the cosmos. For instance, there are three hundred and sixty joints in our frame because the (Chinese) year counts three hundred and sixty days. In this way Heaven and Earth - the macrocosm - is present in the body. This means that human beings also have the primordial breath, the yuanqi, within them. It makes people live and keeps them living. But at this point a pernicious flaw appears. The yuanqi of man gets exhausted and then people die [214].

That people die signifies that multiplicity has triumphed over unity; everything finally falls apart. This leads us to a consequence with a distinctly dualistic character. Daoists are no friends of the Many, of multiplicity and multiformity. They find too much diversity and change in the phenomenal world to take pleasure in it. Therefore, they turn their backs on this world and want to strive back to that primal unity that is the ultimate reality [215]. They start this process by making a sharp differentiation between that 'which is of Heaven', and that 'which is of Man'. Of course, Daoists know that the phenomenal world, including Man, is irrevocably doomed to be multiple, and that this cannot be helped. But hopeless as the situation already is, it can be made still worse. One of the great means to spoil it profoundly, so that people get desperately entangled in multiformity, is learning. To Daoists, 'discursive learning' means 'introducing multiplicity into the soul' [216]. It is for this reason that they utterly abhor and reject Confucian education. In their view, it is wholly artificial, it is 'of Man', and as such wrong, since it is 'the contrived and intentional intrusion of the human mind into Nature' [217].

With the foregoing in mind the reader might reasonably expect that Daoism is profoundly averse to every form of government. To a large extent this was and is true. "I have heard of letting the world alone, but not of governing the world" [218]. Creel supplies us with the following intriguing information on 'the libertinarian tendency of Taoism'. "Only a few years ago (i.e. before 1951) Chen Duxiu (Ch'en Tu-hsiu), the then head of the Chinese Communist Party, complained that the anarchistic influence of the Daoist movement made it difficult to recruit young Chinese for communism" [219]. By the same token this proves that Daoism by no means is a thing of the past but is still a living force. But, as I already stated, this ideology is a paradoxical affair. "Although the law is harsh, it is impossible to dispense with setting it forth", to quote the same Daoist source as before

220). This, and other quotations, even enabled Legalists to appeal to Daoism to justify their advocacy of stern governemental rule.

Understandably enough, many western scholars are thinking here of two different schools of thought in early Daoism. Creel, however, believes that Daoism, as essentially one and indivisible, has two aspects, respectively 'contemplative' and 'purposive'. In the same breath he admits that these two aspects are at variance with each other [221]. Contemplative Daoism is mystical, it is averse to activity, and is wholly concerned with the quest for immortality. No expert on Daoism will deny this. But then Creel goes on to say that true mysticism is a rare phenomenon practised by the happy few only. Other Daoists, more down-to-earth perhaps, were more enraptured with the personal power that Daoism gave them. Such men would willingly engage in official duties while rulers found in them the right type of official [222].

I do not feel qualified to take issue on this point. But it is hardly to be doubted that there have existed two different kinds of Daoists, the true mystics and the common run. So if Creel is right, then the two currents of thought evidently are at loggerheads with each other. Genuine mystics must have accused the more practical ones of utilizing 'an essentially mystical doctrine for the furtherment of personal ambitions and political purposes'. Of course, there is no contemplative quiet for somebody who wants to throw himself into the stream of political affairs [223]. Do we not see Christians too restless to live up to the maxim 'to be in the world but not of the world'? It proves much easier to be 'in the world' than, at the same time, 'not of it'. Of course, Daoists did their utmost to show that at bottom the two states of mind were not incompatible. For did Daoist politicians not exert themselves 'to return people to their natural state' [224].

e. The gods of Daoism

In the opinion of most scholars, Dao essentially is a religion rather than a philosophy, let alone a political ideology, or, like Confucianism, a way of life or a code of ethics. It was the famous Sinologist Maspero who set the tone : "Ancient Taoism is, before all, a religion" [225]. But who is the god, or who are the gods, of Daoism? There is that 'primordial breath', the yuanqi, that, however, is not a god. This breath diversifies itself into a great number of 'breaths' which serve to constitute the phenomenal world. This is the basic cosmogonic process for numerous gods and goddesses originate, but far from being creators, they form part of the creational process. They too, like the world, are made of 'breaths'. So there is no specific creation (neither is there in Confucianism). The host of these gods is immense; the human body alone is inhabited by thousands and thousands of them, thirty thousand, says one Daoist source [226].

These gods play only a very subordinate role in the fabric of the cosmos. They do not govern or regulate it and have no influence on the world or the human body. According to Chinese thought, the world takes care of itself without having need of gods meddling in its course. The purpose the gods serve is not to supply mortals with a doctrine or a creed but with moral prescriptions which will enable man to become immortal [227]. It is in order to receive these prescriptions that Daoists address themselves to their gods rather than venerate them. Daoist gods have nothing mysterious about them; believers are extremely familiar with them. In so far as Daoists knew religious awe, it was inspired by the primordial Dao. Maspero thinks that this familiarity was one of the causes of the decadence of Daoism. Religious minds which did not feel satisfied with these all too common divinities later turned to Buddhism and Confucianism. He supposes that, in a rejuvenated Confucianism, they found 'a more philosophical presentation of the world' [228]. True enough probably, but did these disillusioned Daoists find there the religious satisfaction they wanted?

f. A doctrine of salvation

If Daoism really has to be a religion, it essentially is a doctrine of salvation, or rather, perhaps, a practice of salvation. Its goal is 'illumination', the 'return to a state of tranquillity', and, finally, to

Dao [229]. This really is the other way round, literally, for the way of men does not ascend back to Dao, but goes downward towards Death. Daoist believers are confronted by an iron-clad fact : all people die, even Daoists. Hence the paramount problem becomes how to triumph over Death and thus to reverse the natural order of things. On the face of it, this seems impossible : the Daoists did not have the technical means at their disposal with the help of which the Egyptians secured their bodily survival after their decease. Had the Daoists known it, very probably they would have considered it too materialistic. The method they preferred using was spiritual purification.

We should not think, however, that Daoists believed in a purely spiritual, wholly immaterial existence in the hereafter. Unable as they were to distinguish between spirit and matter as sharply as westerners, they took it for granted that the whole person, with the body, would survive. Survival? In the body? But Daoists were seen to die and to be interred. The Chinese, including the Daoists, do not believe, like Christians, in the resurrection of the body. The adherents found a way out of this dilemma by making these words of the Book of Wisdom their own, albeit in a sense differing from that of the biblical author : "In the eyes of the foolish they seemed to die" [230]. Their death was only apparent. The thing that was enterred was not their body but some object or other, a stick or a sabre, that had assumed the shape of their body. Their real physical presence escaped Death and returned to the dish of the Immortals [231].

g. Daoist practices

Was it really sufficient to be a Daoist believer to triumph over the mortal fiend, the dualistic enemy of Dao? By no means! The road to purification was long and arduous and not open to everyone. The Daoist wishing to achieve immortality, in the form of longevity, had to subject himself to an ascetic way life full of difficult exercises. This way of life consisted of a public and a private cult, of mystical introspection by means of concentration and contemplation, of following moral precepts such as the injunction to give alms, and of bodily discipline as exemplified by following dietary rules, breathing techniques, gymnastics, and so on; such practices were considered very important for securing longevity [232].

One of the corner-stones of the Daoist doctrine is the principle of 'wu wei' or non-action [233]. To be a genuine Daoist one must sense this, or rather, the Daoist himself must become wu wei, inwardly silent and outwardly quiet. "He who acts harms, he who grabs lets slip", is a Daoist maxim [234]. Even promulgating laws does not have the desired effect. "The more laws you make the more thieves there are" [235]. Strange as it sounds, actively doing good too has its drawbacks. "Every straight is doubled by a crook, every good by an ill" [236]. Wu wei, however, does not mean 'doing nothing' but is best translated by 'not doing'. Fond of paradoxes as he is, Laozi says that "the Sage relies on actionless activity" [237]. Doing nothing at all is, of course, impossible; every human being is active in some way or other. Daoists too 'do' things. But they keep their distance. The situation in the phenomenal world is, in their opinion, beyond repair; they have nothing against making the confusion still worse as far as they are forced to take part in it. But as spiritual beings they strive after coming nearer to the innermost mysteries by means of meditation and contemplation.

Daoists believe that everyone has a vital principle, the 'Vital Breath'. Most people neglect this, with the result that they die. It is necessary to tend and to nourish it. This leads to a regime that is as ascetic as it is hygienic. The way Daoists practice sexuality falls on the hygienic side. Many esoteric societies of the kind I am describing here are very reticent with regard to, sometimes averse to, sexuality. By the same token they consider women inferior or downright dangerous. This is not the case in Daoism. The principle of the universe is seen as female; according to Laozi, femininity far surpasses manly virtues [238], doubtless because these manly virtues are much too boisterous. There even is a 'Mysterious Female' that gave birth to Heaven and Earth [239]. Sexual union is not seen as detrimental; only the inconsiderate use of sexual potency is viewed as dangerous, for instance at full moon [240].

The principle of copulation is that it unites yang (male) and yin (female). The Adept has to take certain precautions to avoid wasting the vital essence which is the sexual fluid in the wrong circumstances. But on the whole sexual activity is considered conducive to longevity; it is even sometimes advised to sleep with several women, although in this case the male must take care not to ejaculate every time [241]. There also exist festivities where sexual activity, called 'Union of the Vital Breathes', was practised in common. Such promiscuity was thought to prolong life, to be beneficial to health, to forgive sins, and to avert ills. Everybody, with the exception of the not yet married girls, could take part. One author says that during such orgies men and women 'mixed like animals' [242]. Buddhist and Confucian scholars speak with disgust of these sex festivals [243].

It will be self-evident that Daoists follow a rigorous diet. As far as I know they are no vegetarians; they rather are averse of cereals because their 'breath' is injurious. What really nourishes the 'vital principle' are the 'breathes'; these enter the human organism through the respiratory system. To have the desired profit from the incoming 'breathes', it is necessary to regulate the respiration in a minute way. There are several methods for realizing this; they must all be learned and trained. The bodily position is also important. This leads us to the necessity of special gymnastics; there exist cycles of exercises that must be performed every day [244].

It goes without saying that a Daoist is a contemplative. Aided by keeping aloof from the (in his eyes useless) bustle of daily affairs, and trained by techniques of breathing and postures of sitting, he can easily concentrate himself and ponder on things beyond this world. In doing so he is in harmony with the eternal law of the universe. For Dao itself is quiet, silent, unmoving, far beyond every changing thing. "Realizing the presence of Dao produces wisdom" [245]. No practical wisdom is meant. To start being active would spoil everything. The real wisdom is to know that, in the final stages of contemplation, in the mystical union, the perfect Adept has become one with Dao, even becomes Dao himself. The body is absorbed by the spirit; the

Adept has shed all knowledge, for knowledge is discursive, distinctive, and exterior. He is in Dao now, and since Dao is in everything and everyone, he too, having fused with the Ultimate Reality, is in everything and everyone [246].

h. The Daoist 'Church'

It is to be expected that esoteric and unmistakably elitist people like the Daoists will organize themselves in a closely knit body. There seems, however, to have been no trace of an organization before the period of the Latter Han (ca. 25 - 220 A.D.) [247]. From then on a community became visible that in the Six Dynasties Period (220 - 589) was in full swing; several scholars call it the 'Daoist Church' on account of its solid structure. We find here the same bipartitions we already discovered in other esoteric communities like the Pythagorean fraternity (Vol. I, Ch. I, 5). First there is the dualistic distinction between insiders and outsiders, between the ignorant and the initiated. The Daoists disposed of a mysterious knowledge that was denied to all others; its fruit was Immortality, the Mystical Union with Dao. The others formed the 'massa damnata', of those condemned to death.

In the Church (I don't think that this is quite the appropriate term) there were again two classes. First there was the mass of believers, the 'Dao min', the great majority. They were not too strict, did not strive after perfection, and did not follow all the precepts. The most genuine Daoists were the 'Dao shi', the 'practitioners of Dao'. They worked hard for their own salvation while the Dao min expected their salvation from them [248]. The Daoist community possessed no central authority; Welch calls it 'atomistic' since all its parishes and monasteries were autonomous. The Dao shi acted as priests; among them there were three kinds : low-level priests, high-level priests, and chief priests [249]. Later there was also a Grand Master, or 'Celestial Master'; this, however, was more a honorary position than one of real authority.

26. A final overview

Taken together, the religious picture of ancient China is not very complicated. We have only to do with Confucianism, with Mohism, with Daoism, and with Buddhism (leaving aside the tribal religions). Of these Confucianism is not really a dualist ideology. It secular aim was to make human society more harmonious, but by putting a great deal of emphasis on governmental action, it strengthened the arm of the state rather than raising the status of the common people. At the same time, by giving such a paramount importance to education, it created a wide gap between those were educated and those who remained illiterate.

Mohism may be seen as a reaction to Confucianism. It was more religious and more populist. The relationship of Confucianism and Mohism was undoubtedly dualistic. Then there was Daoism, a distinctly dualistic creed. It not only turned its back on society but rejected the phenomenality and multiformity of the historical world. With regard to the old problem of the precedence of the One or the Many, it resolutely chose for the One; it thought lowly of visible reality and reached after the Ultimate Reality with all its might.

Finally, there was Buddhism. Nearly all that had to be said of this ideology was said in Chapter II of this volume. I need only describe shortly its introduction into China. It was not until the first century A.D. that Buddhism reached China. The missionaries who brought it, armed with Buddhist scripture, made use of the famous Silk Road, and, in consequence, entered the country from the northwest. For a long time the only area of China where Buddhism existed was the north; in the third century A.D. it also gained a foothold in the south. In the sixth century Buddhism had become an essential part of Chinese culture. But even in the north the number of Buddhists during the period of disunion cannot have been impressive. Contact between Buddhist monasteries in China and those in India was, at that time of history, both rare and difficult. A negative factor probably was that the new religion was experienced as foreign. But still more it must have proved confusing to the Chinese that there were so many Buddhist sects and schools. Later the logical Chinese mind tried to elaborate principles of unity and coherent systems.

To Confucians, with their basically secular view of life, Buddhism seemed quaintly otherworldly. Since it had not sprung from Chinese soil, they considered it as something barbarian. Daoists, on the other hand, seem to have believed that Buddhism was in fact a branch of their own religion. Meditation, contemplation, breathing techniques, mystical union, we find them in both systems. But soon enough Daoists discovered that Buddhists abhorred important Daoist tenets and practices. For instance, whereas Daoists propagated sexual promiscuity with a ritual character, Buddhists thought that sex is impure. Furthermore, it was a painful experience for the Daoists that exactly because of this real or supposed kinship between the two ways of thought, Daoism lost far more of its adherents to the new religion than Confucianism. Summing up, we must conclude that, in the period I am covering in this work, Buddhism went through two successive stages that Zürcher dubs 'embryonic' (ca. 50 - ca. 300) and 'formative' (ca. 300 - 589) 250)

NOTES TO CHAPTER III

1) Throughout this chapter I am using the modern and official pinyin spelling. When a name or a Chinese expression is given for the first time, I place the older spelling in brackets behind it.
2) Hulsewé 479.
3) Van der Horst 19.
4) Morton 13.
5) Hulsewé 487.
6) Eberhard 14-16.
7) Hulsewé 491.
8) Morton 15.
9) Morton 15.
10) Reischauer 38.
11) Reischauer 47-49.
12) Hulsewé 499; Reischauer 49/50; Eberhard 29.
13) Hulsewé 500.

14) Li 46/47.
15) Li 48/49.
16) Hulsewé 500; van der Horst 24; Li 49/50.
17) Eberhard 38.
18) Eberhard 39.
19) Reischauer 60.
20) Eberhard 40/41.
21) Li 50.
22) Reischauer 60.
23) Hulsewé 503-506.
24) Li 50.
25) Li 52.
26) Li 53/54.
27) Eberhard 27/28.
28) Morton 25.
29) Morton 28.
30) Van der Horst 27/28.
31) Van der Horst 32 and 106.
32) Li 56.
33) Reischauer 85.
34) Li 59.
35) Hulsewé 521.
36) Bodde 53.
37) Li 97-99.
38) Bodde 54-56.
39) Bodde 57.
40) Bodde 58.
41) Bodde 63.
42) Van der Horst 35.
43) Li 101.
44) Li 102.
45) Bodde 65.
46) Bodde 64/65.
47) Bodde 73.
48) Li 103.
49) Bodde 84; Li 103.
50) Bodde 84/85.
51) Eberhard 77.
52) Cit. Bodde 52.
53) Bodde 80.
54) Bodde 85.
55) Morton 49.
56) Eberhard 76.
57) Canetti, Provinz 138.
58) Canetti, Masse 487.
59) Hoover 43.
60) Hulsewé 528.
61) Li 104.
62) Li 104/105; Hulsewé 529.
63) Li 105.

64) Loewe, Former Han 104/105.
65) Loewe, Former Han 105/106.
66) Loewe, Former Han 106.
67) Loewe, Former Han 106.
68) Reischauer 95.
69) Reischauer 96.
70) Reischauer 42.
71) Reischauer 43.
72) Li 106; Reischauer 96.
73) Li 106.
74) See for a full description Loewe, Structure 463-490.
75) Reischauer 96.
76) Reischauer 98.
77) Yü 384/385.
78) Yü 385.
79) Yü 385/386.
80) Yü 387.
81) Yü 381.
82) Yü 388/389.
83) Reischauer 99.
84) Yü 390.
85) Reischauer 101.
86) Morton 55.
87) Yü 409.
88) Li 111.
89) Li 109.
90) Loewe, Concept 743.
91) Loewe, Concept 743-746.
92) Morton 57/58; van der Horst 47/48.
93) Morton 58/59.
94) Eberhard 117/118.
95) Eberhard 119/120; Morton 62/63.
96) Ch'en 774.
97) Ch'en 776.
98) Ch'en 795.
99) Li 129/130.
100) Eberhard 145/146.
101) Li 140.
102) Li 140.
103) Li 134.
104) Li 135.
105) Li 136.
106) Li 137-140.
107) Eichhorn 19-21.
108) Eichhorn 21-245.
109) Eichhorn 29-31.
110) Fung I 31.
111) Fung I 26.
112) Eichhorn 43; Granet 80-85.
113) Granet 283.

114) Cit. Fung I 178.
115) Fung I 178.
116) Fung I 395.
117) Granet 320.
118) Granet 97. Opera fans very probably will hear at this point the imposing chorus 'Dieci mill' anni al Imperatore' sung to the Emperor in Puccini's opera 'Turandot'.
119) Granet 298.
120) Granet 299/300.
121) Granet 76.
122) Eichhorn 83.
123) Eichhorn 85/86.
124) Cit. Fung I 179.
125) Fung I 165/166.
126) Creel, Confucius IX.
127) Dawson 6.
128) Kaltenmark, Phil.Chin. 11; Ching 38.
129) Creel. Confucius 25; see also his Ch. III 'The China of Confucius'.
130) Creel, Confucius 25.
131) Dawson 6.
132) Wilhelm 2.
133) Creel, Confucius 26/27.
134) Dawson 10.
135) Creel, Confucius 28.
136) His sayings, genuine or not, are collected in the so-called 'Analecta' that appeared many decades after his death. It was the disciples of a later generation who turned out the book, although we also find sayings by his disciples in it. To sum up what Creel says about its authenticity : some passages are wholly irrelevant, others questionable, ranging from the slightly dubious to the clearly false. But another part of it, the earliest chapters, must be considered authentic, Creel, Confucius, Appendix, 'The Authenticity of the Analects', 291-294.
137) Chan 16/17.
138) Liu 18.
139) Creel, Confucius 29.
140) Analecta 7.7, cit. Dawson 17.
141) Creel, Confucius 34.
142) Creel, Confucius 38-40.
143) Hulsewé 508.
144) Liu 25.
145) Analecta 13.30, cit. Creel, Chin.Thought 44.
146) Analecta 7.20, cit. Fung I 59.
147) Cit. by Creel, Confucius 115.
148) Analecta 3.12, cit. by Fung I 58.
149) Creel, Confucius 117.
150) See Creel, Confucius 114-117; Kaltenmark, Phil.Chin. 13/14; Eichhorn 51/52.
151) Creel, Confucius 44.
152) Analecta 6.1.1, cit. Creel, Chin.Thought 51.

153) Wilhelm 111.
154) Dawson 66.
155) Dawson 66 and 68.
156) Creel, Chin.Thought 55.
157) Creel, Confucius 174.
158) Cit. Creel, Confucius 213.
159) Cit. from the Han-Feizi, Creel, Confucius 213.
160) Cit. Creel, Confucius 215/216; see also Creel, Chin.Thought, Ch. VIII 'The Totalitarianism of the Legalists', 146-169.
161) Creel, Chin.Thought 170.
162) Creel, Chin.Thought 178.
163) Mt. 22:21; Mc. 12:17; Lc. 20:25.
164) Creel, Chin.Thought 6/63.
165) Liu 44.
166) Fung I 180.
167) Kaltenmark 48.
168) Kaltenmark 49.
169) Kaltenmark 51.
170) Creel, Chin.Thought 72/73.
171) Fung I 81 and 84; Liu 47.
172) Liu 47/48.
173) See Liu 15 for two theories on the terms of abuse.
174) Kaltenmark 49-51.
175) Fung I 86/87.
176) Fung I 84-87.
177) Hulsewé 516.
178) Mencius IIa 2.22, cit. Fung I 108.
179) Mencius IIb 13, cit. Fung I 108.
180) Mencius VI 1.2, cit. Liu 75.
181) Mencius VIa 6, cit. Fung I 121; see for 'ch'ing' by 'reality' Fung's note 2 on I 126.
182) Fung I 112.
183) Mencius VIa 5.6, cit. Fung I 115.
184) Liu 88.
185) Liu 74.
186) Mencius IIIb 0.9, cit. Fung I 132.
187) Chuangzi 33, cit. Fung I 132. It was these 'Hundred Schools' Mao Zhe Dong (Mao Tze Tung) was referring to when he said "Let a hundred flowers bloom", which the West mistakingly interpreted as an opening towards liberalism.
188) Liu 93.
189) Liu 93.
190) Liu 96; see for Xun, Liu Ch. VI; Fung I 150/151; Hulsewé 518.
191) Kaltenmark 33/34.
192) Nivison 284/285.
193) Nivison 283.
194) Nivison 285.
195) Creel, Taoism 2.
196) Creel, Taoism 1.
197) Creel, Taoism 2.

198) Welch 3; Fung I 413.
199) Creel, Taoism 1/2.
200) Creel, Taoism 2 and 5.
201) Welch 1/2; Kaltenmark, Lao Tseu 10-18.
202) Kaltenmark, Lao Tseu 18.
203) Creel, Taoism 2.
204) Baldrian 291.
205) Nivison 285.
206) Creel, Taoism 29/30.
207) Laozi 25, cit. Fung I 177; Nivison 285.
208) Fung I 178.
209) Laozi 21, cit. Fung I 179.
210) Han-Feizi, cit. Fung I 179.
211) Laozi 40, cit. Fung I 178.
212) Fung I 396; Baldrian 299.
213) Laozi 42, cit. Fung I 178.
214) Baldrian 299.
215) Baldrian 291.
216) Baldrian 291.
217) Nivison 285.
218) Chuangzi I 291, cit. Creel, Taoism 37.
219) Creel, Taoism 37, quoting from Benjamin S. Schwarz, Chinese Communism and the Rise of Mao. Cambridge (Mass.), 1951, 33.
220) Chuangzi I 305, cit. Creel, Taoism 37.
221) Creel, Taoism 38.
222) Creel, Taoism 44/45.
223) Creel, Taoism 44/45.
224) Creel, Taoism 45.
225) Maspero 353. This edition of essays by Maspero (who died in the Nazi concentration camp of Buchenwald is based on this author's 'Mélanges posthumes sur les religions et l'histoire de la Chine' published in 1950.
226) Maspero 470/471.
227) Maspero 473.
228) Maspero 447/448.
229) Baldrian 291.
230) Wisd. 3:2.
231) Maspero 469/470.
232) Maspero 481.
233) See for an excellent exposition of this subject Welch, Part Two, 1 Inaction.
234) Dao De jing 64 w, cit. Welch 20.
235) Dao De jing 57, cit. Welch 20.
236) Dao De jing 58 w, cit. Welch 23.
237) Dao De jing 2 w, cit. Welch 23.
238) Baldrian 291.
239) Dao De jing, cit. Welch 7.
240) See for the seven interdictions Maspero 566.
241) Maspero 553-557; on. p. 557 this scholar describes a Daoist technique of making the 'essence' mount to the brain.

242) Sun En, who died in 402.
243) Maspero 568-577.
244) See for a full description Maspero 479-589.
245) Maspero 314.
246) Maspero 315/316.
247) Lagerwey 306.
248) Maspero 318.
249) Lagerwey 306.
250) For the introduction of Buddhism in China see Zürcher, Enc.Rel. 2, 414-418, and Eichhorn 156-169 and 219-210.

BIBLIOGRAPHY

AGRAWALA, Vasudeva S., Siva Mahadevi. The Great God. An Exposition of the Symbolims of Siva. Varanasi (1966).

ALLCHIN, Bridget, and ALLCHIN, Raymond, The Birth of Indian Civilization. India and Pakistan before 500 B.C. Penguin Books, 1968.

ALTEKAR, A.S., The Position of Women in Indian Civilization from prehistoric times to the present day. Delhi (1962^3)(1938^1).

ALTHEIM, Franz, Das alte Iran. Propyläen Weltgeschichte. II. Berlin-Frankfurt-Wien (1962).

AMBEDKAR, B.R., Who were the Shudras? How they came to be the fourth Varna in the Indo-Aryan society. Bombay, 1970^3(1946^1).

AMMIANUS MARCELLINUS, Rerum Gestarum Libri XVII. Loeb Classical Library, 1956 (1935^1). Ed. John C. Rolfe.

ANANT, Santokh Singh, The Changing Concept of Caste in India. Delhi (1972).

APTE, V.M., Political and Legal Institutions. The History and Culture of the Indian People. Volume I The Vedic Age. London, 1951.

BALDRIAN, Farzeen, Taoism : an overview. Encyclopedia of Religion, Volume 14. New York/London, 1987.

BAREAU, André, Der Indische Buddhismus. II.1. Der Buddha und die frühe Gemeinschaft. II.2. Die Literatur. Die Religionen Indiens, III. Stuttgart (1964).

BASHAM, A.L., The Wonder that was India. A survey of the history and culture of the Indian subcontinent before the coming of the Muslims. London (1969)(1954^1).

BENVENISTE, E., Les Mages dans l'ancien Iran. Publications de la Société des Etudes Iraniennes, no. 15. Paris, 938.

BEVAN, E.R., India in early Greek and Latin literature. The Cambridge History of India. Volume I. Delhi (1955)(1921^1).

BHATTACHARJI, Sukumari, The Indian Theogony. A comparative study of Indian mythology from the Vedas to the Puranas. Cambridge, 1970.

BATTHACHARYA, B., Saivism and the Phallic World. New Delhi (1975).

BODDE, Derk, The state and the empire of Ch'in. The Cambridge History of China. Volume I. Cambridge (1986).

BOYCE, Mary, A History of Zoroastrianism. Volume II. Handbuch der Orientalistik. Erste Abteilung. 8. Bd. 1. Abschnitt. Lieferung 2. Heft 2A. Leiden, 1982².

BUCKLEY, Jorunn Jacobsen, Mandaean Religion. Encyclopedia of Religion. Volume 9. New York, 1987.

BUHLER, Johann George, The Indian Sect of the Jainas. Translated from the German by Ja^s Burgess. Calcutta (1963²)(German edition 1887; English translation 1903¹).

CANETTI, Elias, 1. Masse und Macht. Fischer Taschenbuch 1780. Frankfurt a.M., 1985 (1980)(1960¹).
2. Die Provinz des Menschen. Aufzeichnungen 1942-1972. Fischer Taschenbuch 1677. Frankfurt a.M., 1976(1973¹).

CHALLAYE, Félicien, Les philosophes de l'Inde. Paris, 1956.

CHAN, Wang-Tsit, Confucian Thought. Encyclopedia of Religion, Volume 4. New York/London, 1987.

CHATTERJI, S.K., Race-movements and Prehistoric Culture. The History and Culture of the Indian People. Volume I The Vedic Age. London 1951.

CHATTOPADHYAY, Amalkumar, Slavery in India. Calcutta, 1959.

CH'EN Ch'i-yün, Confucian, Legalist, Taoist Thought in Later Han. The Cambridge History of China. Volume I. Cambridge (1986).

CHILDE, Gordon V., The Aryans. A study of Indo-European origins. London, 1926.

CHING, Julia, Confucius. Encyclopedia of Religion. Volume 4. New York/London, 1987.

CHRISTENSEN, Arthur, L'Iran sous les Sassanides. Copenhague, 1936.

A CLASSICAL DICTIONARY of Hindu Mythology and Religion, Geography, History, and Literature, ed. John Dowson. London, 1957⁹.

CREEL, Herrlee G., 1. Chinese Thought from Confucius to Mao Tsĕ-tung. London, 1954.
2. Confucius. The Man and the Myth. New York (1949).
3. What is Taoism? and Other Essays in Chinese Cultural Studies. Chicago and London (1970).

DAFTARI, K.L., The Social Institutions of India. Nagpur, 1947.

DAWSON, Raymond, Confucius. Oxford, 1981.

DREKMEIER, Charles, Kingship and Community in Ancient India. Stanford (Cal.), 1962.

DUMONT, Louis, 1. The Conception of Kingship in Ancient India. Religion, Politics and History in Ancient India. Paris/The Hague, 1970.
2. Homo hiërarchicus. Essai sur le système des castes. Bibliothèque des sciences humaines. Paris, 1966.
3. Renunciation in Indian Religions. See under 1.

EBERHARD, Wolfgang, Geschichte Chinas von den Anfängen bis zur Gegenwart. Stuttgart (1971, 3. erweiterte Auflage).

EICHHORN, Werner, Die Religion Chinas. Die Religionen der Menschheit. Bd. 21. Stuttgart (1973).

EZNIK von Kolb, Wider die Irrlehren. Der armenischen Kirchenväter ausgewählte Schriften aus dem armenischen übersetzt. Herausgegeben von Dr. Simon Weber. I. Bd. Bibliothek der Kirchenväter. Bd. 57. München, 1927.

FRAUWALLNER, Erich, Geschichte der indischen Philosophie. 2 vols. Salzburg, 1956.

FUNG Yu-lan, A History of Chinese Philosophy. 2 vols. Translated from the Chinese by Derk Bodde. Princeton, 1973^3(1952^2, 1937^1, first Chinese edition 1931).

GHIRSHMAN, R., Iran from the Earliest Times to the Islamic Conquest. Pelican Book A 239. Penguin Books, 1965 (French edition 1951).

GHOSH, B.K., 1. Indo-Iranian Relations. The History and Culture of the Indian People. Volume I The Vedic Age. London, 1951.
2. Vedic Literature - General View. See under 1.

GLASENAPP, Helmuth von, 1. Buddhism - A Non-Theistic Religion. With a selection from Buddhist scriptures, edited by Heinz Bechert. Tanslated from the German (Buddhismus und Gottesidee, 1954) by Irmgard Schloegl. London (1966).
2. Der Jainismus. Eine indische Erlösungsreligion. Nach den Quellen dargestellt ... Hildesheim, 1964. (Reprographischer Nachdruck der Ausgabe Berlin 1925).
3. Die Philosophie der Inder. Eine Einführung in ihre Geschichte und ihre Lehren. Stuttgart, 1949.

GNOLI, Gherardo, 1. Magi, Encyclopedia of Religion. Volume 9. New York, 1987.
2. Mani. See under 1.
3. Manichaeism. See under 1.
4. Mazdakism. See under 1.
5. Zoroastrianism. Encyclopedia of Religion. Volume 15. New York, 1987.
6. Zurvanism. See under 5.

GOKHALE, B.G., Ancient India. History and Culture. Bombay, 1959^4 (1952^1).

GONDA, Jan, 1. De Indische godsdiensten. Servire reeks. Den Haag, 1955 (1974^3).
2. Inleiding tot het Indische denken. Antwerpen, 1948.
3. Die Religionen Indiens. I Veda und älterer Hinduismus. Die Religionen der Menschheit. 11. Stuttgart (1960).

GORDON, D.H., The Pre-Historic Background of Indian Culture. Bombay (1958).

GRANET, Marcel, La pensée chinoise. Paris, 1980 (photostatic reprint of the edition 1968^2 (1934^1).

GUERINOT, A., La religion Djaïna. Histoire, Doctrine, Culte, Coutumes, Institutions. Paris, 1926.

GUPTA, Chitrarekha, The Brahmanas of India. A Study Based on Inscriptions. Delhi (1983).

HÄRTEL, Herbert, Indien. Propyläen Weltgeschichte. Summa historica. Berlin-Frankfurt-Wien (1965).

HEESTERMAN, Jan C., 1. Brahman. Encyclopedia of Religion. Volume 2. New York, 1987.
2. Brahmans and Aranyakas. See under 1.
3. Vedism and Brahmanism. Encyclopedia of Religion. Volume 15. New York, 1987.

HERODOTUS, Historiai. Loeb Classical Library. 4 Vols. Translated by A.D. Godley (cited as Her.).

HILLEBRANDT, Alfred, Vedische Mythologie. I. Hildesheim, 1965 (photostatic reprint of 1927²).

HOPKINS, E. Washburn, 1. The Period of the Sutras, Epics, and Law-Books. Cambridge History of India. Volume I. Delhi (1955, 1921¹).
2. The Princes and Peoples of the Epic Poems. See under 1.

HORST, D. van der, Geschiedenis van China. Utrecht/Antwerpen, 1980² (1977¹).

HULSEWE, A.F.P., China im Altertum. Propyläen Weltgeschichte. II. Berlin-Frankfurt-Wien (1962).

HUMPHREYS, Christmas, A Popular Dictionary of Buddhism. London (1976², 1961¹).

HUTTON, J.H., Les castes de l'Inde. Nature, Fonctions, Origines. Paris, 1949.

INDRA, Prof., The Status of Women in Ancient India. Benares (1955, revised edition).

JACOBI, H., Brahmanism. Encyclopedia of Religion and Ethics. III. Edinburgh, 1909.

KALTENMARK, Max, 1. Lao Tseu et le taoisme. Editions du Seuil.
2. La philosophie chinoise. Que sais-je, no. 707. Paris, 1972.

KAMRISCH, Stella, The Presence of Siva. Princeton, 1981.

KEITH, A. Berriedale, The Age of the Rigveda. The Cambridge History of India. Volume I. Delhi (1955)(1921¹).

KETKAR, Shridhar V., The History of Caste in India. Evidence of the Laws of Manu on the Social Conditions in India during the Third Century A.D., Interpreted and Examined. I. Ithaca, N.Y., 1909.

KOSAMBI, D.D., The Culture and Civilisation of Ancient India in Historical Outline. London (1965).

KUIPER, F.B.J., Ancient Indian Cosmogony. Essays selected and introduced by John Erwin. The Basic Concept of Vedic Religion. New Delhi, 1983.

KUMAR, Pushpendra, Sakti Cult in Ancient India. Varanasi, 1974.

LACOMBE, Olivier, L'Absolu selon le Vedânta. Les notions de Brahman et d'Atman dans les systèmes de Cankara et Ramanoudja. Paris, 1937.

LAGERWEY, John, The Taoist Religious Community. Encyclopedia of Religion. Volume 14. New York, 1987.

LAL, Shyam Kishore, Female Divinities in Hindu Mythology and Ritual. Publications of the Centre of Advanced Study in Sanskrit. Class B. Pune, 1980.

LAMOTTE, Etienne, Histoire du Buddhisme Indien. Des origines à l'ère Saka. Louvain, 1967 (1958).

LI, Dun J., The Ageless Chinese. A History. New York (1971^2, 1965^1).

LIU, Wu-chi, A Short History of Confucian Philosophy. Pelican Book A 333. Penguin Books, 1955.

LOEWE, Michael, 1. The Concept of Sovereignty. The Cambridge History of China. Volume I. Cambridge (1986).
    2. The Former Han Dynasty. See under 1.
    3. The structure and practice of government. See under 1.

MACDONELL, A.A., The Vedic Religion. Encyclopedia of Religion and Ethics (1954^3).

MACMUNN, Sir George, Hidden Cults of India. London, w.d.

MAHONY, William K., 1. (Hindu) Dharma. Encyclopedia of Religion. Volume 4. New York, 1987.
    2. Karman : Hindu and Jain Concepts. Encyclopedia of Religion. Volume 8. New York, 1987.

MAJUMDAR, R.C., RAYCHAUDURI, H.C., and DATTA, Kalininkar, An Advanced History of India. London, 1958.

MAJUMDAR, Ramesh Chandra, Outline of Ancient Indian History and Civilisation (published by the author 1927).

MALIK, S.C., Indian civilization. The formative period. Simla, 1968.

MASPERO, Henri, Le Taoisme et les religions chinoises. Paris, 1971.

MEYER, Johann Jacob, Sexual Life in Ancient India. A study in the comparative history of Indian culture. London, 1930. (Translated from the German edition 'Das Weib im altindischen Epos').

MOOKERJI, Radha Kumud, Hindu Civilization. Part II. Bombay (1951).

MORTON, W. Scott, China. Its History and Culture. New York (1980).

MUKHERJU, Prahbati, Hindu Women. Normative Models. New Delhi, 1978.

NIVISON, S., Tao and Te. Encyclopedia of Religion. Volume 14. New York, 1987.

NYBERG, H.S., Die Religionen des alten Irans. Leipzig, 1938. (Original Swedish edition Uppsala 1937).

O'FLAHERTY, Wendy Doniger, 1. Asceticism and Eroticism in the Mythology of Siva. London, 1973.
2. Brahma. Encyclopedia of Religion. Volume 2. New York, 1987.
3. Horses. Encyclopedia of Religion. Volume 6. New York, 1987.
4. Women, Androgynes, and other Mythical Beasts. Chicago/London (1980).

PAUL, Diana Y., Women in Buddhism. Images of the Feminine in Mahayana Tradition. Berkeley (Cal.), 1979.

PETECH, Luciano, Indien bis zur Mitte des 6. Jahrhunderts. Propyläen Weltgeschichte. Volume II. Berlin-Frankfurt-Wien (1962).

PIGGOTT, Stuart, Prehistoric India to 1000 B.C. Penguin Books, 1952 (1950[1]).

PLUTARCH, De Iside et Osiride. Moralia V, ed. Frank Babbitt. Loeb Classical Library, 1962 (1936[1]).

PRASAD, Beni, The State in Ancient India. A Study in the Structure and Practical Working of Political Institutions in North India in Ancient Times. Allahabad, 1928.

PUSALKAR, A.D., 1. The Indus valley civilization. The History and Culture of the Indian People. I The Vedic Age. London, 1951.
2. The Pali Canon. See under 1.

RADHAKRISHNAN, Indian Philosophy I. London, 1966[8] (1923[1]).

RAJ, Dev, L'esclavage dans l'Inde ancienne d'après les textes palis et sanskrits. Pondichéry, 1957.

RAPSON, E.J., 1. Peoples and Languages. The Cambridge History of India. Volume I. Delhi, 1955 (1921[1]).
    2. The Puranas. See under 1.
    3. The Scythian and Parthian Invaders. See under 1.
    4. The Successors of Alexander the Great. See under 1.

RAYCHAUDHURI, Hemchandra, Political History of Ancient India from the accession of Parikshit to the extinction of the Gupta dynasty. Calcutta, 1923.

REISCHAUER, Edwin Oldfather, East-Asia : The Great Tradition. Boston (1973)(1960).

RENOU, Louis, et FILLIOZAT, Jean, L'Inde classique. Manuel des études indiennes I. Paris, 1947.

RHYS DAVIDS, C.A.F., Economic conditions according to early Buddhist literature. The History and Culture of India. Volume I The Vedic Age. London, 1951.

RHYS DAVIDS, T.V., 1. Buddhist India. Calcutta, 1959[8] (1903[1]).
    2. The earlier history of the Buddhists. The Cambridge History of India. Volume I. Delhi, 1955 (1921[1]).

SENGUPTA, Padmini, Everyday Life in Ancient India. London, 1957 (1950[1]).

SENGURTA, Nilakshi, The Evolution of Hindu Marriage, with special reference to rituals (c. 1000 - A.D. 500). Bombay (1965).

SHARMA, Ram Sharan, Sudras in Ancient India. A Survey of the Position of the Lower Orders down to circa AD 500. Delhi, 1958.

SHASTRI, Shakuntala Rao, Women in the Vedic Age. Bombay, 1960[3] (1951[1]).

SKORUPSKI, Thadeusz, Buddhist Dharma and Dharmas. Encyclopedia of Religion. Volume 4. New York, 1987.

SMITH, Brian K., Samsara. Encyclopedia of Religion. Volume 13. New York, 1987.

SPEAR, Percival, The Oxford History of India. Third edition ed. by Percival Spear. Part I revised by Sir Mortimer Wheeler and A.L. Basham. Oxford (1967)(1958[1]).

SPEYER, J.S., De Indische theosophie en hare beteekenis voor ons. Leiden, 1910.

THOMAS, Edward J., The Life of the Buddha as Legend and History. London (1960, reprinted from the revised edition 1949, 1927[1]).

THOMAS, E.W., The History of Buddhist Thought. London (1967)(1933[1])

THOMAS, F.W., 1. Acoka, the imperial patron of Buddhism. The Cambridge History of India. Volume I. Delhi, 1955 (1921[1]).
2. Chandragupta, the Founder of the Maurya Empire. See under 1.

THOMAS, P., Indian Women thtough the Ages. A Historical Survey of the Position of Women and the Institution of Marriage and Family in India from Remote Antiquity to the Present Day. Bombay (1964).

VETTER, Tilmann, The Ideas and Meditative Practices of Early Buddhism. Leiden, 1988 (first Dutch edition 1980).

WADIA, D.N., The Geological Background of Indian History. The Cambridge History of India. Volume I. Delhi, 1955 (1921[1]).

WELCH, Holmes, The Parting of the Way. Beacon Press, 1965 (revised edition)(1957[1]).

WHEELER, Sir Mortimer, 1. Early India and Pakistan to Ashoka. London (1959).
2. The Indus Civilization. Supplementary Volume of the Cambridge History of India. Cambridge, 1960.

WIDENGREN, Geo, Die Religionen Irans. Die Religionen der Menschheit. Band 14. Stuttgart (1965).

WILHELM, Richard, Kung-tse. Leben und Werk. Stuttgart, 1950[2](1925[1]).

YÜ Ying-shih, Han foreign relations. The Cambridge History of China. Volume I. Cambridge (1986).

ZAEHNER, R.C., The Dawn and Twilight of Zoroastrianism. London (1961).

ZIMMER, Heinrich, Philosophies of India. Edited by Joseph Campbell. Bollingen Series XXVI. Princeton University Press (1951).

ZÜRCHER, Erik, Buddhism in China. Encyclopedia of Religion, Volume 2. New York, 1987.

GENERAL INDEX

Abolition of Slavery Act, 83
Achaemenid, 10, 11, 13, 17, 18, 22, 26, 28, 29, 47
Aditi, 109, 110, 111, 112, 129, 130, 169
Adityas, 109, 111
Adam and Eve, 32
Aegean Sea, 2, 7
Afghanistan, 2, 12, 41, 57, 59, 61, 62, 64, 69
Africa, 1
Agni, 110
Agnistoma, 119
Agnostics, 95
Ahra Mainyu see Angra Mainyu
Ahriman, 21-22, 23-24, 25, 29
Ahura, 111
Ahura Mazdah, 16, 19, 20, 21, 24, 25, 29, 33
Ajasatru, 51, 52, 53
Akbar, 63
Alexander the Great, 1, 2, 7, 8, 9, 13, 47, 53, 54-55, 56, 57, 62, 64, 89
Allahabad, 67, 68
Allchin, Bridget and Raymond, 165
Altekar, A.S., 91, 93, 167
Altheim, Franz, 37
Ambedkar, B.R., 101, 103, 168
America(n)(s), 77, 138, 148, 180, 192, 194, 206, 218, 234
Ammianus Marcellinus, 37
Amritsar, 66
Amsterdam, 168
Amu Darya, 12, 18
Anahita Temple, 10
Ananda, 94
Anant, Santokh Singh, 97, 168
Anatolia, 6
Andhra Pradesh, 54

Androgynous, 108
Anga, 51
Angra Mainyu, 19, 20, 21, 22, 29
Animalism, 160
Anquetil-Duperron, 170
Antioch, 14, 16
Antiochus I, 2
Antiochus II, 2
Antiochus III, 2, 3, 5
Antiochus IV, 3
Antiochus VII Sidetes, 4
Apamea, Peace of, 3
Apamea, 2
Apte, V.M., 166
Arab(ia), 16, 17, 18, 69
Arabian Sea, 40, 68
Aral, Lake, 18, 200
Aramaeic, 31, 32
Arbela, Chronicle of, 30
Ardashir I, 11, 12, 30
Ardewan see Artabanus
Ardhanarisvara, 107
Arians, 34
Armenia(n), 3, 6, 7, 8, 9, 12, 14, 15, 18, 23
Arsacid, 8, 10, 11, 12
Artabanus V, 11
Artakhshatr, 10, 11
Artaxerxes, 10, 11
Arthasastra, 81
Aryan(s), 44, 45-48, 48, 49, 51, 71-73, 81, 83-84,, 85, 99, 102, 107, 110, 112, 113, 125, 160
Ascetic(s), ascetism, 138, 144, 147-148
Asia(n)(s), 1, 2, 3, 5, 9, 17, 40, 198, 201, 202, 204, 234
Asia Minor, 3, 5, 7, 8, 17, 22, 32, 45, 46
Asoka, 58-60, 60, 152

Assam, 67
Asuras, 48, 111-112, 116
Atman, 79, 136, 137, 139, 140, 142
Augustine, saint, 32
Augustus, emperor, 8, 203
Australoids, 41
Avanti, 53
Avesta, 19, 22, 27, 28, 45, 47

Ba, 186
Babylon, 9, 28
Babylonian Captivity, 33
Bactria(n)(s), 2, 5, 50, 60, 61, 62, 63, 64, 65
Bahram II, 14
Bahram V, 34
Baldrian, Farzeen, 249
Balkans, 3, 32, 46
Baluchistan, 42, 57, 59, 65, 69
Ban Chao, 204
Bangladesh, 41, 59, 65
Barbarian(s), 176, 178, 182, 183, 185, 186, 206, 207, 208, 209, 212, 244
Bareau, André, 153, 172, 173
Basham, A.L., 52, 56, 60, 67, 68, 74, 88, 98, 99, 126, 129, 138, 152, 163, 164, 165, 166, 167, 170, 171, 172, 173
Beas, 62
Beijing, 174, 176, 216
Benares, 64, 143
Bengal, 59, 65, 67
Bengali, 46
Benveniste, E., 26, 27, 28, 38
Besarh, 143
Bethlehem, 28
Bevan, E.R., 166
Bhashya, 139
Bhattacharji, Sukumari, 170, 171
Bhattacharya, B., 171
Bichapur, 14
Bihar, 51, 67, 145
Bimsibara, 51, 52, 151
Bindusara, 58
Black Sea, 6, 8
Bodde, Derk, 192, 245
Bodhisattva, 156, 158, 159
Bombay, 69, 135
Bosporus, Kingdom of the, 8
Boyce, Mary, 22, 38

Brāhma(n), 114, 118, 122, 126, 127, 134, 135, 136, 137, 141, 145, 153, 161, 169
Brahmān(s), Brahmin(s), 77, 96, 97, 98, 102, 103, 104, 107, 113, 114, 118, 119, 121-126, 151, 152, 161
Brahmana(s), 109, 114, 117, 130
Brahmanic, 94, 107, 112, 113-126, 135, 169
Brahmanism, 84, 98, 113-126, 127, 152, 160, 161
British see English
British-Indian, 83
British Raj, 63, 65
Bronze Age, 175
Buchenwald, KZ, 249
Buddha, the, 51, 52, 56, 74, 93, 94, 143, 149-151
Buddhism, Buddhist(s), 34, 53, 58, 59, 60, 74, 76, 77, 80, 93-95, 95, 98, 115, 125, 129, 143, 149, 149-160, 160, 161, 206, 238, 241, 243, 244, 250
Buckley, Jorunn Jacobsen, 38
Buhler, Johann George, 172
Burma, Burmese, 41, 50, 152, 158, 174, 202
Byzantine Empire, Byzantium, 16, 17, 34, 193
Byzantines, 17

Caesar, Julius, 7, 40
Cambodia, 158
Cambyses I, 27
Canetti, Elias, 193, 194, 245
Canton see Guangzhou
Cappadocia, 6
Carrhae, battle of 6, 8
Caspian Sea, 4
Caste system, 95-104
Casteless people, 99-101
Cathar, 214
Catholic, Catholicism, 15, 16, 22, 34
Caucasus, 1, 7, 8, 12, 16, 17
Celestial Empire, 174, 185, 189
Census Report 1911, 97
Central Asia, 2, 32, 41, 47, 62
Ceylon see Sri Lanka

Chalcolithic, 42
Chaldees, 28
Challaye, Félicien, 170
Chan, Wing-tsit, 218, 247
Chandragupta I, 66-67
Chandragupta II, 68
Chandragupta Maurya, 55-58, 66, 145
Chang'an, 199
Chaos, 213, 214
Chatterji, S.K., 163
Chattopadhyay, Amalkumar, 166
Ch'en ch'yün, 206, 246
Chen Duxiu, 236
Child marriages, 83, 90
Childe Gordon V., 42, 163
China, Chinese, 5, 14, 32, 50, 62, 63, 64, 152, 159, Ch. III passim, 243
Chorasmia, 18
Chosroes I, 16, 17
Chosroes II, 17
Christensen, Arthur, 30, 33, 37, 38, 39, 164
Christian(ity), 15, 16, 17, 22, 30, 31, 32, 33, 34, 88, 95, 98, 115, 118, 133, 160, 162, 234, 237, 239
Chu, 184, 227, 229
Chuangzi, 213, 233
Chungqiu, 218
Cilicia, 3, 5, 22
Coeurdoux, 45
Communist(s), communism, 236
Communist Party, Chinese, 236
Comorin, Cape, 67
Confucian(s), 178, 188, 189, 191, 192, 197, 203, 206, 218, 219, 221, 222-225, 226, 228, 229, 231, 232, 233, 236, 241, 244
Confucianism, 207, 222-225, 228-229, 231, 232, 237, 238, 243, 244
Confucius, 175, 182, 192, 197, 210, 216, 216-222, 226, 228, 229, 231, 232, 234
Congress, Indian National, 76
Conjeeveram, 67
Constantine I the Great, 15, 33, 34
Constantine II, 15
Constantinople, 17

Cosmogony, cosmogonic(al), 106, 116, 212, 238
Cosmology, cosmological, 212, 213
Crassus, 6, 9
Creel, H.G., 217, 218, 220, 222, 224, 232, 234, 236, 237, 247, 248, 249
Ctesiphon, 9, 11, 17, 18, 32
Cyrus I, 4, 8

Damascus, 38
Danube, 1
Danyan, 202
Dao, 232, 233, 234-235, 239, 241, 242
Dao de jing, 233
Daoism, Daoists, 232-242, 243, 244, 249
Darabgard, Darabjird, 11
Darius I, 8, 10, 15, 46, 52, 53, 54, 59
Daryav, 10
Dasa(s), 71, 81, 82, 99, 102, 112
Dasyu see Dasa
Dawson, Raymond, 217, 221, 247, 248
Deccan, 40, 51, 54, 55, 58, 64, 64, 67, 68, 75
Deistic, 118, 153
Delhi, 50
Demetria, 62
Demetrius, 61
Democritus, 28
Demons, 112-113, 116
Deva(s), 47, 48, 109-110, 112, 116, 117
Dharma, 59, 60, 76, 77-78, 78, 101, 153, 162
Di (godhead), 187
Di (people), 179
Diadochi, 1
Digambara, 148
Digvijaga, 68, 72
Diti, 112
Dongmu, 210
Dravidian, 46, 100
Drekmeier, Charles, 74, 165
Dualism, dualistic, 1, 3, 4, 5, 9, 13, 17, 20, 21, 22, 24, 29, 30, 31, 33, 34, 38, 39, 41, 49,

50, 55, 59, 65, 66, 72, 74, 78, 80, 92-93, 100, 103, 104, 105, 108, 109, 111, 112, 115, 116, 117, 119, 120, 121, 126, 128, 130, 131, 132, 133, 136, 137, 138, 139, 140, 142, 143, 145, 150, 156, 157, 163, 181, 182, 188, 189, 190, 194, 195, 196, 199, 204, 206, 208, 212, 213, 214, 222, 223, 232, 236, 242, 243
Dumont, Louis, 97, 137, 165, 168, 172
Dutch, 45, 46, 65, 96, 138, 142, 171

Earth, 211, 212, 213, 214, 216, 234, 235, 240
Eastern Zhou, 180, 180-215, 244
Eberhard, Wolfgang, 192, 205, 245, 246
Ecbatana, 18
Edessa, battle of, 14
Egypt(ian)(s), 1, 2, 3, 17, 27, 57, 60, 71, 174, 176, 177, 239
Eichhorn, Werner, 210, 215, 246, 247
Eire, 45
Ekam, 106, 107, 117
Endogamy, 97
England, 179
English, 45, 49, 51, 65, 88, 90, 138, 225
Ethiopia, 17
Eucratides, 62
Eudemus of Rhodes, 26
Euphrates, 3, 5, 6, 9, 12, 70
Euripides, 6
Europe(an)(s), 1, 2, 3, 4, 5, 9, 10, 22, 45, 77, 96, 97, 99, 138, 170, 179, 180, 192, 217, 234
European Community, 193
Euthydemia, 62
Euthydemus, 61
Eznik of Kolb, 23, 26, 38

Fars, 10, 11, 14, 18
Fergana, 202
Filliozat, Jean, 163, 164
Firuzabad, 11
Five Rulers, 175, 187
Four Seas, 212, 213
Frauwallner, Erich, 172
French, 45, 46, 65, 170

Fujian, 189
Fung Yu-lan, 211, 233, 246, 247, 248

Gabai, 11
Galatia, 6
Gandhara, 52, 53
Gandhi, Indira, 66
Gandhi, Mahatma, 95
Ganges, 40, 42, 44, 48, 50, 51, 52, 53, 54, 56, 57, 61, 62, 64, 67, 71, 98, 113, 143, 149, 150, 152
Gansu, 174, 200
Gaozu, 200
Gaul, 32, 40
Gautama Buddha see Buddha
Gautami, 150
Gedrosia, 57
Genesis, Book of, 116
Germanic, 45
Germany, German, 46, 51, 96, 111, 142, 195, 198
Ghirshman, R., 2, 5, 6, 10, 14, 16, 37, 38
Ghosh, B.K., 47, 163, 164
Glasenapp, Helmuth von, 105, 108, 115, 144, 149, 154, 155, 166, 168, 169, 170, 172, 173
Gnoli, Gherardo, 28, 29, 30, 38, 39
Gnosis, Gnostic, 31, 32, 34, 35, 38, 39, 137, 141, 146, 152, 155, 214, 234
Gobi desert, 174, 201
Gokhale, B.G., 166
Golden Temple of Amritsar, 66
Golding, William, 163
Gonda, Jan, 110, 112, 113, 131, 166, 168, 169, 170, 171, 172
Gor, 11
Gordon, D.H., 164
Granet, Marcel, 246, 247
Great Britain, 148
Great Vehicle, the, 158-160, 161, 162
Great Wall of China, 63, 177, 189, 200, 201
Greece, 82, 106, 184, 185
Greek(s), 1, 2, 3, 4, 10, 22,

26, 28, 29, 46, 50, 52, 53, 54, 55, 56, 57, 58, 61, 62, 63, 80, 81, 176, 186, 194
Guandong, 190, 202
Guangxi Zhuang, 190, 202
Guangzhou, 190
Guanzi, 216
Guérinot, A., 172
Guha, B.S., 41
Guizhou, 202
Gujarat, 56, 57, 63, 68, 148
Gulf of Bengal, 40, 65
Gupta(s), 64, 66, 66-69, 73, 104, 124, 127, 130
Gupta, Chitrarekha, 124, 125, 170
Guru(s), 95, 126, 138, 147, 150, 160

Hadrian, emperor, 9
Hamadan, 18
Han (empire, period), 188, 190-206, 209, 223, 242
Han (river), 174
Han Fei, 223
Hanoi, 190
Hao, 180
Haotian Shangdi, 211
Hare Krishnas, 127
Härtel, Herbert, 76, 165, 166
Harappa (civilization), 44, 69-71, 83
Heaven, 211, 212, 213, 215, 216, 220, 227, 231, 234, 235, 236, 240
Heesterman, Jan C., 114, 120, 169, 170
Hellenism, Hellenic, Hellenistic, 5, 6, 55, 57
Henan, 176, 180
Hephtalite kingdom, 16
Heraclius, 17
Herat, 12, 57
Hermaeus, 62
Herod I, 7
Herodotus, 27, 38
Himalayas, 40, 41, 42, 52, 59, 67, 132, 133, 149, 150
Hinayana see Lesser Vehicle
Hindi, 132, 139, 154
Hindu(s), 65, 74, 87, 91, 92, 96, 97, 107, 108, 116, 118, 125, 127, 128, 129, 130, 131, 133, 134, 136, 137, 141, 144, 148
Hinduism, 80, 110, 114, 118, 126, 127, 138, 148, 149, 153, 160, 161
Hindu Kush, 40, 59, 61, 64
Hindustan, 40, 57, 60
Hittit(s), 6, 45, 46
Hittite Empire, 47
Holy Roman Empire, 179, 193
Homeric, 49, 50
Honan see Henan
Hoover, Dwight D., 194, 215
Hopkins, E. Washburn, 174
Horner, I.B., Women under Primtive Buddhism. Laywomen and Almswomen. London, 1930, 129, 170
Horst, D. van der, 244, 245, 246
Huai-yi, 179
Huang-di, 186
Huizinga, Johan, 171
Hulsewé, A.F.P., 219, 244, 245, 247, 248
Humphreys, Christmas, 173
Hunas see Huns
Hundred Schools, 231, 248
Huns, 16, 62, 63, 68, 69, 200
Hutton, J.H., 168
Hyphasis, 62

Iliad, 49
Indarpat, 50
India, Indian(s), 1, 2, 9, 12, Ch. II passim, 206, 243
Indian Ocean, 12, 40
Indian Union, 66, 76
Indo-Aryan(s) see Aryans
Indo-European(s), 2, 45, 46, 163, 178
Indo-Germanic, 45
Indra, 47, 72, 73, 110, 111, 112, 117, 154, 169
Indra, Prof., 87, 89, 167
Indus, 1, 2, 7, 12, 13, 40, 42, 48, 52, 53, 54, 55, 56, 57, 61, 62, 64, 67, 69, 70, 71, 113
Indus civilization, 44, 69-71, 129, 160
Ipsus, battle of, 1
Iran(ian)(s), 2, 4, 10, 12, 13, 14, 15, 16, 17, 18, 19, 22, 26, 28, 30, 31, 32, 33, 34, 35, 38, 39, 45, 46, 47, 61, 66, 68, 111, 112, 170, 191

Iraq, 4, 12, 31
Ireland, 45
Irian, 193
Isfahan, 11
Ishvara, 117, 118, 139, 141, 153
Islam(ic)(ites), 17, 37, 69, 98, 115
Israel (biblical), 27, 80, 155, 167, 176
Istakhr, 10, 11
Italy, Italian, 32, 45, 46

Jacobi, H., 169
Jahve, 115
Jainism, Jainist(s), 57, 58, 80, 98, 143-149, 52, 153, 154, 160, 161
Jammu, 65, 66
Japan, 153, 159
Javanese, 50
Jerusalem, 7, 17
Jesuits, 217, 229
Jesus Christ, 34, 224, 225
Jew(s), Jewish, 3, 9, 31, 33, 88, 118, 167
Jhelum, 55
Ji Kangzi, 219
Jia yi, 191
Jin dynasty, 207
Jnatrika, 143
Jona, 65
Jones, Sir William, 45
Jordan (river), 31
Judaism, 31, 32, 115, 160
Julian the Apostate, 15
Justinus, 56, 114

Kabul, 12, 57
Kalinga, 54, 58-59
Kaltenmark, Max, 234, 247, 248, 249
Kama, 106, 134
Kamrisch, Stella, 168
Kanada, 77
Kancheepuram, 67
Kandahar, 57
Kanishka, 64
Kansu, 63
Kapilavasu, 149
Karma(n), 76, 79-80, 101, 105, 106, 144, 146, 148, 162
Kashmir, 64, 65, 66, 152
Kassite(s), 45, 46
Kathiawar, 56, 68

Kausambi, 53
Kawad, 36, 37
Keith, A. Berriedale, 48, 164, 165, 170
Ketkar, Shridar V., 168
Khuzistan, 14
Kirman, 11
Korea, 159, 202
Kosala, 52
Kosambi, D.D., 47, 70, 163, 164, 165
Krishna, 126, 127
Kshatriyas, 56, 96, 102, 110, 125, 126, 143, 149
Kuiper, F.B.J., 116, 117, 169, 170
Kumar, Pushpendra, 171
Kumara Gupta I, 68
Kurukshetra, battle of, 50
Kurus, 50
Kushan(ite)(s), 12, 13, 14, 16, 62, 63, 64, 66, 67, 68
Kusinagara, 151
Kwangsi see Guangxi Zhuang
Kwantung see Guandong
Kweichow see Guizhou

Lacombe, Olivier, 169
Lagerwey, John, 250
Lakshmi, 127
Lal, Shyam Kishore, 171
Lamotte, Etienne, 172
Lanzhou, 174
Laos, 158, 202
Laotius see Laozi
Laozi, 213, 223, 233, 233-234, 235, 240
Latin, 26, 45, 46, 47, 96, 138, 217
Legalism, Legalist(s), 188, 197, 222-223, 224, 237
Lesser Vehicle, the, 157-158, 159, 161
Levirate marriage, 167
Levites, 27
Li, Dun J., 186, 196, 209, 245, 246
Li Si, 189
Licchavi, 67, 143
Linga, 132-135
Lingayat, 133
Li Quangli, 202
Liu Bang, 190-191, 195

Liu Wu-chi, 218, 228, 231, 232, 247, 248
Loewe, Michael, 196, 203, 246
Lok Sabha, 71
London, 148
Lotus position, 141
Loyang, 180, 184, 186, 187, 202, 204, 207, 208, 209, 234
Lu, 217, 219, 225, 229, 231
Lü, 200
Lumbini grove, 149
Lydia, 5

Macbeth, 17
Macdonell, A.A., 169
Macedonia(n)(s), 1, 2, 3, 9, 15, 54, 55, 56, 57, 60, 62, 186
Macmunn, Sir George, 171
Madaraya, 35
Madras, 67
Magadha(n), 50, 51, 52, 53, 54, 55, 56, 61, 66, 73, 151
Magi(ans), 26, 26-29, 29, 30, 32
Magic, 120-121
Magnesia, battle of, 3
Mahabharata, 49, 50, 82, 83, 92, 93, 133, 166, 167
Maha-Devi, 131, 132
Mahapadna Nanda, 54
Mahavira see Vardhamana
Mahavira Brotherhood, 148
Mahayana see Great Vehicle
Mahony, William K., 77, 166
Maitreya, 160
Majumdar, R.C., 49, 58, 67, 164, 165
Malik, S.C., 70, 165
Malwa, 57, 63, 68
Manchuria, 200, 201, 208
Mandaeism, Mandaean(s), 30, 31, 32, 34, 35
Mandarins, 225
Mandate of Heaven, Celestial Mandate, 178, 187, 189, 201, 202, 202-203, 203, 204, 221, 230
Mani, 32, 35, 38
Manichaeism, Manichaean(s), 30, 31, 32-33, 34, 35, 38, 39, 214
Mantra, 86
Mao Zhe Dong, 248

Maodun, 200, 201
Marathi, 46
Marc Antony, 7, 9
Marx, Karl, 175
Marxist, 97, 175, 176, 177, 195
Maspero, Henri, 233, 238, 249, 250
Matthew, Gospel of, 28
Maurya(n)(s), 56, 57, 60, 62, 65, 66, 67, 73, 80, 81, 104, 152
Mauryan Empire, 55-60, 61, 62, 65, 68, 81, 104
Mazdaites, 24
Mazdak, 35, 36
Mazdakism, Mazdakite(s), 30, 35-37
Media(n)(s), 4, 7, 18, 27, 46
Mediterranean Sea, 202
Megasthenes, 80, 81
Menander, 62
Mengzu (Mencius), 229-230, 230, 231
Merv, 6, 12, 18
Mesopotamia(n)(s), 3, 4, 5, 6, 13, 14, 15, 17, 18, 28, 33, 35, 45, 46, 47, 49, 181
Metempsychosis see Migration of souls
Meyer, Johann Jacob, 166, 167
Miao-yao, 191
Middle Ages, 50
Middle East, 9, 10
Migration of souls, 84, 105, 146, 162
Milinda, 62
Mitanna, 47
Mithra, 30, 47, 50, 110
Mithraism, 30
Mithridates I, 4
Mithridates II, 5
Mo Di, 225-229
Moghul Empire, 65
Mohenjo-daro, 44, 70
Mohism, Mohist(s), 225-229, 243
Moksa, 78, 122
Mongolia, 159, 189, 200, 201
Mongolian(s), Mongoloid, Mongols, 63, 68, 163, 191, 205, 208, 209
Monier Williams, Monier, Relig-

ious Thought and Life in India. New Delhi (1974)(1881¹), 108, 121, 128, 136, 169, 170, 171
Monism, monists, 20, 21, 22, 24, 106, 108, 117, 118
Monogamy, 83, 87
Monophysite, 34
Monotheism, monotheistic, 19, 20, 154
Mookerji, Radha Kumud, 106
Mopsuestia, 22
Morton, W. Scott, 192, 204, 244, 246
Moslim(s), 65, 115
Mother-Goddess(es), 44, 109, 129-130, 131
Mukherjee, Prahbati, 128, 170

Nairanjara, 150
Nanda(s), 50, 51, 54, 56, 73
Nanjing (Nanking), 207
Napoleonic Wars, 9
Narseh, 14
Nazi ideology, 45
Nellore, 59
Neolithic, 49
Nepal, 67, 149
Nestorians, 34
Netherlands, the, 177
New Delhi, 66
New Guinea, 193
Nihawand, battle of, 18
Nile, 1, 17, 70
Ninxia, 201
Nirrti, 130
Nirvana, 59, 78, 105, 122, 142, 144, 145, 146, 156, 157, 158, 159, 162
Nivison, S., 248, 249
Nomads, nomadic, 42, 62, 185
Normans, 179
North Africa, 32
Nyberg, H.S., 38, 39

Odyssey, 49
O'Flaherty, Wendy Doniger, 130, 131, 134, 136, 138, 169, 171, 172
Omar, 17
One, the -- and the Many, 106, 156, 213, 235-237, 243
Ordos region, 200, 201
Oriental, 41

Orissa, 51, 54
Ormizd see Ormuzd
Ormuzd, 16, 21-22, 23-24, 25, 29
Orodes II, 7
Otto, Rudolf, 155
Oudh, 67
Outcastes see casteless
Oxus see Amu Darya

Pacific Ocean, 174
Pahlevi, Pahlava, 22, 63, 64
Pakistan, 2, 12, 13, 32, 41, 57, 59, 65, 66, 101
Palestine, 3, 5, 7, 17, 3
Pali, 46, 151, 157
Pamir, 174, 202
Pandavas see Pandus
Pandu, 83
Pandus, 50
Pantheism, pantheistic, 118, 121
Papak, Papek, Pabagh, 10, 11
Papua, 193
Paraiyar, 100
Pariahs, 95, 97, 100, 104
Parmenides, 106, 137, 142
Parshva (person), 143-145, 145
Parshva (creed, sect), Parshvaites, 143-145, 145
Parthia(n)(s), 2, 3, 4-10, 11, 12, 32, 47, 61, 63, 64, 204
Parthian Empire, 4-10, 29, 31, 191, 204
Parthizeites, 27
Parvati, 132, 133
Pasargadae, 11
Pataliputra (Patna), 53, 56, 62, 67, 68, 143
Patanjali, 139
Patna (Pataliputra), 53, 62, 143, 149, 150
Pattala, 12
Paul, Diana, 94, 168, 170
Peking see Beijing
Peking man, 175
Pergamum, 5
Peroz, 16
Persepolis, 11
Persia(n)(s), Ch. I passim, 41, 45, 46, 47, 52, 53, 54, 55, 61, 67, 73, 110, 170, 181, 188

Persian Empire, 1, 4, 12, 28, 29, 30, 57
Persian Gulf, 9, 10, 11
Peshawar, 13
Petech, Luciano, 40, 44, 49, 54, 102, 106, 108, 148, 163, 164, 168, 169, 172
Philosophy (Indian), 104-109
Phraates II, 4, 5
Piggott, Stuart, 45, 70, 163, 165
Plato, 28, 227
Plutarch, 26, 38, 56, 164
Pohkar, 169
Polish, 45
Polyandry, 87
Polygamy, 86-88
Polygyny, 87
Pontus, 6
Portuguese, 96
Porus, 55
Prasad, Beni, 165
Prostitution, 92, 171
Prussia, 51
Ptahil, 31
Ptolemaic(s), 2, 3
Puccini, Giacomo, 247
Punjab, 48, 53, 56, 61, 70
Punjabi, 46
Puranas, 130
Purohita, 122-123
Pururava, 85
Purusha, 140, 142
Pusalkar, A.D., 171, 172
Pythagoras, 28
Pythagoreanism, Pythagorean, 155, 218, 242

Qadisya, battle of, 18
Qi, 182, 184, 219
Qin (Ch'in) (empire, period), 181, 185-190, 190, 191, 192, 194, 198, 199, 206, 223-224
Qufu, 217

Radhakrishnan, 104, 116, 118, 168, 169, 170, 171
Raj, Dev, 166
Rajahigra, 51
Rajasthan, 148
Rajputs, 50

Raksasas, 112
Ranke, Leopold von, 194
Rapson, E.J., 41, 63, 98, 163, 165, 171
Raychaudhuri, Hemchandra, 51, 164
Realm of the Middle, 186
Red Eyebrows, 204
Reischauer, Edwin Oldfather, 177, 198, 244, 245, 246
Renou, Louis, 163, 164, 168
Rhys Davids, C.A.F., 81, 137, 164, 166, 170
Rigveda, 48, 77, 85, 90, 98, 106, 107, 110, 114, 117, 129, 139, 165, 166, 168, 169
Rijupalika, 145
Risley, 163
Ritualism, 119
Roman(s), 3, 5, 6, 7, 8, 9, 10, 12, 13, 14, 15, 16, 17, 31, 33, 203
Roman Empire, Rome, 3, 6, 7, 8, 9, 10, 13, 14, 15, 16, 30, 32, 33, 34, 181, 188, 191, 192, 193, 197, 202, 204
Romance, 45
Rome (city), 8, 204
Russia(n), 45, 46, 47
Rustam, 17, 18

Saka(s), 63, 64, 67, 68
Sakti(s), 131, 135
Saktism, Saktist, 131, 135, 136, 161
Sakhyas, 52, 149
Samarkand, 13
Samkhya, 139-141, 153
Samkhya-karika, 139
Samsara, 76, 77, 78, 79, 94, 122, 162
Samudragupta, 67, 68
Sandrocottos, 56
Sangha, 59
Sanskrit, 45, 46, 77, 78, 79, 114, 130, 157
Sanskritist, 171
Sarda Act, 90
Sasan (Sassan), 10
Sasanian(s), 10-19, 22, 29, 30, 31, 33, 36, 47

Sasanian Empire, 10-18, 29, 33, 37, 66
Sassanid see Sasanian
Schwarz, Benjamin S., 249
Scipio Africanus, 3
Scythians, 12, 62, 63, 64
Seleucid(s), 2, 24, 47, 61, 64, 80
Seleucus I, 2, 57
Seleucid Empire, 1-3
Semitic, 9, 45
Senate of Rome, 6
Sengupta, Padmini, 166, 167
Septimius Severus, 10
Seven Kings', Seven States Rebellion, 196, 199
Shaanxi, 178
Shakra see Indra, 154
Shandong, 181, 187, 189, 191, 217
Shang dynasty, period, 176-178, 178, 187, 210, 222
Shangdi, 210
Shantung see Shandong
Shanxi, 182
Shapur I, 12, 13, 14, 29, 37
Shapur II, 14, 15
Sharma, Ram Sharan, 102, 103, 168
Shastri, Shakuntala Rao, 86, 166
She, 212
Sheji, 211
Shiva, 44, 107, 108, 118, 127, 130, 131, 132, 133, 134, 135, 136, 161
Shivaism, 127, 161
Shu, 186
Shudras, 96, 101-104, 113, 125
Sichuan, 186, 205, 206
Siddharta (Buddha), 94
Siddharta (father of Vardhamana), 143
Sikhs, 66, 98, 160
Silk Road, 202, 243
Sinanthropus pekinensis, 175
Sind(h), 42, 53, 5⁻
Sisunaga, 53
Skanda Gupta, 69
Skorupski, Thadeusz, 166
Slavery, 80-83, 166
Slavonic, 45
Smith, Brian K., 166
Söderblom, Nathan, 155
Soma, 119
Son of Heaven, 179, 180, 181, 185, 187, 198, 202-203, 212, 214, 221

Song, 227
Southern Russia, 12
Spain, 32
Spaniards, 96
Spear, Percival, 50, 164
Spenta Mainyu, 19, 20, 29
Speyer, J.S., 137, 171
Sri Gupta, 66
Sri Lanka, 40, 41, 60, 65, 152, 158
Stone Age, 41, 42, 69, 174
Strabo, 62, 165
Sui dynasty, 209
Sulla, Lucius, 5
Sumer(ian), 13, 45, 52, 174
Sun En, 250
Sun god, 212
Sung, 225
Susa, 11
Sutras, 77
Syr Darya, 13
Syria, 3, 5, 6, 7, 9, 14, 17, 33, 57, 60
Swetateku, 84
Szech'uan, Szechwan see Sichuan

Taishan, 187
Taksasila, 52
Tamil, 46, 59, 60, 100
Tantras, 131, 135
Tantrism, 131, 161
Tao see Dao
Taoism, Taoists see Daoism, Daoists
Tapas, 106, 134
Tarim Basin, 202, 204
Tashkent, 13
Taurus, 3
Taxila, 3 (see also Taksasila)
Te, 183, 203
Teilhard de Chardin, Pierre, 176
Telugu, 46
Texas, 179
Thailand, 152, 158
Theism, theistic, 118, 141, 153 - 155
Theodorus of Mopsuestia, 22, 23
Theogony, 106
Theravada, 95, 151
Thomas of Aquinas, 169
Thomas, E.J., 172
Thomas, E.W., 173
Thomas, F.W., 152, 157, 164, 165

Thomas, P., 83, 92, 166, 167, 198
Three Sovereigns, 175
Tian see Heaven
Tianan-men, 216
Tiberius, 203
Tibet(an)(s), 152, 159, 191, 205, 208
Tigris, 3, 9, 14, 17, 32, 35, 70
Toynbee, Arnold, 4, 61, 191
Trajan, 8, 9
Tree of Enlightenment, 150, 152
Trisala, 143
Trombay, 135
Tulu, 46
Tunisia, 32
Turcmenia, 6
Turco-Mongolian, 68, 178, 200
Turkestan, 14, 32, 63, 202

Universal states, 4, 13
Untouchables see pariahs
Upanayana, 91, 103, 125, 126
Upanishads, 73, 116, 117, 118, 130, 136, 152, 165, 169, 170
Uttar Pradesh, 148
Uzbekistan, 13

Vaisali, 143
Vaishekika-sutra, 77
Vaishyas, 96, 125, 126
Valerian (Roman emperor), 13, 14
Vardhamana, 143, 145
Varna(s), 96, 98-99, 101, 114, 115, 121
Varuna, 47, 110, 111
Vedas, 47, 68, 83, 85, 113, 125, 126, 127, 129, 130, 133, 141, 160, 166
Vedic (mythology, period, religion, ritual), 48-50, 77, 83, 84, 85, 87, 91, 92, 98, 102, 103, 109-113, 114, 115, 116, 117, 119, 120, 124, 129, 132, 166
Vedism, 98, 111, 113, 126, 160
Vegetarian(ism), 144, 145, 147
Vetter, Tilmann, 172
Vietnam, 190, 202
Vindhya Mountains, Range, 40, 41, 49, 53, 57, 59, 60, 64, 65, 68, 71, 72
Vishnu, 110, 118, 126, 127, 130, 136, 141, 153, 161
Vishnuism, Vishnuites, 127, 153, 161
Vrijji, 52
Vyasa, 139, 141

Wang Mang, 203, 204
Wadia, D.N., 163
Waley, Arthur, 233
Warring States, the, 184, 222, 227, 228, 230
Wessex, 51
Wei (river), 176, 180, 186
Welch, Holmes, 242, 249
Wendi, 201, 224
Western Zhou, 180
Wheeler, Sir Mortimer, 44, 163
Wisdom, Book of, 239
Widengren, Geo, 25, 30, 38, 39
Widows, Indian, 88-90
Wilhelm, Richard, 248
Wilhelmina (queen), 193
Wolfe, Thomas, 61
Women, Position of -- in India, 83-95
Wu (king), 178, 179, 180
Wudi, 196, 198, 199, 200, 201, 224

Xerxes I, 3, 15, 52
Xia dynasty, 175
Xiamu, 210
Xiang Yu, 190
Xinjiang (Sinkiang), 202
Xianyang, 186
Xianyuan, 179
Xiongnu, 199-208
Xunzi (Xun Qing), 231-232, 248

Yangzi (Yangtze), 174, 179, 182, 184, 186
Yasoda, 143
Yasodhara, 94
Yazgard, 17
Yellow Emperor, 187
Yellow River, 176, 177, 178, 182, 186, 200, 204, 206
Yellow Sea, 174, 182
Yellow Turbans, 205
Yemen, 16

Yin and Yang, 215-216, 235
Yoga, 138-142, 143
Yoga-sutras, 139
Yogi(s), 139, 141-142
Yoni, 132-135
Yu (king), 180, 226
Yü Ying-shih, 246
Yuezhi, 63, 178
Yunnan, 202

Zaehner, R.C., 26, 36, 38, 39
Zarathustra see Zoroaster
Zervan, 22, 43, 24, 25-26
Zervanism, Zervanite(s), 21-30, 33, 42
Zhang Ling, 205
Zhao, 231
Zhou dynasty, period, 178-215, 186, 195, 197, 198, 210, 215, 219, 222, 232
Zhuangzu, 213, 216
Zimmer, Heinrich, 140, 172
Zoroaster, 18-30, 36
Zoroastrianism, Zoroastrian(s), 18-30, 32, 33, 34, 35, 37, 39, 59, 142, 155, 160
Zou, 217
Zürcher, Erik, 244, 250
Zurvan see Zervan